THINE
IS MY HEART

THINE
IS MY HEART

Devotional Readings from the
Writings of John Calvin

Compiled by
John H. Kromminga

Reformation Heritage Books
Grand Rapids, Michigan
2006

Published by
Reformation Heritage Books
2965 Leonard St., NE
Grand Rapids, MI 49525
616-977-0599 / Fax 616-285-3246
e-mail: orders@heritagebooks.org
website: www.heritagebooks.org

Originally published
Grand Rapids: Zondervan, 1958

10 digit ISBN 1-892777-95-9
13 digit ISBN 978-1-892777-95-9

*For additional Reformed literature, both new and used, request a free
book list from Reformation Heritage Books at the above address.*

INTRODUCTION

As anyone who reads his writings must come to recognize, there is a strong devotional strain in John Calvin. This devotional spirit stands out clearly in his many *Sermons*, a number of which are represented in these selections. Here Calvin is seen as the true pastor, bringing the full message of the Word of God with a genuine concern for the needs of his hearers. The spirit of devotion is strongly present also in his *Commentaries*, especially in the practical applications of the truths he expounds. Somewhat more surprising, however, are the brilliant flashes of devotional insight which are present in Calvin's major doctrinal work, the *Institutes of the Christian Religion*. Christian doctrine was not for him a mere intellectual exercise, but a pathway to the presence of God. And devotion is also clearly present in the tender concern, the Scriptural consolation, and the brotherly reproof which abound in Calvin's extensive *Correspondence*.

Among students of John Calvin it is common knowledge that the Reformer has been a badly misunderstood man. The perverted conception of his character, which is of long standing and continues to the present day, pictures him as a cold, impractical, one-track theologian.

That this popular picture is untrue is evidenced by the selections contained in this volume. It is a manly Christianity which is reflected in these writings. The practical application of Christian truth is never far from Calvin's mind. The Reformer exhibits everywhere a deep consciousness of the sovereignty of God. He engages in searching examinations of human frailties, speaking plainly and without compromise about the depravity of man. But throughout he manifests also a sturdy confidence in the grace of God which overcomes human sin.

It is hoped that through these selections the reader will gain a new appreciation of a truly great man. The selections will also carry the one who uses them into living contact with the faith of the Christian Church throughout the ages. But it is especially desired and expected that the use of this book will bring the reader into the presence of the living God. This is most in keeping with the purpose of the man whose motto included this truly devotional element: "My heart I offer to Thee, O Lord."

The selections from the *Commentaries* are taken from the edition prepared for the Calvin Translation Society. Readings from Calvin's *Correspondence* are taken from the four-volume English translation prepared by Jules Bonnet. The selections from the *Institutes* are from the translation by John Allen. Excerpts from *Sermons on Isaiah* are from the version of T. H. L. Parker, and are used by permission of James Clarke & Co. of London. Selections from *Sermons on Job* have been adapted from an old English version translated from the French by Arthur Golding and published in London in 1584, and the sermon excerpts on *I and II Timothy* are from a similar volume printed in 1579.

John H. Kromminga

Calvin Seminary
November, 1958

Thine Is My Heart

*Except the Lord build the house, they labour in vain
that build it: except the Lord keep the city, the
watchman waketh but in vain.*   Psalm 127:1

In affirming that God governs the world and the life of man,
the Psalmist does so for two reasons. First, whatever prosperous
event may fall out to men, their ingratitude is instantly manifested by their ascribing it wholly to themselves; and thus God
is defrauded of the honor which is his due. Solomon, to correct such a perverse error, declares that nothing happens prosperously to us except in so far as God blesses our proceedings.
Secondly, his purpose was to beat down the foolish presumption of men, who, setting God aside, are not afraid to undertake
to do anything, whatever it may be, in exclusive reliance upon
their own wisdom and strength. Stripping them, therefore, of
that which they groundlessly arrogate to themselves, he exhorts
them to modesty and the invocation of God.

He does not, however, reject either the labor, the enterprises,
or the counsels of men; for it is a praiseworthy virtue diligently
to discharge the duties of our office. It is not the will of the
Lord that we should be like blocks of wood, or that we should
keep our arms folded without doing anything; but that we
should apply to use all the talents and advantages which he
has conferred upon us. It is indeed true that the greatest part
of our labors proceeds from the curse of God; and yet although
men had still retained the integrity of their primitive state,
God would have had us to be employed, even as we see how
Adam was placed in the Garden of Eden to dress it. Solomon,
therefore, does not condemn watchfulness, a thing which God
approves; nor yet men's labor, by which when they undertake
it willingly, according to the commandment of God, they offer
him an acceptable sacrifice; but lest, blinded by presumption,
they should forcibly appropriate to themselves that which belongs to God, he admonishes them that their being busily occupied will profit them nothing, except in so far as God blesses
their exertions.—*Commentaries*

*Thou therefore endure hardness, as a good soldier
of Jesus Christ.*   II Timothy 2:3

We have two points to consider. The one is, seeing the Son
of God has called us to be his soldiers, we must at least do him
as much honor as the soldiers of the world do to their captains.
How shall we do this? We must be free from all hindrances,
we must not be entangled in things that might hold us back,
but we must walk boldly and do our duty, seeing we are no
more our own men.

But especially and before all things we must expect that
which we have heard of; namely, that our condition is such
that we must fight, seeing we are called to be the flock of
Christ. And again, let us know this, that our warfare is not
to fight either against flesh or blood, but against powers of the
air, against all lusts of the flesh, and against all temptations of
the world. And therefore we must be in readiness to do it.

And again, because we have to suffer many afflictions, we
must also be ready to bear them. And let us know especially
that our issue is certain and cannot deceive us; we do not fight
in a lost cause. We are not as they that take great pains and
disquiet themselves to get a crown of leaves, and are often deceived. For many, he says, run in a race, and there is but one
that is crowned. He that gets the prize deprives all the others.
But for our part, we have a far better condition; for we are so
far from hindering one another and depriving each other of
the prize and crown which is promised us, that we help one
another. — *Sermons*

And I say unto you, Ask, and it shall be given you; seek, and ye shall find; knock, and it shall be opened unto you.   Luke 11:9

The saints have an excellent stimulus to calling upon God when their necessities and perplexities harass and disquiet them, and they are almost despairing in themselves, till faith opportunely relieves them. Because, amidst such troubles, the goodness of God is so glorious in their view, that though they groan under the pressure of present calamities, and are likewise tormented with the fear of greater in the future, yet a reliance on it relieves the difficulty of bearing them, and encourages a hope of deliverance.

The prayers of a pious man, therefore, must proceed from both these dispositions, and must also contain and discover them both. Though he groan under present evils, and is anxiously afraid of new ones, yet at the same time he must resort for refuge to God, not doubting his readiness to extend the assistance of his hand. For God is highly incensed by our distrust, if we supplicate him for blessings which we have no expectation of receiving. There is nothing, therefore, more suitable to the nature of prayers, than that they be conformed to this rule — not to rush forward with temerity, but to follow the steps of faith. — *Institutes,* III, xx, xi

JANUARY 4

Then they that feared the Lord spake often one to another: and the Lord hearkened, and heard it, and a book of remembrance was written before him for them that feared the Lord, and that thought upon his name.   Malachi 3:16

But the prophet says not only that individuals were touched with repentance, but also that they spoke among themselves, by which he intimates that our efforts ought to be extended to our brethren. And it is an evidence of true repentance when each one endeavors as much as he can to unite himself to as many friends as possible, so that they may with one consent return to the way from which they had departed; yes, that they may return to the God whom they had forsaken. This then is what we are to understand by the words spoken mutually by God's servants. — *Commentaries*

JANUARY 5

He shall feed his flock like a shepherd: he shall gather the lambs with his arm, and carry them in his bosom, and shall gently lead those that are with young.   Isaiah 40:11

He will feed his flock . . . He will carry them in his bosom. Now, although by the word "flock" he describes an elect people, whom he had undertaken to govern, yet we are reminded that God will be a shepherd to none but to those who, in modesty and gentleness, shall imitate the sheep and lambs. We must therefore lay aside our fierceness, and permit ourselves to be tamed, if we wish to be gathered into the fold of which God promises that he will be the guardian.

These words describe God's wonderful condescension; for not only is he moved by a general feeling of regard to his whole flock, but in proportion to the weakness of any one sheep, he shows his carefulness in watching, his gentleness in handling, and his patience in leading it. Here he leaves out nothing that belongs to the office of a good shepherd; for the shepherd ought carefully to observe every sheep, so as to treat it according to its capacity; and especially they ought to be supported if they are exceedingly weak. In a word, God will be mild, kind, gentle, and compassionate, so that he will not drive the weak harder than they are able to bear.

—*Commentaries*

6   JANUARY 6

My tongue shall speak of thy word: for all thy commandments are righteousness.   Psalm 119:172

"My tongue shall speak of thy word." Here the Psalmist says that when he shall have profited in God's law he will also employ himself in teaching it to others. This order is undoubtedly to be observed; that divine truth take root in our hearts before we engage in the work of teaching it to others. Yet every man, according to the measure of his faith, ought to communicate to his brethren what he has received, that the doctrine, whose use and fruit God would have to be displayed for the common edification of the Church, may not be buried. There is added the reason which ought to stir up all the godly to declare the law of God — namely, that by this means righteousness is spread abroad through the whole world. —*Commentaries*

*Humble yourselves therefore under the mighty hand
of God, that he may exalt you in due time: Casting
all your care upon him; for he careth for you.*

I Peter 5:6, 7

It is consoling to recognize that not only he tries our faith,
but also that, in withdrawing us from the allurements and delights of the world, which deceive us, he lets us taste his
bounty and feel his aid, by gathering us as it were under his
wings, that we may say with David that our supreme good is
to cleave to him.

Indeed, when all goes well with us, it is hard to prevent
our minds in their wantonness from going astray; and it is
a miracle, which seldom happens, that those who have long
basked in prosperity hold on in the fear of the Lord. And
that is the reason why, to keep his children in restraint, he
sends them divers afflictions.

Doubtless though we feel that what are called adversities are
common to us with unbelievers and profane people entirely
given up to the world, nevertheless God blesses those which we
have to suffer, turning them to such account that we have always matter for consolation and rejoicing in our sorrows. You
cannot but recognize, also, that he has been pleased to spare
you, for you see how much more harshly he deals with many
others, who have not for all that any mitigation in their afflictions. — *Correspondence*

8 JANUARY 8

Then Job arose, and rent his mantle, and shaved his head, and fell down upon the ground, and worshipped. And said, Naked came I out of my mother's womb, and naked shall I return thither: the Lord gave, and the Lord hath taken away; blessed be the name of the Lord. Job 1:20, 21

This present text is as excellent as any in all the holy Scripture to show us what this word *patience* means. And it behooves us to be taught if we will have God to acknowledge us to be patient in our afflictions. We commonly say a man is patient although he has no true patience in him. For men call anyone patient who suffers adversity. But let us hold this for a rule, that to be considered patient, it behooves us to moderate our sorrow. If there be any adversity, it must be assuaged by confidence that God does not cease to procure our welfare; and that we ought to be subject to him; and that it is reasonable that he should govern us according to his good pleasure. This is how patience manifests itself.

But there is nothing better or more necessary than to look in the mirror that is set before us here. We have seen that Job might have been overwhelmed by the report of so many evil tidings. But it is said that he arose and tore his clothes and sheared his head, and cast himself on the ground to humble himself before God.

Here we see first of all that those who are patient are sure to endure some grief and feel some sorrow and anguish; for if we were as stocks or stones it would be no virtue at all in us. We sometimes see a poor madman laugh and scorn the whole world, even when he is at death's door. But that is because he has no awareness of his misery. This does not deserve to be taken for patience; it is mere stupidity. Brute beasts sometimes have no feeling, but they are not patient for all that.

So then let us note that the word *patience* does not mean that men should become brutish, so that they should have no heaviness at all, or be burdened with grief when they feel adversities; but the virtue is when they moderate themselves, and so control themselves that they do not cease to glorify God in the midst of all their miseries, nor be so overburdened and swallowed up with sorrow and anguish as to give up altogether; but fight against their own passions until they are able to conform themselves to the will of God, and to conclude as Job does here, finally saying that God is righteous in every respect. — *Sermons*

9   JANUARY 9

For all flesh is as grass, and all the glory of man as the flower of grass. The grass withereth, and the flower thereof falleth away: But the word of the Lord endureth for ever. And this is the word which by the gospel is preached unto you.   I Peter 1:24, 25

Therefore being illuminated by him, we now believe the divine original of the Scripture, not from our own judgment or that of others, but we esteem the certainty that we have received it from God's own mouth by the ministry of men, to be superior to that of any human judgment, and equal to that of an intuitive perception of God himself in it. We seek not arguments or probabilities to support our judgment, but submit our judgments and understandings as to a thing which it is impossible for us to judge; and that not like some persons, who are in the habit of hastily embracing that which they do not understand, which displeases them as soon as they examine it; but because we feel the firmest conviction that we hold an invincible truth; nor like those unhappy men who surrender their minds captives to superstitions, but because we perceive in it the undoubted energies of the Divine power, by which we are attracted and inflamed to an understanding and voluntary obedience, but with vigor and efficacy superior to the power of any human will or knowledge. — *Institutes*, I, vii, v

And though after my skin worms destroy this body,
yet in my flesh shall I see God: Job 19:26

Let us not say, "I believe in God because he maintains me, because he gives me health, and because he nourishes me"; but "I believe in God because he has allowed me to taste of his goodness in preserving this body, which is but rottenness, so that I see him show himself to me as a Father in that I have being through the power of his Spirit. I believe in him alone because he calls me to heaven, and has not created me as an ox or ass to live here a little while, but has formed me after his own image, to the intent that I should hope for the inheritance of his kingdom and be partaker of the glory of his Son. I believe that he daily allures me thither, so that I should not doubt but that when my body is laid in the grave, and there consumed to nothing, notwithstanding it shall be restored again at the last day; and in the meantime my soul shall be in safe and sure keeping, because when I am dead God will have it in his protection."

And when we are so well disposed, we may say with Job, "Well, now, I see my body must go to decay. Look, whatever freshness was in it, it diminishes day by day, and I need not go far to seek death. For I see no infirmity in my flesh which is so small that it is not a messenger of death. But yet for all that I shall see my God." If we could speak thus when we see that our strength diminishes and vanishes away little by little; then although it pleased God to smite us in such a way that, so to speak, we would rot above the ground, as Job did (for he says that his skin was worm-eaten and consumed, and he was as good as dead, and yet he protests that he will not cease looking unto his God), yet we should not cease to trust God after the example of Job. This, then, is how the greatness of the afflictions that God sends us will not be to astonish us, provided that we are taught to recognize him as he is toward us; namely, to consider well to what end he has created us and maintains us in this world. — *Sermons*

A new commandment I give unto you, That ye love one another; as I have loved you, that ye also love one another. By this shall all men know that ye are my disciples, if ye have love one to another.

John 13:34, 35

"That you love one another." Brotherly love is indeed extended to strangers, for we are all of the same flesh, and are all created after the image of God; but because the image of God shines more brightly in those who have been regenerated, it is proper that the bond of love among the disciples of Christ should be far more close. In God brotherly love seeks its cause, from him it has its root, and to him it is directed. Thus in proportion as it perceives any man to be a child of God, it embraces him with the greater warmth and affection. Besides, the mutual exercise of love cannot exist but in those who are guided by the same Spirit. It is the highest degree of brotherly love, therefore, that is here described by Christ; but we ought to believe, on the other hand, that as the goodness of God extends to the whole world, so we ought to love all, even those who hate us.

"By this all men will know." Since Christ lays down this mark for distinguishing between his disciples and strangers, they who lay aside brotherly love and adopt new and invented modes of worship labor in vain. Nor is it superfluous that Christ dwells so largely on this subject. There is no greater agreement between the love of ourselves and the love of our neighbor than there is between fire and water. Self-love keeps all our senses bound in such a manner that brotherly love is altogether banished. And yet we think that we fully discharge our duty, because Satan has many enticements to deceive us that we may not perceive our faults. Whoever, then, desires to be truly a disciple of Christ and to be acknowledged by God, let him form and direct his whole life to love the brethren, and let him pursue this object with diligence.

—*Commentaries*

Thy righteousness is like the great mountains; thy judgments are a great deep: O Lord, thou preservest man and beast. Psalm 36:6

It is obvious from the context that the language of the Psalmist is to be understood in such a sense that however great the depth of wickedness which there is among men, and though it seems like a flood which breaks forth and overflows the whole earth, yet still greater is the depth of God's providence, by which he righteously disposes and governs all things. Whenever, therefore, our faith may be shaken by the confusion and disorder of human affairs, and when we are unable to explain the reasons of this disorder and confusion, let us remember that the judgments of God in the government of the world are with the highest propriety compared with a great depth which fills heaven and earth, that the consideration of its infinite greatness may ravish our minds with admiration, swallow up all our cares, and dispel all our sorrows.

—Commentaries

13   J ANUARY 13

Wherefore seeing we also are compassed about with so great a cloud of witnesses, let us lay aside every weight, and the sin which doth so easily beset us, and let us run with patience the race that is set before us, Looking unto Jesus the author and finisher of our faith; who for the joy that was set before him endured the cross, despising the shame, and is set down at the right hand of the throne of God. Hebrews 12:1, 2

There, then, it behooves you to turn your eyes during these great troubles, and to rejoice that he has esteemed you worthy of suffering affliction for his word rather than of chastisement for your sins, which we would all deserve did he not support us by his grace. And if he promises to console poor sinners who received patiently correction from his hand, be confident that the aid and comfort of his Holy Spirit will not fail you, when reposing your trust on him you shall accept the condition to which he has subjected his children.

And wait not until the great ones of this world point out to you the way, who most frequently corrupt their brethren and cause them to backslide rather than further their progress. What is more, let not each man look on his fellow to say like Peter, And this man, what of him? But let each man follow as he shall be called, seeing that each must give an account for himself. Look rather at the invincible courage of so many martyrs who have been set before us an example, and take heart to join yourself to so goodly a company; which for this reason the Apostle compares to an immense and thick cloud, as if he said that their numbers are so vast as in a manner to blind our eyes.

Moreover, according as each is placed in a higher station, let him reflect that he is so much the more bound to take the lead, and on no occasion to yield to dissimulation. Let not the noble and rich and people of rank think that they are privileged, but on the contrary let them acknowledge that God has chosen them, to be more highly glorified in them. When you shall march with such simplicity, invoking God to look upon you with compassion, it is certain that you will thus feel more relief than if each thought of escaping by subterfuge. We do not mean to say that you should with your eyes open, or without discretion, expose yourselves to the jaws of the wolf; only beware of withdrawing from the flock of our Lord Jesus Christ in order to avoid the cross, and fear more than all the deaths in the world the dispersion of the church. Otherwise what excuse will you be able to plead when our Lord Jesus Christ, his Father, and all the angels of paradise shall bring against you this reproach, that having made a profession of confessing God in life and in death, you have betrayed the faith which you had pledged?

—*Letter* (to persecuted Christians in France)

*And the Lord said unto Moses, I will do this thing
also that thou hast spoken: for thou hast found grace
in my sight, and I know thee by name. And he said,
I beseech thee, shew me thy glory.*

Exodus 33:17, 18

So the eye, accustomed to see nothing but black, judges
that to be very white which is but whitish, or perhaps brown.
Indeed, the senses of our bodies may assist us in discovering
how grossly we err in estimating the powers of the soul. For
if at noonday we look either on the ground, or at any sur-
rounding objects, we conclude our vision to be very strong
and piercing; but when we raise our eyes and steadily look at
the sun, they are at once dazzled and confounded with such
a blaze of brightness, and we are constrained to confess that
our sight, so piercing in viewing terrestrial things, when
directed to the sun is dimness itself. Thus also it happens in
the consideration of our spiritual endowments. For as long
as our views are bounded by the earth, perfectly content with
our own righteousness, wisdom, and strength, we fondly flatter
ourselves, and fancy we are little less than demigods. But if
we once elevate our thoughts to God, and consider his nature,
and the consummate perfection of his righteousness, wisdom,
and strength, to which we ought to be conformed — what before charmed us in ourselves under the false pretext of righteousness will soon be loathed as the greatest iniquity; what
strangely deceived us under the title of wisdom, will be despised as extreme folly; and what wore the appearance of
strength will be proved to be most wretched impotence. So
very remote from the divine purity is what seems in us the
highest perfection. — *Institutes*, I, i, ii

So after he had washed their feet, and had taken his garments, and was set down again, he said unto them, Know ye what I have done to you? John 13:12

"When then he had washed their feet . . ." Had it not been for the opposition made by Peter, Christ would not have spoken on that subject. Now, therefore, he discloses the reason of what he had done; namely, that he who is the Master and Lord of all gave an example to be followed by all the godly, that none might grudge to descend to do a service to his brethren and equals, however mean and low that service might be. For the reason why the love of the brethren is despised is that every man thinks of himself more highly than he ought, and despises almost every other person. Nor did he merely intend to inculcate modesty, but likewise to lay down this rule of brotherly love, that they should serve one another; for there is no brotherly love where there is not a voluntary subjection in assisting a neighbor.

"Know you what I have done?" We see that Christ for a short time concealed his intention from his disciples, but that, after having tried their obedience, he seasonably revealed to them that which it was not expedient for them previously to know. Nor does he now wait till they ask, but of his own accord anticipates them. The same thing will be experienced by us also, provided that we suffer ourselves to be guided by his hand, even through unknown ways.

—*Commentaries*

He was oppressed, and he was afflicted, yet he opened not his mouth: he is brought as a lamb to the slaughter, and as a sheep before her shearers is dumb, so he openeth not his mouth. He was taken from prison and from judgment: and who shall declare his generation? for he was cut off out of the land of the living: for the transgression of my people was he stricken.

Isaiah 53:7, 8

Since the *age* of our Lord Jesus Christ never comes to an end, and no change will ever prevent him from being careful to guard his Church, even were the temptations much greater and more violent than they are, we may be full of assurance. And that needs to be applied, not only to the whole community of the faithful, but also to each individual. Let us then know and be well persuaded that, even though our life be but a breath and we are ready each moment to vanish away, yet we have an unending life, because we are members of our Lord Jesus Christ. And moreover, let us learn to pass by this world, since what we enjoy at present is not our life but a road along which we must run swiftly, until we arrive at the rest in our inheritance. Hoping for life eternal, we must leave all this, which is nothing but a shadow; and our senses must not be wrapped up in all the things that are apparent to us and which can make us settle down in the world. For all who keep themselves to this world certainly separate themselves from the Son of God and become unworthy of any part or lot in his eternity. So then, let us withdraw from this world if we would be joined to the Son of God. — *Sermons*

JANUARY 17

*No lion shall be there, nor any ravenous beast shall
go up thereon, it shall not be found there; but the redeemed shall walk there:*   Isaiah 35:9

"There shall not be a lion . . ." We may draw from this
a profitable doctrine, namely, that God not only begins, but
conducts to the end, the work of our salvation, that his grace
in us may not be useless and unprofitable. As he opens up
the way, so he paves it, and removes obstacles of every description, and is himself the leader during the whole journey.
In short, he continues his grace towards us in such a manner
that he at length brings it to perfection. And this ought to be
applied to the whole course of our life. Here we walk as on
a road, moving forward to that blessed inheritance. Satan
presents numerous obstructions, and dangers surround us on
every side; but the Lord, who goes before and leads us by
the hand, will not leave us in the midst of the journey, but at
length will perfectly finish what he has begun in us by his
Spirit (Phil. 1:6). Yet it ought to be observed that the very
beasts, through God's kindness, shall be tamed, so as not to
direct their rage and cruelty against us, as it is said, "I will
make a covenant for you with the fowls of the heaven and
with the beasts of prey" (Hosea 2:18). — *Commentaries*

*Ye have not chosen me, but I have chosen you, and
ordained you, that ye should go and bring forth fruit,
and that your fruit should remain: that whatsoever
ye shall ask of the Father in my name, he may give it
you.*   John 15:16

"That your Father may give you all that you ask in my
name." This clause was not added abruptly, as many might
suppose; for since the office of teaching far exceeds the power
of men, there are added to it innumerable attacks of Satan,
which never could be warded off, but by the power of God.
That the apostles may not be discouraged, Christ meets them
with the most valuable aid; as if he had said, "If the work assigned to you be so great that you are unable to fulfill the
duties of your office, my Father will not forsake you; for I
have appointed you to be ministers of the Gospel on this condition, that my Father will have his hand stretched out to
assist you whenever you pray to him *in my name,* to grant you
assistance." And indeed that the greater part of teachers either
languish through indolence or utterly give way through despair, arises from nothing else than that they are sluggish in
the duty of prayer. — *Commentaries*

*He openeth also their ear to discipline, and com-
mandeth that they return from iniquity.*

Job 36:10

We must be moved to think upon our sins and be sorry for
them, and then to note that Elihu adds that God then opens
our ears. That saying can mean two things in Scripture.
Sometimes it merely means to speak to us: and sometimes it
means to touch our hearts in such a way that we hear what is
said to us. God therefore opens our ears when he sends us
his Word and causes it to be set before us; and again he opens
our ears, or uncovers them (for that is what the Hebrew word
means), when he does not allow us to be deaf to his doctrine,
but causes it to find entrance into us that we may receive it,
and be moved by it, and that its power may show itself. These
are the two ways of opening our ears which we see that God
daily uses toward us.

Also he opens the ears of those whom he afflicts, in that he
gives them some sign of his wrath, thereby to teach them to
bethink themselves better than they have done. If a man ask,
"What then; does not God speak to us in prosperity?" Yes,
surely he does, but his voice cannot reach us, because we are
preoccupied with our own delights and worldly affections. And
undoubtedly we see that when men have their fill of good
cheer and make merry at their own good pleasure, and live
in health and wealth, they are overjoyed. There is then no
other conversation but about pleasure. God is no longer heard
among them. But afflictions are messengers of his wrath, and
then we are touched with his wrath, so that we come to our
senses again. So afflictions in general ought to serve for instruction to those that receive them, so that they may draw near to
God, from whom they had previously been estranged.

. . . Yet, however, men do not let themselves be governed
by God until he has softened their hearts by his Holy Spirit
and opened the passage for the warnings that he gives and

pierced men's ears in order that they may dedicate themselves
to his service and obedience . . . But since we are hard to
prick, and, what is more, we are utterly stubborn and deaf
to all the warnings that he gives us, it behooves us to pray to
him to pierce our ears and to open them in such a way to his
instructions that the same may turn to our profit: and that
he suffer not the air to be beaten without touching our heart;
but that he move us to come and return to him. Otherwise let
us know that we shall do nothing but provoke him and reject
his corrections, as experience shows in most men that those
who are beaten with God's rods do not improve thereby, but
rather grow worse. — *Sermons*

20   JANUARY 20

*If we confess our sins, he is faithful and just to forgive
us our sins, and to cleanse us from all unrighteous-
ness.*   I John 1:9

For in the Scripture one method of confession is prescribed;
which is, that since it is the Lord who forgives, forgets, and
obliterates sin, we should confess our sins to him, that we may
obtain pardon. He is a physician; to him, then, let us discover
our wounds. He is injured and offended; let us pray to him for
peace. He is the searcher of hearts, and privy to all thoughts;
let us hasten to pour out our hearts before him. Finally, it is
he who calls sinners; let us not delay to approach him. David
says, "I acknowledge my sin unto thee, and mine iniquity have
I not hid. I said, I will confess my transgressions unto the Lord,
and thou forgavest the iniquity of my sin."
Whoever from the heart makes this confession before God,
will also, without doubt, have a tongue prepared for confession, as often as it shall be necessary to proclaim the Divine
mercy among men; and not only to whisper the secret
of his mind once into the ear of an individual, but frequently
and publicly, and in the hearing of the whole world, in-
genuously to declare, both his own shame and the magnificence
and glory of God. — *Institutes*, III, iv, ix

*Sing unto the Lord a new song, and his praise from
the end of the earth, ye that go down to the sea, and
all that is therein; the isles, and the inhabitants
thereof.*   Isaiah 42:10

"Sing to Jehovah a new song . . . ." *New* is here contrasted
with what is ordinary, and thus he extols the infinite mercy of
God, which was to be revealed in Christ, and which ought
therefore to be sung with the highest praises. Hence we infer
that each of us ought to be the more zealous in proclaiming the
praises of God in proportion to the greater number of favors
which we have received. It is indeed the duty of all men to
sing praise to God, for there is no person who is not bound
to it by the strongest obligations; but more lofty praises ought
to proceed from those on whom more valuable gifts have been
bestowed. Now, since God has laid open the fountain of all
blessings in Christ, and has displayed all spiritual riches, we
need not wonder if he demand that we offer to him an unusual
and excellent sacrifice of praise.

It ought to be observed that this *song* cannot be sung but
by renewed men; for it ought to proceed from the deepest feeling of the heart, and therefore we need the direction and influence of the Spirit, that we may sing those praises in a proper
manner. Besides, he does not exhort one or a few nations to
do this, but all the nations of the world; for to all of them
Christ was sent. — *Commentaries*

*Thy children shall make haste; thy destroyers and
they that made thee waste shall go forth of thee.*

Isaiah 49:17

We ought also to pray not only that he may "send forth
laborers into his harvest" (Matthew 9:38) but that he may
recruit their strength and efficaciously direct them, so that
they may not labor in vain; for when the doctrine of the
Gospel is preached with any advantage, it arises from his extraordinary goodness. But even this would not be enough, if he
did not "drive destroyers far away." For Satan, by innumerable arts, invades and assails the Church, and is in no want
of servants and attendants, who direct their whole energy to destroy, or spoil, or hinder the Lord's building. We ought, therefore, constantly to entreat that he would ward off their attacks; and if the result be not entirely according to our expectations, let us blame our own sins and ingratitude; for the
Lord was ready to bestow those blessings abundantly upon us.

—*Commentaries*

*The Lord doth build up Jerusalem: he gathereth to-
gether the outcasts of Israel.*   Psalm 147:2

Here the Psalmist would comfort those miserable exiles
who had been scattered in various quarters, with the hope of
being recovered from their dispersion, as God had not adopted
them without a definite purpose into one body. As he had
ordered his temple and altar to be erected at Jerusalem, and
had fixed his seat there, the Psalmist would encourage the
Jews who were exiles from their native country, to entertain
good hope of a return, intimating that it was no less properly

God's work to raise up his Church when ruined and fallen down, than to found it at first. It was not, therefore, the Psalmist's object directly to celebrate the free mercy of God in the first institution of the Church, but to argue from its original, that God would not suffer his Church altogether to fall, having once founded it with the design of preserving it forever; for he forsakes not the work of his own hands. This comfort ought to be improved by ourselves at the present period, when we see the Church on every side so miserably rent asunder, leading us to hope that all the elect who have been adjoined to Christ's body will be gathered into the unity of the faith, although now scattered like members torn from one another, and that the mutilated body of the Church, which is daily distracted, will be restored to its entireness; for God will not suffer his work to fall. — *Commentaries*

24   JANUARY 24

As it is written, For thy sake we are killed all the day long; we are accounted as sheep for the slaughter. Nay, in all these things we are more than conquerors through him that loved us.   Romans 8:36, 37

It is certainly true that the whole family of believers, as long as they dwell on the earth, must be "accounted as sheep for the slaughter," that they may be conformed to Christ their Head. Their state, therefore, would be extremely deplorable, if they did not elevate their thoughts towards heaven, rise above all earthly things, and look beyond present appearances. On the contrary, when they have once raised their heads above this world, although they see the impious flourishing in riches and honors, and enjoying the most profound tranquillity; though they see them boasting of their splendor and luxury, and behold them abounding in every delight; though they may also be harassed by their wickedness, insulted by their pride, defrauded by their avarice, and may receive from them any other lawless provocations — yet they will find no difficulty in supporting themselves even under such calamities as these. For they will keep in view that day when the Lord will receive his faithful servants into his peaceful kingdom; will wipe every tear from their eyes, invest them with robes of joy, adorn them with crowns of glory, entertain them with his incomparable delights, exalt them to fellowship with his majesty, and, in a word, honor them with a participation of his happiness. But the impious, who have been great in this world, he will cast down to the lowest disgrace; he will change their delights into torments, and their laughter and mirth into weeping and gnashing of teeth; he will disturb their tranquillity with dreadful agonies of conscience, and will punish their delicacy with inextinguishable fire, and even put them in subjection to the pious, whose patience they have abused. For, according to Paul, "it is a righteous thing with God to recompense tribulation to them that trouble" the saints, "and to them who are troubled, rest, when the Lord Jesus shall be revealed from heaven." This is our holy consolation; and deprived of this, we must of necessity either sink into despondency of mind, or solace ourselves to our own destruction with the vain pleasures of the world. For even the Psalmist confesses that he staggered when he was too much engaged in contemplating the present prosperity of the impious; and that he could not otherwise establish himself, till he entered the sanctuary of God, and directed his views to the last end of the godly and of the wicked. To conclude in one word, the cross of Christ triumphs, in the hearts of believers, over the devil and the flesh, over sin and impious men, only when their eyes are directed to the power of the resurrection. — *Institutes,* III, ix, vi

*Trust in the Lord, and do good; so shalt thou dwell
in the land, and verily thou shalt be fed.*   Psalm 37:3

"Put thy trust in Jehovah and do good." It is not without
good reason that he begins with the doctrine of faith, or
trust in God. For there is nothing more difficult for men than
to preserve their minds in a state of peace and tranquillity;
undisturbed by any disquieting fears, while they are in this
world, which is subject to so many changes. On the other
hand, while they see the wicked becoming rich by unjust means,
extending their influence, and acquiring power by unrestrained
indulgence in sin, it is no less difficult for them steadily
to persevere in a life of piety and virtue. Nor is it sufficient
merely to disregard those things that are commonly sought
after with the greatest eagerness. Some of the philosophers of
antiquity were so noble-minded that they despised riches
unjustly acquired, and abstained from fraud and robbery; nay,
they held up to ridicule the vain pomp and splendor of the
wicked, which the common people look upon with such high
admiration. But as they were destitute of faith, they defrauded God of his honor, and so it happened that they never
knew what it was to be truly happy. Now, as David places
faith first in order, to show that God is the author of all
good, and that by his blessing alone prosperity is to be
looked for; so it ought to be observed that he connects this
with a holy life; for the man who places his whole confidence
in God, and gives himself up to be governed by him, will live
uprightly and innocently, and will devote himself to doing
good. — *Commentaries*

I beseech you therefore, brethren, by the mercies of God, that ye present your bodies a living sacrifice, holy, acceptable unto God, which is your reasonable service. And be not conformed to this world: but be ye transformed by the renewing of your mind, that ye may prove what is that good, and acceptable, and perfect, will of God.   Romans 12:1, 2

Even so, Madame, consider, I beseech you, if hitherto you have taken pains to serve and honor so good a master, how you can strive more earnestly than ever to arm yourself against opposition, to take courage against all difficulties in order to surmount them; for, since the worldly often manifest invincible constancy in the pursuit of their vanities, patiently enduring so many labors, troubles, and dangers, it would be too shameful if we were to grow weary in the way of salvation; although this is by no means all that is required of us, that we show ourselves steadfast in the midst of persecutions; for, even if there were no enemies to make open war upon us, we find enough of aversion and indisposedness in ourselves and all around to hinder us in making our calling sure, which all those who have a true zeal to devote themselves to God experience more fully than any one could tell them. Inasmuch, then, as I hold you to be of the number, I entreat you to exercise yourself continually in the doctrine of renouncing the world yet more and more, in order to come nearer to our Lord Jesus, who has once for all purchased us to separate us unto himself. I mean the world, such as we carry it within ourselves, before we are made again after his likeness. And seeing that our whole nature, inasmuch as by the corruption of the plague it has been depraved, is enmity against God, the kingdom of our Lord Jesus Christ cannot be duly established, until all which is ours has been beaten down; and not only the open vices which are condemned of men, but also our own reason and wisdom. I am aware that I do not speak to you of any new thing, and that by the grace of God you have long ago begun to follow in the way of the holy heavenly calling. But the study of holiness is one of which we must avail ourselves even to the end. — *Correspondence*

27   JANUARY 27

And they, continuing daily with one accord in the temple, and breaking bread from house to house, did eat their meat with gladness and singleness of heart.   Acts 2:46

The knowledge of God's love toward us, and the hope of his protection, bring us this goodness with them, that we praise God with quiet minds, no matter how the world threatens. And as Luke said earlier, speaking of the public estate of the Church, so he declares now what form and what manner of life the faithful used; that we may learn by their example a thrifty fellowship of living, and in all our whole life to embrace singleness, to enjoy the spiritual joy, and to exercise ourselves in the praises of God. Furthermore, the singleness of heart reaches far; but if you join it in this place with breaking of bread, it shall signify as much as sincere love, where one man deals plainly with another, neither does any man craftily hunt after his own profit. Yet I had rather set the same against that carefulness wherewith worldly men torment themselves too much. For when we do not cast our care upon the Lord, this reward hangs over our heads, that we tremble and quake even when we take our rest. — *Commentaries*

*I made a covenant with mine eyes; why then should I
think upon a maid?*   Job 31:1

When Saint James speaks of sin, he uses the figure of childbearing. For he says that lust conceives and afterward brings forth sin, and that sin is accomplished when it comes to the actual execution of a deed. But I say there are three degrees of fault in a sin although it does not come to an outward deed. The first is a fleeting imagination or thought which a man conceives by beholding anything; it will come to him in a fantasy here or there; or else, though he sees nothing, his mind is so inclined to evil that it runs here and there and causes many fantasies to come into his head. And without doubt, this is a fault, and yet it is not imputed to us as sin. The second degree is, that upon conceiving such a fantasy, we be somewhat interested, and feel that our will bends in that direction; and though there may be no consent or agreement to it, yet there is some inward pricking to provoke us unto it. Now that is a serious sin, and as it were, already conceived. Afterward follows consent, when we settle our wills upon it, so that there is no hindrance in us for the performance of evil but the lack of occasion and opportunity. There you see the third degree, and then the sin is finally formed in us, although there be no outward deed at all. And this is well worthy to be noted; for although it may seem a hard matter, yet notwithstanding there is no man or woman who does not have some experience from day to day with that of which I speak.

—Sermons

And she shall bring forth a son, and thou shalt call his name JESUS: for he shall save his people from their sins. Matthew 1:21

Since we see that the whole of our salvation, and all the branches of it, are comprehended in Christ, we must be cautious not to alienate from him the least possible portion of it. If we seek salvation, we are taught by the name of JESUS that it is in him; if we seek any other gifts of the Spirit, they will be found in his unction; strength in his dominion; purity in his conception; indulgence discovers itself in his nativity, by which he was made to resemble us in all things, that he might learn to condole with us; if we seek redemption, it will be found in his passion; absolution, in his condemnation; remission of the curse, in his cross; satisfaction, in his sacrifice; purification, in his blood; reconciliation, in his descent into hell; mortification of the flesh, in his sepulchre; newness of life and immortality, in his resurrection; the inheritance of the celestial kingdom, in his entrance into heaven; protection, security, abundance, and enjoyment of all blessings, in his kingdom; a fearless expectation of the judgment, in the judicial authority committed to him. Finally blessings of every kind are deposited in him; let us draw from his treasury, and from no other source, till our desires are satisfied. For they who, not content with him alone, are carried hither and thither into a variety of hopes, although they fix their eyes principally on him, nevertheless deviate from the right way in the diversion of any part of their attention to another quarter. This distrust, however, cannot intrude, where the plenitude of his blessings has once been truly known. — *Institutes,* II, xvi, xix

Neither was there any among them that lacked: for as many as were possessors of lands or houses sold them, and brought the prices of the things that were sold. Acts 4:34

Hereby it appears what it means that no man counted anything as his own, but they had all things common. For no man had his own privately to himself, that he alone might enjoy it, neglecting others; but as need required, they were ready to bestow upon all men. And now we must needs have more than flinty hearts, seeing that we are no more moved with the reading of this history. The faithful at that day gave abundantly even of that which was their own, but we are not only content at this day wickedly to suppress that which we have in our hands, but also rob others. They simply and faithfully brought forth their own; we invent a thousand subtle shifts to draw all things unto us by hook or crook. They laid it down at the apostles' feet; we fear not with sacrilegious boldness to convert that to our own use which was offered to God. They sold in times past their possessions; there reigns at this day an insatiable desire to buy. Love made that common to the poor and needy which was proper to every man; such is the unnaturalness of some men now that they cannot abide that the poor should dwell on the earth and that they should have the use of water, air, and heaven. — *Commentaries*

But as many as received him, to them gave he power
to become the sons of God, even to them that believe
on his name: John 1:12

The many words which the Evangelist has employed tend more to magnify the excellence of grace than if he had said in a single word that all who believe in Christ are made by him sons of God. For he speaks here of the unclean and profane, who, having been condemned to perpetual ignominy, lay in the darkness of death. Christ exhibited an astonishing instance of his grace in conferring this honor on such persons, so that they began, all at once, to be sons of God; and the greatness of this privilege is justly extolled by the Evangelist, as also by Paul, when he ascribes it to God, who is rich in mercy, for his great love with which he loved us (Eph. 2:4). But if any person shall prefer . . . Christ gave to the unclean and the uncircumcised what appeared to be impossible; for an incredible change took place when out of stones Christ raised up children to God (Matt. 3:9). The power, therefore, is that fitness which Paul mentions when he gives thanks to God, who hath made us fit to be partakers of the inheritance of the saints (Col. 1:12). — *Commentaries*

*Laying up in store for themselves a good foundation
against the time to come, that they may lay hold on
eternal life.*   I Timothy 6:19

We must aspire to this everlasting life, as Paul says, to conclude the matter. And when we are so minded, it is certain
that riches can hinder us no more to turn to God. Yes,
that is to say, they will be good aids and means for us, to set
us forward to our salvation; for, for this cause and for this
purpose God gave them to us. Why does God give men more of
the world's goods than they need? He wishes to test their charity, whether they be courteous or not, when he has given them
material with which to do good. And when the faithful are
rich, they have wherewith to go forward; for they are stirred up
to thank God, knowing that he has showed himself so bountiful
to them. Moreover they have to fight against pride, against the
pomp and vanity of this world, and when they resist them
through the virtue of the Holy Spirit, this is another advancement for them. And again, they consider this with themselves; I have wherewith to help my neighbors, if there be
any that want; I am bound to do them good. This is another
witness for us. And thus we see how by all means riches are
to better the children of God, and to make them draw near to
the heavenly inheritance. And therefore they that aim at everlasting life will beware that they be not held or entangled in this
world's goods; they will not turn to their confusion what God
has given them for their salvation. — *Sermons*

Go, and say to Hezekiah, Thus saith the Lord, the
God of David thy father, I have heard thy prayer,
I have seen thy tears: behold, I will add unto thy days
fifteen years.   Isaiah 38:5

"I have heard thy prayer." Having opened the door of
hope, he tells Hezekiah that God has heard his prayers. This
ought greatly to encourage us to earnestness in prayer; for,
although God of his own accord takes a deep interest in our
salvation, and anticipates us by his kindness, not only while
we are asleep, but before we were born (Rom. 9:11), yet
when he testifies that all the benefits which he bestows are
granted in answer to our prayers, our negligence is altogether
inexcusable if, after having received such large invitations,
we neglect to perform the duty of prayer. And yet we must not
imagine that prayers, to which God so graciously listens, are
meritorious; but, in giving freely what he freely promised, he
adds this as the crowning excellence of his kindness, in order
more strongly to stimulate our faith. It is no ordinary privilege to be able to approach him freely, and in a familiar
manner to lay our cares on his bosom. If Hezekiah had not
prayed, God would undoubtedly have secured that, in one way
or another, some government of the kingdom should be preserved in the posterity of David; but what he would do from a
regard to his truth, he says that he will give in answer to the
prayers of Hezekiah, that he may acknowledge that he has
obtained very abundant fruit from his faith which he exercised in prayer. — *Commentaries*

And lest, when I come again, my God will humble me among you, and that I shall bewail many which have sinned already, and have not repented of the uncleanness and fornication and lasciviousness which they have committed.   II Corinthians 12:21

It is not necessary in all cases publicly to make men witnesses of our repentance; but a private confession to God is a branch of true penitence which cannot be omitted. For nothing is more unreasonable than that God should pardon sins, in which we encourage ourselves, and which, lest he should bring them to light, we conceal under the garb of hypocrisy. And it is not only necessary to confess the sins which we commit from day to day; more grievous falls ought to lead us further, and to recall to our remembrance those which appear to have been long buried in oblivion . . . . It is further to be remarked that the repentance we are commanded constantly to practise differs from that which arouses, as it were, from death, those who have either fallen into some great enormity, or abandoned themselves to a course of sin with unrestrained license, or by any rebellion shaken off the Divine yoke . . . . The special repentance, therefore, which is only required of some whom the devil has seduced from the fear of God and entangled in his fatal snares, does not supersede that ordinary repentance which the corruption of our nature obliges us to practise during the whole course of our lives.

—*Institutes,* III, iii, xviii

FEBRUARY 4

*Paul, an apostle of Jesus Christ by the commandment
of God our Saviour, and Lord Jesus Christ, which is
our hope; Unto Timothy, my own son in the faith:
Grace, mercy, and peace, from God our Father and
Jesus Christ our Lord.* I Timothy 1:1, 2

Are we beloved of God? Are we grounded and stayed fast
upon his grace? He will send us what he shall think meet for
us . . . . He will send his children what he knows is good for
them, and if they have any want or need, he will comfort them,
so that they may rejoice in the midst of their miseries; as Saint
Paul says, that when we have this assurance of the love of
God, that our souls rest on him, we may rejoice not only for
the hope which he gives us of everlasting life, but also in
this present life, because we know that he loves us; although we
are afflicted, yet we rejoice, because we know that he will turn
all to our salvation, seeing he already gives us the feeling
that he takes care of us. See how miseries shall serve the
children of God, and by this means they may rejoice in them.
Now then we see how the grace of God is the beginning of all
goodness and of all blessedness. And it is not without cause
that Saint Paul joins them together. And thereby we also are
taught not to set the cart before the horse when we ask of
God that which is good for us. — *Sermons*

*Then Jesus turned, and saw them following, and saith
unto them, What seek ye? They said unto him, Rabbi,
(which is to say, being interpreted, Master,) where
dwellest thou?*   John 1:38

Here we see how small and low the beginning of the Church
was. John, indeed, prepared disciples for Christ, but it is only
now that Christ begins to collect a Church. He has no more
than two men who are mean and unknown, but this even contributes to illustrate his glory, that within a short period, without human aid, and without a strong hand, he spreads his
kingdom in a wonderful and incredible manner. We ought also
to observe what is the chief object to which John directs the
attention of men; it is, to find in Christ the forgiveness of sins.
And as Christ had presented himself to the disciples for the
express purpose that they might come to him, so now, when
they come, he gently encourages and exhorts them; for he does
not wait until they first address him, but asks, "What do you
seek?" This kind and gracious invitation, which was once
made to two persons, now belongs to all. We ought not therefore to fear that Christ will withdraw from us, or refuse to us
easy access, provided that he sees us desirous to come to him;
but, on the contrary, he will stretch out his hand to assist our
efforts. And how will he not meet those who come to him, who
seeks at a distance those who are wandering and astray, that
he may bring them back to the right road? — *Commentaries*

Though the Lord be high, yet hath he respect unto the lowly: but the proud he knoweth afar off.

                                     Psalm 138:6

    The meaning is, that though God's glory is far above all heavens, the distance at which he is placed does not prevent his governing the world by his providence. God is highly exalted, but he sees afar off, so that he needs not change place when he would condescend to take care of us. We on our part are poor and lowly, but our wretched condition is no reason why God will not concern himself about us. While we view with admiration the immensity of his glory as raised above all heavens, we must not disbelieve his willingness to foster us under his fatherly care. The two things are, with great propriety, joined together here by David, that, on the one hand, when we think of God's majesty we should not be terrified into a forgetfulness of his goodness and kindness, nor, on the other, lose our reverence for his majesty in contemplating the condescension of his mercy. — *Commentaries*

*Then the eyes of the blind shall be opened, and the
ears of the deaf shall be unstopped.*   Isaiah 35:5

"Then shall the eyes of the blind be opened . . ." The eyes
cannot see what is right and the ears cannot hear, and the
feet cannot guide us in the right way, till we are united to
Christ. Though the senses of men are abundantly acute whenever they are impelled by sinful passions; though the tongue is
eloquent for slander, lying, and every kind of foolish speaking; though the hands are too ready for thefts, extortions, and
cruelty; though the feet are swift to do injury; and, in short,
though the whole of our nature is not only willing but strongly
bent on doing what is evil; yet we are altogether slothful and
dull to do what is good, and therefore every part of us must
be created anew by the power of Christ, that it may begin to
understand aright, to feel, to speak, and to perform its offices;
for "no man can say that Jesus is the Lord, but by the Holy
Spirit" (I Cor. 12:3). — *Commentaries*

*Behold, my servant shall deal prudently, he shall be
exalted and extolled, and be very high.*   Isaiah 52:13

And we ought not to think it strange that he is called the
Servant of God, seeing that he has not refused to be even our
Servant, which is far more wonderful. For if we take not of
ourselves, we are but vanity, mere worms of the earth; ruled,
even, by the devil and sin. Yet God's only Son abases himself
to the extent of employing himself as our Servant — as St.
Paul says: "He is the minister of the circumcision." Furthermore, the Prophet particularly used this word to teach us that
everything he relates here is for the common good and salvation of the whole Church. Now we must look at the task
to which Jesus Christ has been called — to be the Redeemer
of all believers and all the elect of God. Since it is true then,

that this is the work committed to him and to which he is
called, let us not doubt that all that is said of this person is
common also to us and that we also profit from what follows.

—Sermons

40 FEBRUARY 9

*By whom we have received grace and apostleship,
for obedience to the faith among all nations, for his
name:* Romans 1:5

The same divine word is the foundation by which faith is
sustained and supported, from which it cannot be moved without an immediate downfall. Take away the word, then, and
there will be no faith left. We are not here disputing whether
the ministry of men be necessary to disseminate the word of
God, by which faith is produced, which we shall discuss in
another place; but we assert, that the word itself, in whatever
way it may be conveyed to us, is like a mirror, in which faith
may behold God. Whether, therefore, God in this instance uses
the agency of men, or whether he operates solely by his own
power, he always discloses himself by his Word to those whom
he designs to draw to himself. From this Paul defines faith
as an obedience rendered to the gospel, and praises the service
of faith. For the understanding of faith is not confined to our
knowing that there is a God, but chiefly consists in our understanding what is his disposition towards us. For it is not of so
much importance to us to know what he is in himself, as what
he is willing to be to us. We find, therefore, that faith is a
knowledge of the will of God respecting us, received from his
word. And the foundation of this is a previous persuasion of
the Divine reliability; if we entertain any doubt of this in the
mind, the authority of the word will be dubious and weak, or
rather it will be no authority at all. Nor is it sufficient to believe that the veracity of God is incapable of deception or
falsehood, unless you also admit, as beyond all doubt, that
whatever proceeds from him is sacred and inviolable truth.

—Institutes, III, ii, vi

Doth not behave itself unseemly, seeketh not her own,
is not easily provoked, thinketh no evil;
I Corinthians 13:5

Here, then, we must rest, that our life will then be governed according to the will of God, and the prescriptions of his law, when it is in all respects most beneficial to our brethren. But we do not find in the whole law one syllable that lays down any rule for a man respecting those things which he should practise or omit for his carnal convenience. And surely, since men are born in such a state that they are entirely governed by an immoderate self-love — a passion which, however great their departure from the truth, they always retain — there was no need of a law which would inflame that love, already of itself too violent. Whence it plainly appears that the observance of the commandments consists not in the love of ourselves, but in the love of God and of our neighbor; that his is the best and most holy life who lives as little as possible to himself; and that no man leads a worse or more iniquitous life than he who lives exclusively to himself, and makes his own interest the sole object of his thoughts and pursuits. Moreover the Lord, in order to give us the best expression of the strength of that love which we ought to exercise towards our neighbors, has regulated it by the standard of our self-love, because there was no stronger or more vehement affection.

—Institutes, II, viii, liv

*Hold fast the form of sound words, which thou hast
heard of me, in faith and love which is in Christ Jesus.
That good thing which was committed unto thee keep
by the Holy Ghost which dwelleth in us.*

II Timothy 1:13, 14

They that have received any grace are so much the more
bound to God, and their burden is so much the greater. And
if a man should give his friend all his goods to keep, and the
key of his strongbox where all his treasure is, and should deliver all his writings into his hands, this is a charge committed
to a man. So God commits to us that which he has, and that
which pertains to him only; he commits it to us, not that we
should be lords of it and keep it to ourselves. Truth it is that
the graces which we have received of God are ours, and we
may also call them so; but it is not to be said that he has given
up all his rights to us, that he must not always be glorified by
them, and that we must not refer them all to him. We see
then how Paul warns them here, which have received graces,
which have any charge and commission, that they must give up
an account to God. And therefore let them not think that
they may apply them to whatever use they wish, but they must
make them serve their neighbors, that God may be honored by
them, and that Jesus Christ may always have the pre-eminence.
And if they do not shoot at this mark, they are sacrilegious, and
God will plead the matter with them. For if a man should deceive his friend when he has delivered his goods into his hands,
putting his trust in him, if such a one be a thief and keep
away that which was committed to his charge, or waste that
which was committed to him, shall we not be guilty before God
if we abuse his graces? — *Sermons*

Seeing then that we have a great high priest, that is passed into the heavens, Jesus the Son of God, let us hold fast our profession. For we have not an high priest which cannot be touched with the feeling of our infirmities; but was in all points tempted like as we are, yet without sin. Let us therefore come boldly unto the throne of grace, that we may obtain mercy, and find grace to help in time of need.

Hebrews 4:14-16

The vast importance of this we are taught by that solemn oath which "the Lord hath sworn, and will not repent; Thou art a priest forever, after the order of Melchizedek." For there is no doubt that God intended to establish that capital point, which he knew to be the principal hinge on which our salvation turns. And as we have observed, there is no access to God, either for ourselves or our prayers, unless our Priest sanctify us by taking away our sins, and obtain for us that grace from which we are excluded by the pollution of our vices and crimes. Thus we see it is necessary to begin with the death of Christ, in order to experience the efficacy and utility of his priesthood. Hence it follows that he is an eternal intercessor, and that it is by his intervention that we obtain favor with God. Hence proceeds not only confidence in prayer, but also tranquillity to the consciences of the faithful; while they recline in safety on the fatherly mercy of God, and are certainly persuaded that he is pleased with whatever is consecrated to him through the Mediator. — *Institutes*, II, xv, vi

*Which executeth judgment for the oppressed: which
giveth food to the hungry. The Lord looseth the
prisoners: The Lord openeth the eyes of the blind:
the Lord raiseth them that are bowed down: the
Lord loveth the righteous.*   Psalm 146:7, 8

We learn from this that he is not always so indulgent to
his own as to lead them with abundance, but occasionally withdraws his blessing, that he may help them when reduced to
hunger. Had the Psalmist said that God fed his people with
abundance, and pampered them, would not those in want or in
famine have immediately desponded? The goodness of God is
therefore properly extended farther to the feeding of the
hungry. What is added is to the same purpose — that he looses
them that are bound, and enlightens the blind. As it is the
fate of his people to be pressed by anxiety, or oppressed by
human tyranny, or reduced to extremity, in a manner equivalent to being shut up in the worst of dungeons, it was necessary to announce, by way of comfort, that God can easily find
a way out for us when brought into such trouble. To enlighten
the blind is the same as giving light in the midst of darkness.
When at any time we know not what to do — are in perplexity,
and lie confounded and dismayed, as if the darkness of death
had fallen upon us — let us learn to ascribe this title to God,
that he may dissipate the gloom and open our eyes. So when
he is said to raise up the bowed down, we are taught to take
courage when weary and groaning under any burden. Nor is
it merely that God would here have his praises celebrated; he
in a manner stretches out his hand to the blind, the captives,
and the afflicted, that they may cast their griefs and cares upon
him. There is a reason for repeating the name of Jehovah
three times. In this way he stimulates and excites men to seek
him who will often rather chafe and pine away in their miseries than betake themselves to this sure refuge. What is
added in the close of the verse — that Jehovah loves the right-

eous — would seem to be a qualification of what was formerly said. There are evidently many who, though they are grievously afflicted, and groan with anxiety, and lie in darkness, experience no comfort from God; and this because in such circumstances they provoke God more by their stubbornness, and by failing for the most part to seek his mercy; thus they reap the just reward of their unthankfulness. The Psalmist therefore very properly restricts what he had said in general terms of God's helping the afflicted, to the righteous — that those who wish to experience his deliverance may address themselves to him in the sincere exercise of godliness. — *Commentaries*

45   FEBRUARY 14

Who hath believed our report? and to whom is the
arm of the Lord revealed?   Isaiah 53:1

And therefore we must be equipped and armed against this sight — put before our eyes by the devil — of so many men resisting the Gospel, even the greatest men and those with some reputation in the world. For then it seems to us not to be God's Word. And why? Because we pay too much regard to men. In this way our faith is shaken. So let us rise above all that is earthly and know that when God speaks we must submit to him, and though none should be on our side but all against us, let us not fail to accept with a sincere faith what God declares. And, moreover, lest we should be surprised that men are so perverse as to fight against their God, against him who has created them, even him who has declared that he is their Redeemer, let us know that faith is not given to all, but is a singular gift that God keeps as a treasure for those he has chosen; and let us know that our duty is to cleave to him, knowing the while that none of us gains faith by his own effort, but God has enlightened us and given us eyes by his Holy Spirit, and in so doing has declared his power — that is to say, he has given us a lively feeling of it in our hearts, so that we know that the Gospel comes, not from men, but from him.

—*Sermons*

Verily, verily, I say unto thee, We speak that we do
know, and testify that we have seen; and ye receive
not our witness.   John 3:11

"You receive not our testimony." This is added, that the
gospel may lose nothing on account of the ingratitude of men.
For since few persons are to be found who exercise faith in the
truth of God, and since the truth is everywhere rejected by the
world, we ought to defend it against contempt, that its majesty
may not be held in less estimation, because the world despises
it, and obscures it by impiety. Now though the meaning of
the words be simple and one, still we must draw from this
passage a twofold doctrine. The first is, that our faith in
the gospel may not be weakened, if it have few disciples on
earth; as if Christ had said, "Though you receive not my doctrine, it remains nevertheless certain and durable; for the unbelief of men will never prevent God from remaining always
true." The other is, that they who, in the present day, dis-
believe the gospel, will not escape with impunity, since the
truth of God is holy and sacred. We ought to be fortified with
this shield, that we may persevere in obedience to the gospel
in opposition to the obstinacy of men. True indeed, we must
hold by this principle, that our faith be founded on God. But
when we have God as our security, we ought, like persons
elevated above the heavens, boldly to tread the whole world
under our feet, or regard it with lofty disdain, rather than
allow the unbelief of any person whatever to fill us with alarm.
As to the complaint which Christ makes, that his testimony
is not received, we learn from it that the word of God has in
all ages been distinguished by this peculiar feature, that they
who believed it were few; for the expression — you receive
not — belongs to the greater number, and almost to the whole
body of the people. There is no reason, therefore, that we
should now be discouraged if the number of those who believe
be small. — *Commentaries*

The sun shall be turned into darkness, and the moon into blood, before that great and notable day of the Lord come: Acts 2:20

We must first note that because men are too slow to receive Christ, they must be constrained by divers afflictions, as it were with whips. Secondly, forasmuch as Christ calls to himself all those who labor and are heavy laden, we must first be tamed by many miseries, that we may learn humility. For through great prosperity men set up the horns of pride. And he cannot but despise Christ fiercely, whoever he be that seems to himself to be happy. Thirdly, because we are, more than we ought, set upon seeing the peace of the flesh, whereby it comes to pass that many tie the grace of Christ to the present life, it is expedient for us to be accustomed to think otherwise, that we may know that the kingdom of Christ is spiritual. Therefore, to the end that God may teach us that the good things of Christ are heavenly, he exercises us, according to the flesh, with many miseries; whereby it comes to pass that we seek our happiness outside the world. — *Commentaries*

But thou, when thou prayest, enter into thy closet, and when thou hast shut thy door, pray to thy Father which is in secret; and thy Father which seeth in secret shall reward thee openly. Matthew 6:6

It is highly worthy of observation that whoever engages in prayer should apply all his faculties and attention to it, and not be distracted, as is commonly the case, with wandering thoughts; nothing being more contrary to a reverence for God than such levity, which indicates a licentious spirit, wholly unrestrained by fear. In this case our exertions must be great in proportion to the difficulty we experience. For no man can be intent on praying, but he may perceive many irregular thoughts intruding on him, and either interrupting, or by some oblique digression retarding him in the course of his devotions. But here let us consider what an indignity it is when God admits us to familiar intercourse with him, to abuse such great condescension by a mixture of things sacred and profane, while our thoughts are not confined to him by reverential awe; but as if we are conversing with a mean mortal, we leave him in the midst of our prayer, and make excursions on every side. We may be assured, therefore, that none are rightly prepared for the exercise of prayer, but those who are so affected by the Divine Majesty as to come to it divested of all earthly cares and affections. — *Institutes*, III, xx, iv

And he said unto me, Son of man, I send thee to the children of Israel, to a rebellious nation that hath rebelled against me: they and their fathers have transgressed against me, even unto this very day.

Ezekiel 2:3

We must bear in mind, then, this principle; when God wishes to stir us up to obedience, he does not always promise a happy result of our labor; but sometimes he so puts our obedience to the test, that he wishes us to be content with his command, even if our labor should be deemed ridiculous before men. Sometimes, indeed, he indulges our infirmity, and when he orders us to undertake any duty, he at the same time bears witness that our labor shall not be in vain, and our industry without its recompense. Then indeed God spares us.

But he sometimes proves his people as I have said, providing that whatever is the result of their labors, it is sufficient for them to obey his commands. And from this passage we readily see that our prophet was dispirited. And we read the same of Isaiah; for when he is sent by God, he is not only told that he must speak to the deaf, but what God proposes to him is still harder. Go, says he, render the eyes of this people blind, and their ears dull, and their heart obstinate (Is. 6:9, 10). Not only therefore does Isaiah see that he would be exposed to ridicule and thus lose the fruit of his labors, but he sees that his address has but one tendency, and that the blinding of the Jews: . . . God sometimes so wishes his servants to acquiesce in his government that they should labor even without any hope of fruit; and this must be diligently marked.

For as often as we are called upon by God, before we apply ourselves to our work, these thoughts come into the mind: "What will be the result of this?" and "What shall I obtain by my labor?" And then when the event does not turn out according to our wish, we despond in our minds: but this is wresting from God a part of his government. For although our labor should be in vain, yet it is sufficiently pleasing to God himself; therefore let us learn to leave the event in the hand of God when he enjoins anything upon us; and although the whole world should deride us, and despair itself should render us inactive, yet let us be of good cheer and strive to the utmost, because it ought to suffice us that our obedience is pleasing to God. — *Commentaries*

50   FEBRUARY 19

And shewing mercy unto thousands of them that love me, and keep my commandments.   Exodus 20:6

God gives a promise to extend his mercy to a thousand generations; which also frequently occurs in the Scripture, and is inserted in the solemn covenant with the Church, "I will be a God unto thee and to thy seed after thee." In allusion to this, Solomon says that "the children of the just man are blessed after him;" not only as the effect of a religious education, which is of no small importance, but also in consequence of the blessing promised in the covenant, that the grace of God shall perpetually remain in the families of the pious. This is a source of peculiar consolation to the faithful, but to the impious of great terror; for if, even after death, the memory of righteousness and iniquity has so much influence with God, that the curse of the one and the blessing of the other will redound to posterity, much more will it remain on the persons of the actors themselves. Now it is no objection to our argument that the descendants of the impious sometimes grow better, while those of the faithful degenerate; since the Legislator never intended to establish in this case such an invariable rule as would derogate from his own free choice. For it is sufficient for the consolation of the righteous and the terror of the sinner that the denunciation is not vain or ineffective, although it be not always executed . . . . He also gives a brief suggestion of the greatness of his mercy, which he extends to a thousand generations, while he has assigned only four generations to his vengeance. — *Institutes*, II, viii, xxi

Then Jesus turned, and saw them following, and saith
unto them, What seek ye? They said unto him,
Rabbi, (which is to say, being interpreted, Master,)
where dwellest thou?   John 1:38

"Where dwellest thou?" By this example we are taught that
from the first rudiments of the Church we ought to draw such a
relish for Christ as will excite our desire to profit. And next, that
we ought not to be satisfied with a mere passing look, but that
we ought to seek his dwelling, that he may receive us as
guests. For there are very many who smell the gospel at a distance only, and thus allow Christ suddenly to disappear, and all
that they have learned concerning him to pass away.

The circumstance of Andrew immediately bringing his
brother expresses the nature of faith, which does not conceal or
quench the light, but rather spreads it in every direction.
Andrew has scarcely a spark, and yet, by means of it, he enlightens his brother. Woe to our indolence, therefore, if we do
not, after having been fully enlightened, endeavor to make
others partakers of the same grace.

We may observe in Andrew two things which Isaiah requires from the children of God; namely, that each should take
his neighbor by the hand; and next, that he should say, "Come,
let us go up into the mountain of the Lord, and he will teach
us" (Is. 2:3). For Andrew stretches out the hand to his
brother, but at the same time he has the object in view that he
may become a fellow disciple in the school of Christ. We
ought also to observe the purpose of God, which determined
that Peter, who was to be far more eminent, was brought to
the knowledge of Christ by the agency of Andrew; that none
of us, however excellent, may refuse to be taught by an inferior; for that man will be severely punished for his peevish-
ness, or rather for his pride, who, through his contempt of a
man, will not deign to come to Christ. — *Commentaries*

52   FEBRUARY 21

*And I thank Christ Jesus our Lord, who hath enabled
me, for that he counted me faithful, putting me into
the ministry;*   I Timothy 1:12

True it is that it pleased God that his gospel should be
preached by men, which are frail creatures, and oftentimes of
small account; but is it therefore to be said that because the
pot is not worth a farthing the treasure which is hidden in it
is the worse, or to be accounted of less value? Is the gold of
less value because of the vessel wherein it is? We know this
is not so. So then, although our Lord sent us his word by
mortal man, yet must we not therefore take occasion to make
no account of it. And why so? Because it is always a glorious
word. If there be majesty in God, it must needs be known in
this, and whosoever scoffs and jests at this word, it is just the
same as if he spat in God's face or cast stones against his
kingly seat. — *Sermons*

53   FEBRUARY 22

*Surely he hath borne our griefs, and carried our sor-
rows: yet we did esteem him stricken, smitten of God,
and afflicted. But he was wounded for our transgressions, he was bruised for our iniquities: the chastisement of our peace was upon him; and with his
stripes we are healed.*   Isaiah 53:4, 5

So then it is impossible that God should have mercy on us
and that we should be assured of finding favour before him
until the correction be made. Not that God demands vengeance in the same way as men. A man who is angry will want
reparation made for the injury and some amends, and punish-

ment meted out, so that he may be avenged. God has not passions like these. But all the same, in order that we may be the more horrified by our sins and that we may learn to detest them, he wishes us to be aware of his righteousness and the severity of his judgment. If God pardoned us without Jesus Christ interceding for us and being made our pledge, we should think nothing of it. We should all shrug our shoulders and make it an opportunity for giving ourselves greater license. But when we see that God did not spare his only Son, but treated him with such an extreme severity that in his body he underwent all the sorrows that it would be possible to suffer and that even in his soul he was afflicted to the limit, to the point of crying out, "My God, my God, why hast thou forsaken me?" — when we hear all this, it is impossible for us, unless we are harder than stone, not to shudder and be filled with such a fear and amazement as will utterly put us to confusion; impossible not to detest our offences and iniquities seeing that they provoke the anger of God against us in this way. This, then, is why it was necessary for all the correction of our peace to be laid upon Jesus Christ that we might find grace before God his Father; that is to say, that we might have a settlement with him, so that we today may have boldness and liberty to call upon God as our Father, although with good cause he is our enemy and abhors us so far as our nature is concerned. So now we see what the Prophet means by saying that our Lord Jesus Christ was afflicted by the hand of God, that he was disfigured, that everyone turned his back on him and did not condescend to look upon him, because he was without beauty.

—*Sermons*

*Now the end of the commandment is charity out of a
pure heart, and of a good conscience, and of faith
unfeigned:*   I Timothy 1:5

Let us conclude, then, that faith is not merely in the brain,
that it is no simple and bare knowledge, but it is an assurance
which we have of the goodness of our God. And this it is
that Saint Paul says in another place, for he compares the
gospel to a looking glass, where God's face shows itself in the
person of our Lord Jesus Christ, and it is said that in beholding his face we are changed from glory to glory to resemble
God. And Saint James also, when he shows how we ought
to profit in the word of God, says that we must not have as it
were a looking glass wherein a man goes and beholds his face,
but as soon as he has turned his back sees it no more; we
must not, says Saint James, have such a knowledge which vanishes away, and has no constancy in it, nor sure ground. For
there is indeed a figure in a looking glass, but it is nothing but a
representation. How then? Let us have that looking glass of
which Saint Paul speaks; that is to say, that in beholding God's
face in it, we may be changed into it, and be made like unto
him. And because this cannot be done in one day, we must
grow up therein; and therefore he says from glory to glory. If
we cannot at the first attempt be fully made like to the image
of our God, let us at least strive unto it, and let us be more and
more like it all the days of our life. — *Sermons*

*And they shall be mine, saith the Lord of hosts, in
that day when I make up my jewels; and I will spare
them, as a man spareth his own son that serveth him.*
Malachi 3:17

See how all our works, if estimated according to the rigor
of the law, are subject to its curse. How, then, could unhappy
souls apply themselves with alacrity to any work for which they
could expect to receive nothing but a curse? On the contrary,
if they are liberated from the severe exaction of the law, or
rather from the whole of its rigor, and hear God calling them
with fatherly gentleness, then with cheerfulness and prompt
alacrity they will answer to his call and follow his guidance.
In short, they who are bound by the yoke of the law are like
slaves who have certain daily tasks appointed by their masters.
They think they have done nothing, and presume not to enter
into the presence of their masters without having finished the
work prescribed to them. But children, who are treated by
their parents in a more liberal manner, hesitate not to present
to them their imperfect and in some respects faulty works, in
confidence that their obedience and promptitude of mind will
be accepted by them, though they have not performed all that
they wished. Such children ought we to be, feeling a certain
confidence that our services, however small, rude, and imperfect,
will be approved by our most indulgent father. This he also
confirms to us by the prophet; "I will spare them," says he,
"as a man spareth his own son that serveth him." It is evident
from the mention of *service,* that the word *spare* is used to denote indulgence, or an overlooking of faults. And we have
great need of this confidence, without which all our endeavors
will be vain; for God considers us as serving him in none of
our works, but such as are truly done by us to his honor. But
how can this be done in the midst of those terrors, where it is a
matter of doubt whether our works offend God or honor him?
—*Institutes,* III, xix, v

*All we like sheep have gone astray; we have turned
every one to his own way; and the Lord hath laid on
him the iniquity of us all.*   Isaiah 53:6

In his wound we have healing. He again directs us to
Christ, that we may betake ourselves to his wounds, provided
that we wish to regain life. Here the Prophet draws a contrast
between us and Christ; for in us nothing can be found but destruction and death; in Christ alone is life and salvation. He
alone brought medicine to us, and even procures health by his
weakness and life by his death; for he alone has pacified the
Father, he alone has reconciled us to him. Here we might bring
forward many things about the blessed consequences of Christ's
sufferings, if we had not determined to expound rather than to
preach; but let us be satisfied with a plain exposition. Let
everyone, therefore, draw consolation from this passage, and
let him apply the blessed result of this doctrine to his own
use, for these words are spoken to all in general, and to
individuals in particular. — *Commentaries*

*Charge them that are rich in this world, that they be
not highminded, nor trust in uncertain riches, but in
the living God, who giveth us richly all things to
enjoy;*   I Timothy 6:17

Whereby we protest that it is God's part to feed us, as a
father cherishes his children. God has so referred this to
himself, that he will have us crave our nourishment at his
hands. And Paul says that he gives us all things richly.
Not that we have all that we wish for, and that God fills us; for
we know that our appetites will never be satisfied; and if God
should give us whatever we would ask, it would be enough to
choke us, for we are unsatiable whirlpools, and the question is
not only to content us in measure and soberly, but every one of
us would swim in the pleasures of this world and play the glut-
tons without measure, yes, and we would not only cram in without all order and excessively, but we would have and scrape
goods together such as to put our eyes out, and to stifle us
with abundance. Such we are by nature.

Therefore God does not give us richly according to our
own desire whatever we want, but yet he is not so niggardly
but that he nourishes us his children as he knows is best and
most suitable for us. Thus we see God's bounty, that he does
not fail the poor world, but feeds them that commit themselves
to him and call upon him. And if he has a care over all, will
he despise his faithful? Will he forget them? — *Sermons*

But he, willing to justify himself, said unto Jesus,
And who is my neighbour? Luke 10:29

Now, since Christ has demonstrated in the parable of the
Samaritan that the word "neighbor" comprehends every man,
even the greatest stranger, we have no reason to limit the commandment of love to our relations or friends. I do not deny
that the more closely a person is united to us, the greater
claim he has to the assistance of our kind offices. For the
condition of humanity requires that men should perform more
acts of kindness to each other, in proportion to the closeness
of the bonds by which they are connected, whether of relation-
ship, or acquaintance, or vicinity; and this without any offense
to God, by whose providence we are constrained to it. But I
assert that the whole human race, without any exception, should
be comprehended in the same affection of love, and that in this
respect there is no difference between the barbarian and the
Grecian, the worthy and the unworthy, the friend and the foe;
for they are to be considered in God, and not in themselves,
and whenever we deviate from this view of the subject, it is no
wonder if we fall into many errors. Wherefore if we wish to
adhere to the true law of love, our eyes must chiefly be directed, not to man, the prospect of whom would impress us with
hatred more frequently than with love, but to God, who commands that our love to him be diffused among all mankind; so
that this must always be a fundamental maxim with us, that
whatever be the character of a man, yet we ought to love him
because we love God. — *Institutes*, II, viii, lv

*Now consider this, ye that forget God, lest I tear you
in pieces, and there be none to deliver.*   Psalm 50:22

Now consider this, ye that forget God . . . . While the
Psalmist threatens and intends to alarm them, he would, at
the same time, hold out to them the hope of pardon, upon their
hastening to avail themselves of it. But to prevent them from
giving way to delay, he warns them of the severity, as well as
the suddenness, of the divine judgments. He also charges
them with base ingratitude, in having forgotten God. And
here what a remarkable proof we have of the grace of God in
extending the hope of mercy to those corrupt men, who had so
impiously profaned his worship, who had so audaciously and
sacrilegiously mocked at his forbearance, and who had abandoned themselves to such scandalous crimes!

In calling them to repentance, without all doubt he extends
to them the hope of God being reconciled to them, that they
may venture to appear in the presence of his majesty. And can
we conceive of greater clemency than this, thus to invite to himself, and into the bosom of the Church, such guilty apostates
and violators of his covenant, who had departed from the doctrine of godliness in which they had been brought up? Great as
it is, we would do well to reflect that it is no greater than what
we ourselves have experienced. We, too, had fallen away from
the Lord, and in his singular mercy he has brought us again
into his fold. It should not escape our notice that the Psalmist
urges them to hasten their return, as the door of mercy will not
always stand open for their admission — a needful lesson to us
all! lest we allow the day of our merciful visitation to pass
by, and be left, like Esau, to indulge in unavailing lamentations.

— Commentaries

*Have pity upon me, have pity upon me, O ye my
friends; for the hand of God hath touched me.*

Job 19:21

Whoever thinks of himself shall find himself worthy to be
punished as grievously as those whom he sees distressed. And
therefore we ought to look on them with pity and compassion; and so our vices and sins must cause us to humble
ourselves. Behold a poor wretch; I see that God punishes
him; it is a terrible thing. But what of it? There is good
reason that God should punish me as well. Then it behooves
me to humble myself, and to behold myself as in a mirror in
the person of this man.

Again when we see a man sorely punished by God's hand,
let us consider not only that he was created after the image
of God, but also that he is our neighbor, and in a sense one
with us. We are all of one nature, all one flesh, all one
mankind, as it may be said that we have all issued out of one
spring. Since it is so, should we not be considerate of one
another? I see moreover a poor soul that is going to destruction. Ought I not to pity him and to help him, if it
be in my power to do so? And even if I should not be able,
I ought to desire to do it.

These, I say, are two reasons which ought to move us to
pity when we see that God afflicts those who are worthy of it.
If we think on ourselves, either we are hard hearted and dull
witted, or else we shall pity those who are like ourselves. We
shall consider, "Here is a man formed after the image of
God; he is of the selfsame nature as I; here is one purchased
with the blood of the Son of God. If he perishes, ought we not
to be grieved?" — *Sermons*

He shall see of the travail of his soul, and shall be satisfied: by his knowledge shall my righteous servant justify many; for he shall bear their iniquities.

Isaiah 53:11

We know that man's sin involves not only that temporal death which is the separation of the body from the soul, but also it means feeling that God is against us and dreading his judgment. And what is that? The most unbearable and horrible thing that exists. So it was necessary that our Lord Jesus should go even to those lengths to deliver us, and it is this the Prophet now declares. And here we see again how greatly God has loved us and what are the treasures of his grace and infinite goodness that he has displayed towards us. And we should certainly also know what care and zeal our Lord Jesus Christ had for our salvation, when he did not spare himself, and was not only willing in his body to be answerable for making satisfaction for our sins, but even to be terrified as one who had to feel the judgment of God, and who fears what this curse deserves that God himself pronounces — that it is to swallow us in hell and that it is a chasm to engulf us entirely. So it was necessary that Jesus Christ should feel that. And indeed when we see that he sweated blood and water, that he needed angels to descend and comfort him, we must certainly say that this was an extreme sorrow; never was its like in all the world.

So this is the meaning of this word *labour* or *trouble* of the soul of our Lord Jesus Christ. Now it is true, as St. Peter says, that he could not be holden of the sorrows of hell; but he had to do battle with them. He won the victory, but not without bitter fighting and much difficulty. — *Sermons*

I thank God, whom I serve from my forefathers with pure conscience, that without ceasing I have remembrance of thee in my prayers night and day;

II Timothy 1:3

We see moreover that when God has put forward a man and has bestowed the grace of his Holy Ghost upon him, we may not say therefore that we may not always pray for him. For there will never be such perfection in this world but we shall have need to be better and better, and to have God's helping hand always, praying him that he would augment his gifts and cut off those corruptions that are in us. Therefore when we have an excellent man among us, and such a one as seems to be half an angel, true it is that we have great occasion to give thanks to God that he has poured the gifts of his Holy Ghost upon him so abundantly; but yet we must pray to God for him, that he would go on to increase him, until he have brought him to perfection.

Now if we have need to pray for one whom God has so highly advanced, what must we do for the poor silly ones who are but beginning, who are yet weak, who have only some little taste of the truth? Ought we not to be so much the more careful for them? Yes, no doubt. And therefore let us make this our reckoning, that there was never mortal creature in this world, but had need to be commended to God, that that might be brought to completion which was begun in him. Why so? Because men are always on their way while they live upon the earth. And this may teach us to humble ourselves, that no man esteem himself, that no man content himself with his estate, to say, "I have come as far as I should come." But let us always go on, and let us pray to God that he would bring us forward, knowing well that we have not yet gotten to the mark. — *Sermons*

*Therefore I love thy commandments above gold; yea,
above fine gold.*   Psalm 119:127

This is a message deserving of special attention, for the baneful influence of evil example is well known, every man thinking that he may lawfully do whatever is commonly practised around him. Whence it comes to pass that evil company carries us away like a tempest. The more diligently then ought we to meditate on this doctrine; that when the wicked claim to themselves an unbridled liberty, it behooves us to contemplate with the eyes of faith, the judgments of God, in order to our being thereby quickened to the observance of the divine law. If attention to this doctrine has been needful from the beginning, at the present day it is necessary to exert ourselves, that we may not be involved in violating the law of God with the wicked conspiracy which almost the whole world have formed to violate it. The more outrageously the wicked vaunt themselves, let our respect for and our love of the divine law proportionately increase. — *Commentaries*

MARCH 4

Lord, hear my voice: let thine ears be attentive to the voice of my supplications. Psalm 130:2

As the miseries to which there is no prospect of a termination commonly bring despair in their train, nothing is more difficult than for persons, when involved in grievous and deep sorrow, to stir up their minds in the exercise of prayer. And it is amazing, considering that while we enjoy peace and prosperity we are cold in prayer (because then our hearts are in a state of infatuated security), how in adversities, which ought to quicken us, we are still more stupified. But the Prophet derives confidence in coming to the throne of grace, from the very troubles, cares, dangers, and sorrow into which he was plunged. He expresses his perplexity and the earnestness of his desire both by the word *cry* and by his repetition contained in the second verse. — *Commentaries*

Rebuke not an elder, but intreat him as a father;
and the young men as brethren.   I Timothy 5:1

Though we speak to them who have charge of teaching, showing them what their duty is toward the people, yet this admonition belongs to us all. For if we are gently dealt with when we have done amiss, and feel that we are kindly handled, and that others seek our salvation; if we should play the rebels we should not show that unkindness to any man, but to God whom we despise, and grieve his Holy Spirit as much as we are able. And why? Because we see that God has appointed this agency, so that we should profit in his doctrine and not be hardened in our sins. He will not have our sins covered and lie smothering so that they may not be known, nor found fault with. And therefore God will not have men use such flattering, for that creates a rottenness which can never be healed. But he will have sins reproved, he will have us beaten down; yes, though sins be lovingly and gently reproved, yet if we cannot endure such loving admonitions when they are made to us, this is not to despise men, but to make war against God.

If this were well observed, we would see another obedience than we do. For no man can now endure to have his fault told him, but as soon as a man opens his mouth to reprove someone, then begins an open war, then we have deadly hatred. And why? Because we do not consider that to refuse the admonitions that are made us in God's name, and by his commandment, is to resist God. And therefore we must take so much the more notice of this place, where we are told that God will not have sins nourished by acting as if we do not see them, but that we must be corrected gently and modestly. And we have yet another point to gather out of this place, namely that as we are all commanded to reprove and rebuke our neighbors, so we follow the rule that is stated here, that because all correction is sharp and loathsome, we moderate it, and sweeten it the best we can, that it may be the better received and profit more. — *Sermons*

Let Israel hope in the Lord: for with the Lord there is
mercy, and with him is plenteous redemption.

Psalm 130:7

It is to be noticed that the foundation upon which he would
have the hope of all the godly to rest is the mercy of God,
the source from which redemption springs. In the first clause
he reminds them that although they bring with them no
worth or merits of their own, it ought to suffice them that God
is merciful. This mutual relation between the faith of the
Church and the free goodness of God is to be attentively
marked, to the end we may know that all those who, depending
upon their own merits, persuade themselves that God will be
their rewarder, do not have their hope regulated according to
the rule of Scripture. From this mercy, as from a fountain, the
Prophet derives redemption; for there is no other cause which
moves God to manifest himself as the redeemer of his people
but his mercy.

The true use of the present doctrine is, first, that the faithful,
even when plunged in the deepest gulf, should not doubt of
their deliverance being in the hand of God, who, whenever
it proves necessary, will be able to find means, which are now
hidden and unknown to us; and, secondly, that they should
hold it as certain, that as often as the Church shall be afflicted,
he will manifest himself to be her deliverer. — *Commentaries*

*For he shall grow up before him as a tender plant,
and as a root out of a dry ground: he hath no form nor
comeliness; and when we shall see him, there is no
beauty that we should desire him. He is despised and
rejected of men; a man of sorrows, and acquainted
with grief: and we hid as it were our faces from him;
he was despised, and we esteemed him not.*

Isaiah 53:2, 3

If I am troubled and worried when I think of the only Son
of God being, as it were, trampled underfoot and hated by
men, I must enter into myself. For if I look only at Jesus Christ
I shall turn away from him and hold him of no account. But
if I first of all look at myself and then come to him, what he
has suffered will be laudable to me. Why? Because I shall
consider that I am a poor sinner and have provoked the wrath
of God against me so terribly that he is my adversary and
judge. If I think of my sins and so become aware of how fearful
and appalling is the wrath of God and that he is my judge to
cast me into hell, then I shall come to say, "What means have
you for coming to an agreement with God? Can you bring
him something to satisfy his demands, even for the least
sin you have committed?" Alas, no! When I shall have scoured
earth and sea, shall I have discovered anything to make amends
with? Can the angels in paradise help me? Therefore it is
necessary that Jesus Christ shall appear in my name and stand
as my pledge and surety.

This is how the death and passion of our Lord Jesus Christ
ceases to be foolishness to us. But we shall conceive that,
since we are accurst like this, and there is no means of finding
grace before God since we have so provoked him and he was
against us and our enemy, we had to be subject to Satan and his
tyranny until Jesus Christ delivered us from him. The way to
begin to glorify the infinite goodness of our God is to hate our
sins and be utterly confounded. This also is how the scandal

that we imagine and that each of us weaves around the death and passion of our Lord Jesus Christ will soon be taken away—namely, when we enter into ourselves and make a thorough examination of our sins, and recognize that we are so detestable to God that he had to come in the person of his Son to make satisfaction and reparation for our sins so that by this means we might be reconciled to him. — *Sermons*

68   MARCH 8

Then Peter said unto them, Repent, and be baptized every one of you in the name of Jesus Christ for the remission of sins, and ye shall receive the gift of the Holy Ghost.   Acts 2:38

When they ask us what faith we had for many years after our baptism, in order to show that our baptism was vain, since baptism is not sanctified to us except by the word of promise received in faith — to this inquiry we answer, that being blind and unbelieving for a long time, we did not embrace the promise which had been given us in baptism, yet that the promise itself, as it was from God, always remained steady, firm, and true. Though all men were false, yet God ceases not to be true; though all men were lost, yet Christ remains a Saviour. We confess, therefore, that during that time we received no advantages whatever from baptism because we totally neglected the promise offered to us in it, without which baptism is nothing.

Now since by the grace of God we have begun to repent, we accuse our blindness and hardness of heart for our long ingratitude to his great goodness; yet we believe that the promise itself never expired, but, on the contrary, we reason in the following manner: — By baptism God promises remission of sins, and will certainly fulfill the promise to all believers; that promise was offered to us in baptism; let us, therefore, embrace it by faith; it was long dormant by reason of our unbelief; now, then, let us receive it by faith. — *Institutes,* IV, xv, xvii

He sheweth his word unto Jacob, his statutes and his judgments unto Israel.   Psalm 147:19

How little would it avail the Church that it were filled with the perishing enjoyments of time and protected from hostile violence, if its hope did not extend beyond this world! This, accordingly, is the grand proof of his love, that he has set before us in his word the light of eternal life. On this account it is appropriately mentioned here as the crowning part of true solid happiness. And let us learn from this, that we should not only receive the doctrine of God with reverential and holy obedience, but embrace it with affection, for we can conceive of nothing more delightful and desirable than that God should undertake our salvation, and give testimony to this by stretching out his hand to bring us to himself. For this is the design with which the doctrine has been given to us, that amidst the thick darkness of this world, and the devious errors into which Satan misleads the children of men, the great Father of us all may by it cast a foregoing light upon our path before gathering us to the inheritance of heaven.

We are to notice that the part played by Moses and the Prophets according to divine appointment is here ascribed to God himself, for we only put due honor upon the doctrine of religion, and estimate it at its proper worth, when we rise to the consideration of God, who, in using the instrumentality of men, still claims to be considered our chief and only teacher. Thus its due majesty is assigned to the word from the person of its author. — *Commentaries*

*Now is my soul troubled; and what shall I say? Father,
save me from this hour: but for this cause came I unto
this hour.*   John 12:27

"Father, save me from this hour." It may be thought that it
is unbecoming in the Son of God to utter rashly a wish which
he must immediately retract, in order to obey his Father. I
readily admit that this is the folly of the cross, which gives
offence to proud men; but the more the Lord of Glory humbled
himself, so much the more illustrious is the manifestation of
his vast love to us.

Besides, we ought to recollect what I have already stated,
that the human feelings of Christ were in him pure and free
from sin. The reason is that they were guided and regulated
in obedience to God; for there is nothing to prevent Christ
from having a natural dread of death, and yet desiring to
obey God. This holds true in various respects; and hence he
corrects himself by saying, "For this cause came I unto this
hour." For though he may lawfully entertain a dread of death,
yet, considering why he was sent, and what his office as Redeemer demands of him, he presents to his Father the dread
which arose out of his natural disposition, in order that it
may be subdued, or rather, having subdued it, he prepares
freely and willingly to execute the command of God.

Now, if the feelings of Christ, which were free from all
sin, needed to be restrained in this manner, how earnestly
ought we to apply to this object, since the numerous affections
which spring from the flesh are so many enemies of God in us.
Let the godly, therefore, persevere in doing violence to themselves, until they have denied themselves. — *Commentaries*

All we like sheep have gone astray; we have turned every one to his own way; and the Lord hath laid on him the iniquity of us all.   Isaiah 53:6

And now we have to conclude that all those who wander about here and there turn away from our Lord Jesus Christ; for the Prophet declares that there has never been a patriarch or a prophet, or single one of all the holy Fathers and martyrs, who has not had need to be reconciled to God by the death and passion of our Lord Jesus Christ. If Abraham, the father of believers, if David, the mirror of all righteousness, if others like them, Job and Daniel, who are named as mirrors of all sanctity and perfection, if they, say I, were poor sheep, strayed and lost until they were gathered by our Lord Jesus Christ — alas! how shall it be with us? So then, when we go to seek them as our mediators and imagine that by their means we shall escape from the perdition we are in, do we not show that we are altogether ungrateful to our Lord Jesus Christ? Do we not show that we have lost our senses when we go to beg from those who also need to have recourse to the death and passion of our Lord Jesus Christ? For if necessity constrains us to seek a remedy, we must go to him in whom believers of all time have found their refuge. For neither St. Peter, nor St. Paul, nor the Virgin Mary, nor anyone else, is an exception. So then, let us learn to come to the source and fountain and to draw thence what we lack. For our Lord Jesus has enough to satisfy us all; and we need never fear that the fullness of grace which he has in himself will be exhausted; to each one he will give his part and portion when we come to seek it of him. — *Sermons*

It is like the precious ointment upon the head, that ran down upon the beard, even Aaron's beard: that went down to the skirts of his garments; As the dew of Hermon, and as the dew that descended upon the mountains of Zion: for there the Lord commanded the blessing, even life for evermore. Psalm 133:2, 3

There can be no doubt that the Holy Spirit is to be viewed as commending in this passage that mutual harmony which should subsist amongst all God's children, and exhorting us to make every endeavor to maintain it. So long as animosities divide us, and heart-burnings prevail amongst us, we may be brethren no doubt still by common relation to God, but cannot be judged one so long as we present the appearance of a broken and dismembered body. As we are one in God the Father, and in Christ, the union must be ratified amongst us by a reciprocal harmony and fraternal love.

Let us then, as much as lies in us, study to walk in brotherly love, that we may secure the divine blessing. Let us even stretch out our arms to those who differ from us, desiring to bid them welcome if they will but return to the unity of the faith. Do they refuse? Then let them go. We recognize no brotherhood, as I have said already, except amongst the children of God. — *Commentaries*

*But he was wounded for our transgressions, he was
bruised for our iniquities: the chastisement of our
peace was upon him; and with his stripes we are
healed.* Isaiah 53:5

But all the same, the Prophet shows that without the wounds
of our Lord Jesus Christ, there is nothing but death in us and
that we must certainly look to him for healing. So when we
want to partake of the fruit that the death and passion of our
Lord Jesus Christ brings us, let us understand that the many
vices rooted in our nature are so many wounds and mortal sick-
nesses, even though they may not be apparent. If a man thinks
he is healthy because he cannot see his sickness, he must be
quite out of his mind. Our illnesses may be the more deadly
when they are secret. Now besides our deep-rooted sins, there
are faults that we commit every day, and which show clearly
enough that our nature is perverse and accursed and that we
are all perverted. Since then there is in us nothing but spiritual
infection and leprosy and that we are corrupt in our iniquities,
what shall we do? What remedy is there? Shall we go seek
help from the angels in Paradise? Alas! they can do nothing
for us. No, we must come to our Lord Jesus Christ, who was
willing to be disfigured from the top of his head even to the
sole of his feet and was a mass of wounds, flogged with many
stripes and crowned with thorns, nailed and fastened to the
cross and pierced through the side. This is how we are healed;
here is our true medicine, with which we must be content, and
which we must embrace whole-heartedly, knowing that otherwise we can never have inward peace but must always be tormented and tortured to the extreme, unless Jesus Christ comforts us and appeases God's wrath against us. When we are
certain of that, we have cause to sing his praises, instead of
being capable of nothing but trembling and confusion. This,
in brief, is what we have to remember from these words of the
Prophet. — *Sermons*

*Nevertheless the foundation of God standeth sure,
having this seal, The Lord knoweth them that are his.
And, Let every one that nameth the name of Christ depart from iniquity.*   II Timothy 2:19

It is true that we do not presume to enter into the secret
counsel of God, to know thoroughly his wonderful secrets; but
if we do not know that God chose us before the world was made,
this deprives us of a comfort which is not only profitable for
us, but more than necessary. The devil could find no better
means to destroy our faith than to hide this article from us.
Why? I ask you, what kind of situation would we be in? And
especially nowadays, when there are so many rebels, so many
hypocrites, yes, and such as look for wonders at men's hands,
might we not think that the like might befall us? But then
how should we be constant to rest ourselves upon God, and
commit ourselves to him with settled hearts, not doubting that
he will care for us to the end? How could we do this unless
we flee to this election as our only refuge? For it would seem
that God breaks his promise to us which he gives us touching
his gospel, and that Jesus Christ is hunted out of the world.
This is the chiefest cause and best means that Satan could
find to bring us out of touch with the gospel.

Therefore let us hold fast these weapons in spite of Satan's
teeth. For these must be our defense; let us be confirmed, I
mean, in the election of our God, and let us make it available,
and see that it be not taken from us, if we value and love the
salvation of our souls. And let us take these weapons all from
our deadly enemies who would hide such a doctrine from us,
knowing that the devil stirs them up to deprive us of a comfort
which if we lack we cannot be assured of our salvation; which,
notwithstanding, we have to desire more than anything else.

—*Sermons*

And ye have forgotten the exhortation which speaketh
unto you as unto children, My son, despise not thou
the chastening of the Lord, nor faint when thou art
rebuked of him: Hebrews 12:5

It is very true, as you say, that while clinging from worldly
fear to the superstitions which in the world reign paramount,
you are still very far from that perfection to which our gracious
God calls us. But yet it is a mark of some progress even to
acknowledge our sins, and to be displeased with them. You must
now advance farther, and condemning your own weakness, set
yourself in earnest about getting rid of it; and if you cannot
succeed all at once in accomplishing your wish, yet nevertheless you must persevere in seeking the remedy for it, until you
have been completely cured. To do this, you will find it to
your advantage to call yourself to account day by day, and while
acknowledging your faults, to groan within yourself, and
mourn over them before God, so that your displeasure against
whatsoever is evil may become more intense, until you are
quite confirmed and resolved to renounce it as you ought, even
as indeed I feel assured you labor hard to do.

And it is not in vain that you beg of me to join my prayers
with yours, to seek with importunity to God that he would
be pleased to have compassion on you, and to deliver you from
this unhappy captivity. Let us continue then with one accord
to put up this request, and he will at length make manifest
that you have not altogether wasted your time.

True, sometimes he lets us grow faint, and before declaring
effectually that he has heard our prayers, he seems to keep at
a distance, as much to sharpen our desire as to make trial of
our patience; and, therefore, you need not reckon that hitherto
your prayers to him have been in vain, but much rather take
encouragement, and strive even more and more, knowing that
if perseverance be required throughout our whole life, it is
specially desired in prayer. And, besides, you must also take
care in real earnest to fan the flame which God has already

begun to kindle in you; for all the gracious affections he breathes into us are just so many sparks which we must not extinguish, or allow to go out by our heedlessness.

Since, then, God has already opened your eyes so far, that you admit we ought to be his peculiar ones, and dedicated to him in righteousness, so as to glorify him as well in our bodies as in our souls; seeing also that he has touched your heart so that you have some feeling of our unhappiness in alienation from him, unquestionably you must not now go to sleep or trifle away at your ease, but even as we stir fire when it does not burn as it ought to do, it is quite right that you be stirred up yet more and more, until the longing desire to devote yourself wholly to him and to his righteousness, overcomes all hindrances either from the flesh or from the world.

—*Correspondence*

76 MARCH 16

Where they crucified him, and two others with him, on either side one, and Jesus in the midst. John 19:18

"And two others with him, on either side one, and Jesus in the midst." As if the severity of the punishment had not been sufficient of itself, he is hanged in the midst between two robbers, as if he not only had deserved to be classed with other robbers, but had been the most wicked and the most detestable of them all.

And if there were the best reasons for the purpose of God in all those things which he determined that his Son should suffer, we ought to consider on the one hand the dreadful weight of his wrath against sin, and on the other hand his infinite goodness towards us. In no other way could our guilt be removed than by the Son of God becoming a curse for us. We see him driven out into an accursed place, as if he had been polluted by a mass of all sorts of crimes, that there he might appear to be accursed before God and men. Assuredly we are terribly stupid if we do not plainly see in this mirror with what abhorrence God regards sin; and we are harder than stones if we do not tremble at such a judgment as this.

When on the other hand God declares that our salvation was so dear to him that he did not spare his only-begotten Son, what abundant goodness and what astonishing grace do we here behold! Whoever, then, takes a just view of the causes of the death of Christ, together with the advantage which it yields to us, will not, like the Greeks, regard the doctrine of the cross as foolishness, nor, like the Jews, will he regard it as an offence, but rather as an invaluable token and pledge of the power and wisdom and righteousness and goodness of God. — *Commentaries*

77   MARCH 17

If ye will not hear, and if ye will not lay it to heart, to give glory unto my name, saith the Lord of hosts, I will even send a curse upon you, and I will curse your blessings: yea, I have cursed them already because ye do not lay it to heart.   Malachi 3:2

We see then that the prophet shows how God had a just cause for severely punishing them; for it was an impiety not to be borne when he could obtain no hearing from men. But the prophet shows at the same time what it is to hear God; he therefore adds the latter clause as a definition or an explanation of the former; for God is not heard if we receive his words with levity, so that they soon vanish away; but we hear them when we lay them on the heart, or as the Latins say, when we apply the mind to them. There is then required a serious attention, otherwise it will be the same as if our ears were closed against God.

Let us further learn from this passage that obedience is of so much account with God that he considers nothing worse than a contempt of his word or a careless attention to it, as though we regarded not its authority. We must also notice that our guilt before God is increased when he recalls us to the right way and seeks to promote our welfare by warning and exhorting us. When therefore God is thus kindly careful for our salvation, we are doubly inexcusable if we perversely reject his teachings, warnings, counsels, and other remedies which he may apply. — *Commentaries*

> *Who hath believed our report? and to whom is the*
> *arm of the Lord revealed?*   Isaiah 53:1

For if we are ashamed to receive our Lord Jesus Christ crucified, we are most certainly excluded from all hope of salvation. For how are we saved by him? How does the inheritance of heaven belong to us, if not because he has been made a curse for us — and that not only before men, but even at the mouth of God his Father? Look how Jesus Christ, who is the fountain of all blessing, has yet borne our sins and become like the ancient sacrifices which were called "sin" because the wrath of God had to be declared there, so that men might be set free and absolved from it! And how is it that Jesus Christ is our life, save in that he has swallowed up death in dying? And how is it that we are raised by him, save in that he has gone down even to the depths of hell — that is to say, that he has carried the horrors which were upon us because of our sins and which would have crushed us? For we should have had to have God always as our Judge; and it is the most appalling thing that could happen, to have God against us. It was necessary that Jesus Christ should come forward as our pledge and make atonement for us, and bear our condemnation so as to absolve us from it. So then, let us not find it strange when we see that he was so disfigured. — *Sermons*

*Wherefore the Lord said, Forasmuch as this people
draw near me with their mouth, and with their lips do
honour me, but have removed their heart far from me,
and their fear toward me is taught by the precept of
men: Therefore, behold, I will proceed to do a marvellous work among this people, even a marvelous work
and a wonder: for the wisdom of their wise men shall
perish, and the understanding of their prudent men
shall be hid.* Isaiah 29:13, 14

It is clearly evident that neither voice nor singing, if used
in prayer, has any validity, or produces the least benefit with
God, unless it proceed from the inmost desire of the heart . . .
We do not here condemn the use of the voice, or singing, but
rather highly recommend them, provided they accompany the
affection of the heart. For they exercise the mind in Divine
meditation, and fix the attention of the heart; which by its
versatility is easily relaxed and distracted to a variety of objects,
unless it be supported by various helps. Besides, as the glory
of God is in some respect to be manifested in every part of
our bodies, to this service, both in singing and in speaking,
it is especially fitting to us to devote our tongues, which were
created for the express purpose of declaring and celebrating the
Divine praises. Nevertheless the principal use of the tongue
is in the public prayers which are made in the congregations
of believers; the design of which is that with one common
voice, and as it were with the same mouth, we may all at once
proclaim the glory of God, whom we worship in one spirit and
with the same faith; and this is publicly done, that all inter-
changeably, each one of his brother, may receive the confession of faith and be invited and stimulated by his example.
—Institutes, III, xx, xxxi

And he sent Eliakim, who was over the household, and Shebna the scribe, and the elders of the priests covered with sackcloth, unto Isaiah the prophet the son of Amoz.   Isaiah 37:2

King Hezekiah rent his clothes. Scarcely do we find one man in a hundred who does not murmur if God treats him with any degree of severity, who does not bring forward his good deeds as a ground of complaint, and remonstrate that he has been unjustly rewarded. Other men, when God does not comply with their wishes, complain that their worship of God has served no good purpose.

We see nothing of this kind in Hezekiah, who, though he is conscious of possessing uncommon piety, does not shrink from a confession of guilt, and therefore if we desire to turn away God's anger, and to experience his favor in adversity, we must testify our repentance and sincerely acknowledge our guilt; for adversity does not happen to us by chance, but is the method by which God arouses us to repentance. True, indeed, sackcloth and ashes will be of little avail if they are not preceded by the inward feelings of the heart; for we know that hypocrites are abundantly liberal in the use of ceremonies; but the Holy Spirit justly commends those exercises when they are directed to their proper object. And indeed it was a proof of uncommon piety and modesty that the pious king and the whole nation excited themselves in this manner to fear God, and that he made a voluntary acknowledgment of guilt in a form attended by wretched filthiness; for we know how unwilling kings are to let themselves down from their rank.

—*Commentaries*

He that walketh righteously, and speaketh uprightly;
he that despiseth the gain of oppressions, that shaketh
his hands from holding of bribes, that stoppeth his
ears from hearing of blood, and shutteth his eyes
from seeing evil;   Isaiah 33:15

"He that walketh in righteousness." He explains that they
who provoke his anger, and thus drive away from them his
forbearance, have no right to complain that God is excessively
severe. Thus he convinces them of their guilt and exhorts
them to repentance, for he shows that there is a state of
friendship between God and men, if they wish to follow and
practise "righteousness," if they maintain truth and integrity,
if they are free from all corruptions and act inoffensively towards their neighbors. But because they abound in every
kind of wickedness, and have abandoned themselves to malice,
calumny, covetousness, robbery, and other crimes, it is impossible that the Lord should not strike them down with fear, by
showing that he is terrible to them. In short, the design of
the Prophet is to shut the mouths of wicked babblers, that
they may not accuse God of cruelty in their destruction; for the
whole blame rests on themselves. By evasions they endeavor
to escape condemnation. But the Prophet declares that God is
always gracious to his worshippers, and that in this sense Moses
calls him "a fire," (Deut. 4:24 and 9:3) that men may not despise his majesty and power; but that every one who shall approach to him with sincere piety will know by actual experience that nothing is more pleasant or delightful than his
presence. Since, therefore, God shines on believers with a
bright countenance, they enjoy settled peace with him through
a good conscience; and hence it follows that God is not naturally
terrible, but that he is forced to it by our wickedness.

—Commentaries

*Be silent, O all flesh, before the Lord: for he is raised
up out of his holy habitation.*　　　Zechariah 2:13

By silence we are to understand, as elsewhere observed,
submission. The ungodly are not indeed silent before God,
so as willingly to obey his word, or reverently to receive what
he may bid or command, or humbly to submit under his
powerful hand; for these things are done only by the faithful.
Silence, then, is what especially belongs to the elect and the
faithful; for they willingly close their mouth to hear God
speaking. But the ungodly are also said to be silent when God
restrains their madness; and however much they may inwardly
murmur and rage, they yet cannot openly resist; so that he
completes his work, and they are at length made ashamed of
the swelling words they have uttered, when they pass off in
smoke. This is the sense in which the Prophet says now,
silent be all flesh. He means, in short, by these words, that
when God shall go forth to deliver his Church, he will be
terrible; so that all who had before furiously assailed his
chosen people shall be constrained to tremble.—*Commentaries*

MARCH 23

Come, and let us return unto the Lord: for he hath
torn, and he will heal us; he hath smitten, and he will
bind us up.   Hosea 6:1

Notwithstanding, we shall not give up praying to God that
it would please him to confirm you entirely, with thanksgiving
that he has brought you back from the brink of the grave. Besides, I hope, from the present appearances, that he is minded
yet to make use of you in health, since he has employed you in
sickness. For although laid powerless on a bed, we are by no
means useless to him, if we testify our obedience by resigning
ourselves to his good pleasure — if we give proof of our faith
by resisting temptation — if we take advantage of the consolation which he gives us in order to overcome the troubles of the
flesh. It is in sickness, especially when prolonged, that patience
is most needful; but most of all in death. Nevertheless, as I
have said, I confide in this good God, that after having exercised you by sickness he will still employ your health to some
good purpose. Meanwhile, we must beseech him that he
would uphold us in steadfast courage, never permitting us to
fall away because of lengthened waiting. — *Correspondence*

MARCH 24

All we like sheep have gone astray; we have turned
every one to his own way; and the Lord hath laid on
him the iniquity of us all.   Isaiah 53:6

Every one has turned to his own way. By adding the term
"every one," he descends from a universal statement, in which
he included all, to a special statement, that every individual
may consider in his own mind if it be so; for a general statement produces less effect upon us than to know that it belongs
to each of us in particular. Let "everyone," therefore, arouse
his conscience, and present himself before the judgment seat

of God, that he may confess his wretchedness. Moreover, what is the nature of this "going astray" the Prophet states more plainly. It is, that every one has followed the way which he had chosen for himself, that is, has determined to live according to his own fancy; by which he means that there is only one way of living uprightly, and if any one "turn aside" from it, he can experience nothing but "going astray."

He does not speak of works only, but of nature itself, which always leads us astray. For if we could by natural instinct or by our own wisdom, bring ourselves back into the path, or guard ourselves against going astray, Christ would not be needed by us. Thus in ourselves we are all undone unless Christ (John 8:36) sets us free; and the more we rely on our wisdom or industry, the more dreadfully and the more speedily do we draw down destruction on ourselves. And so the Prophet shows what we are before we are regenerated by Christ; for all are involved in the same condemnation. "There is none righteous, none that understandeth, none that seeketh God. All have turned aside, and have become unprofitable. There is none that doeth good, no, not one" (Ps. 14:3). All this is more fully explained by Paul (Rom. 3:10).

And Jehovah hath laid on him. Here we have a beautiful contrast. In ourselves we are scattered; in Christ we are gathered together. By nature we go astray, and are driven headlong to destruction; in Christ we find the course by which we are conducted to the harbor of salvation. Our sins are a heavy load; but they are laid on Christ, by whom we are freed from the load. Thus when we were ruined and, being estranged from God, were hastening to hell, Christ took upon him the filthiness of our iniquities, in order to rescue us from everlasting destruction; This must refer exclusively to guilt and punishment; for he was free from sin (Heb. 4:15; I Peter 2:22). Let every one, therefore, diligently consider his own iniquities, that he may have a true relish of that grace, and may obtain the benefit of the death of Christ.

—Commentaries

He was taken from prison and from judgment: and who shall declare his generation? for he was cut off out of the land of the living: for the transgression of my people was he stricken.   Isaiah 53:8

Now, it was very necessary that our Lord Jesus should descend into the depths of the abyss before being exalted into the glory of the heavens; for if he had appeared only in his majesty, how could we today be assured that our sins were forgiven? We should indeed see the Son of God who is the fountain of life, but he would be, as it were, separated from us, and we should have nothing in common with him, nor be able to draw near him. Moreover, we should always have cause for despair, in that we are guilty of infinite faults. And if our Lord Jesus had descended into the abyss without being raised to the heavens, where should we be then? We should be always wretched creatures, petrified with fear and in endless and ceaseless anxiety; we should be in a horrible torment, for the wrath of God would ever be upon us. But when it is said in the first place that he was condemned, and suffered terrible pangs that we might be delivered from them, and that, having peace with God, we now know that he loves us, is favorable to us and receives us in mercy; when we know that Jesus Christ was raised on high, we can also conclude that it was to draw us to him that we might share in the glory given to him by his Father. — *Sermons*

*Therefore will I divide him a portion with the great,
and he shall divide the spoil with the strong; because
he hath poured out his soul unto death: and he was
numbered with the transgressors; and he bare the sin
of many, and made intercession for the transgressors.*
Isaiah 53:12

And let us realize that if we come flocking to our Lord Jesus
Christ, we shall not hinder one another and prevent him being
sufficient for each of us. It is a different matter when we seek
relief in a mortal man. If, after one man has said: "Will you
please carry such and such a load," a second comes, and a
hundred all together, however greatly he may wish to help
them individually, yet his shoulders would give way, for he
would not have the strength to carry everything upon him.
Or again, if it is a question of borrowing when we are hungry
and thirsty, we may come and ask a man to give us something
to eat and drink, and perhaps he could cater for a dozen; but
if there came such a great crowd that all the food gave out,
he would find himself short. So then, as far as men are concerned, we need to receive help and assistance from many if we
come in such a great multitude. But when we come to Jesus
Christ we must not be afraid that his power will fail. When
each has received his portion from him, there is no lessening
in Him, so that there is not enough for others. For the greater
number we are who come to him, the more shall we find him
rich to supply our need. Thus, we have to note that not without
cause does the Prophet say *he bore the sin of many* — that we
may not envy our neighbours, as if we were balked of assistance
because there were too many others. This, in sum, is what we
have to remember from this passage. — *Sermons*

*And there came also Nicodemus, which at the first
came to Jesus by night, and brought a mixture of
myrrh and aloes, about an hundred pound weight.*
John 19:39

"Joseph of Arimathaea besought Pilate." It is certain that
this was effected by a heavenly impulse, so that they who,
through fear, did not render the honor due to him while he
was alive, now run to his dead body as if they had become
new men.

They bring their spices to embalm the body of Christ; but
they would never have done so if they had been perfumed
with the sweet savor of his death. This shows the truth of
what Christ had said, "Unless a grain of corn die, it remaineth
alone; but when it is dead, it bringeth forth much fruit." For
here we have a striking proof that his death was more quickening than his life; and so great was the efficacy of that sweet
savor which the death of Christ conveyed to the minds of those
two men, that it quickly extinguished all the passions belonging
to the flesh. So long as ambition and the love of money reigned
in them, the grace of Christ had no charms for them; but now
they begin to lose their taste for the whole world.

—*Commentaries*

*But now is Christ risen from the dead, and become the
firstfruits of them that slept.*   I Corinthians 15:20

But when we pass from his death to his resurrection we
recognize that our Lord Jesus has won the victory for us. And
this is what St. Paul says in that other passage in II Corinthians
that he died in the weakness of his flesh, but was raised in
the power of God his Father. So this order that the Prophet

observes aims at making us certain that our Lord Jesus has possession of his life and is Lord and Master over it, seeing that this has been declared in his person. Let us understand, then, that the Son of God was brought to nothing for us, but was nevertheless not stript of his power; and that though he kept himself hidden for a little while, his resurrection bears such certain witness to him, that we have no excuse for not putting our trust completely in him and boldly scorning the devil and sin. For Jesus Christ has triumphed over them and the hand of God upheld him to free him from his bonds; and likewise he was exalted to be the vicegerent of God his Father, and, as I have already said, to bear sovereign rule over the world. This then, in a word, is what we have to remember when it is said that *he was raised from prison and from judgment.* — *Sermons on Isaiah*

89   MARCH 29

Jesus said unto her, I am the resurrection, and the life: he that believeth in me, though he were dead, yet shall he live: John 11:25

Christ rose again that we might be the companions of his future life. He was raised by the Father, inasmuch as he was the head of the Church, from which he does not suffer him to be separated. He was raised by the power of the Spirit, who is given to us also for the purpose of quickening us. In a word, he was raised that he might be "the resurrection and the life." But this mirror exhibits to us a lively image of our resurrection, and so it will furnish us a firm foundation for our minds to rest upon, provided we are not wearied or disturbed by the long delay.

But that no doubt might be entertained of the resurrection of Christ, on which the resurrection of us all is founded, we see in how many and various ways he has caused it to be attested to us . . . . As to the people at large and the governor himself, it is no wonder that after the ample conviction they had, they were denied a sight of Christ, or any other proofs. The sepulchre is sealed, a watch is set, the body is not found on the third day. The soldiers, corrupted by bribes, circulate a rumor that he was stolen away by his disciples; as if they had power to collect a strong force, or were furnished with arms, or were even accustomed to such a daring exploit. But if the soldiers had not courage enough to repulse them, why did they not pursue them, that with the assistance of the people they might seize some of them? The truth is, therefore, that Pilate by his zeal attested the resurrection of Christ; and the guards who were placed at the sepulchre, either by their silence or by their falsehood, were in reality so many heralds to publish the same fact. — *Institutes*, III, xxv, iii

90   **MARCH 30**

The Lord was ready to save me: therefore we will sing my songs to the stringed instruments all the days of our life in the house of the Lord.   Isaiah 38:20

"All the days of our life." He declares that he will do his endeavor that the favor of God may be known to all, and that the remembrance of it may be preserved, not only for one day or for one year, but as long as he shall live. And indeed at any time it would be exceedingly base to allow a blessing of God so remarkable as this to pass away or be forgotten; but, being forgetful, we continually need spurs to arouse us. At the same time, he takes a passing notice of the reason why God appointed holy assemblies. It was that all with one mouth might praise him, and might excite each other to the practise of godliness. — *Commentaries*

And he hath put a new song in my mouth, even
praise unto our God: many shall see it, and fear, and
shall trust in the Lord.   Psalm 40:3

"And he hath put into my mouth a new song." In the first
clause of this verse he concludes the description of what God
had done for him. By God's putting a new song into his
mouth he denotes the consummation of his deliverance. In
whatever way God is pleased to succor us, he asks nothing
else from us in return but that we should be thankful for and
remember it. As often, therefore, as he bestows benefits upon
us, so often does he open our mouths to praise his name. Since
God, by acting liberally towards us, encourages us to sing his
praises, David with good reason reckons that having been so
wonderfully delivered, the matter of a new song had been furnished him. He uses the word new in the sense of exquisite and
not ordinary, even as the manner of his deliverance was singular and worthy of everlasting remembrance. It is true that
there is no benefit of God so small that it ought not to call
forth our highest praises; but the more mightily he stretches
forth his hand to help us, the more does it become us to stir
up ourselves to fervent zeal in this holy exercise, so that our
songs may correspond to the greatness of the favor which has
been conferred upon us.

"Many shall see it." Here the Psalmist extends still farther
the fruit of the aid which he had experienced, telling us that
it will prove the means of instruction common to all. And certainly it is the will of God that the benefits which he bestows
upon any individual of the faithful should be proofs of the
goodness which he constantly exercises towards all of them, so
that the one, instructed by the example of the other, should
not doubt that the same grace will be manifested towards himself. — *Commentaries*

Verily, verily, I say unto thee, When thou wast young, thou girdedst thyself, and walkedst whither thou wouldest: but when thou shalt be old, thou shalt stretch forth thy hands, and another shall gird thee, and carry thee whither thou wouldest not.

John 21:18

In Peter we have a striking mirror of our ordinary condition. Many have an easy and agreeable life before Christ calls them; but as soon as they have made profession of his name, and have been received as his disciples, or at least some time afterwards, they are led to distressing struggles, to a troublesome life, to great dangers, and sometimes to death itself. This condition, though hard, must be patiently endured. Yet the Lord moderates the cross by which he is pleased to try his servants, so that he spares them a little while, until their strength has come to maturity; for he knows well their weakness, and beyond the measure of it he does not press them. Thus he forbore with Peter so long as he saw him to be as yet tender and weak. Let us therefore learn to devote ourselves to him to the latest breath, provided that he supply us with strength. — *Commentaries*

*Then saith Pilate unto him, Speakest thou not unto
me? knowest thou not that I have power to crucify
thee, and have power to release thee?*   John 19:10

"Knowest thou not that I have power to crucify thee?" We
see in Pilate an image of a proud man, who is driven to madness by his ambition; for when he wishes to exalt his power,
he deprives himself of all praise and reputation for justice.
He acknowledges that Christ is innocent, and therefore he
makes himself no better than a robber when he boasts that
he has power to cut his throat. Thus wicked consciences, in
which faith and the true knowledge of God do not reign, must
necessarily be agitated, and there must be within them various
feelings of the flesh, which contend with each other; and in
this manner God takes signal vengeance on the pride of men,
when they go beyond their limits, so as to claim for themselves infinite power. By condemning themselves for injustice,
they stamp on themselves the greatest reproach and disgrace.
No blindness, therefore, is greater than that of pride; and
we need not wonder, since pride feels the hand of God, against
which it strikes, to be armed with vengeance. Let us therefore
remember that we ought not rashly to indulge in foolish boast-
ings, lest we expose ourselves to ridicule; and especially that
those who occupy a high rank ought to conduct themselves
modestly, and not be ashamed of being subject to God and to
his laws. — *Commentaries*

*Likewise the Spirit also helpeth our infirmities: for
we know not what we should pray for as we ought:
but the Spirit itself maketh intercession for us with
groanings which cannot be uttered. And he that
searcheth the hearts knoweth what is the mind of the
Spirit, because he maketh intercession for the saints
according to the will of God.*   Romans 8:26, 27

By means of prayer, then, we penetrate to those riches which
are reserved with our heavenly Father for our use. For between
God and men there is a certain communication; by which
they enter into the sanctuary of heaven, and in his immediate
presence remind him of his promises, in order that his declarations, which they have implicitly believed, may in time of
necessity be verified in their experience. We see, therefore,
that nothing is revealed to us, to be expected from the Lord,
for which we are not likewise enjoined to pray; so true is it,
that prayer digs out those treasures, which the gospel of the
Lord discovers to our faith.

Now the necessity and various utility of the exercise of
prayer no language can sufficiently explain. It is certainly
not without reason that our heavenly Father declares that the
only fortress of salvation consists in invocation of his name;
by which we call to our aid the presence of his providence,
which watches over all our concerns; of his power, which supports us when weak and ready to faint; and of his goodness,
which receives us into favor, though miserably burdened with
our sins; in which, finally, we call upon him to manifest his
presence with us in all his attributes. Hence our consciences
derive peculiar peace and tranquillity; for when the affliction
which oppressed us is represented to the Lord, we feel abundant
composure even from this consideration, that none of our
troubles are concealed from him whom we know to possess
both the greatest readiness and the greatest ability to promote
our truest interest. — *Institutes*, III, xx, ii

*He that loveth his life shall lose it; and he that hateth
his life in this world shall keep it unto life eternal.*
John 12:25

"He who hateth his soul." This expression is used com-
paratively; because we ought to despise *life*, so far as it hinders
us from living to God; for if meditation on the heavenly life
were the prevailing sentiment of our hearts, the world would
have no influence in detaining us. Hence, too, we obtain a
reply to an objection that might be urged. "Many persons,
through despair, or for other reasons, and chiefly from weariness of life, kill themselves; and yet we will not say that such
persons provide for their own safety, while others are hurried
to death by ambition, who also rush down to ruin." But here
Christ speaks expressly of that hatred or contempt of this fading life, which believers derive from the contemplation of a
better life. Consequently, whoever does not look to heaven
has not yet learned in what way life must be preserved. Besides, this latter clause was added by Christ, in order to strike
terror into those who are too desirous of the earthly life; for if
we are overwhelmed by the love of the world, so that we cannot easily forget it, it is impossible for us to go to heaven. But
since the Son of God arouses us so violently, it would be the
height of folly to sleep a mortal sleep. — *Commentaries*

*Make me to hear joy and gladness; that the bones
which thou hast broken may rejoice. Hide thy face
from my sins, and blot out all mine iniquities.*
Psalm 51:8, 9

Our faith is weak, and we cannot at once apprehend the
full extent of the divine mercy; so that there is no reason to
be surprised that David should have once and again renewed
his prayers for pardon, the more to confirm his belief in it. The

truth is that we cannot properly pray for pardon of sin until we have come to a persuasion that God will be reconciled to us. Who can venture to open his mouth in God's presence unless he be assured of his fatherly favor? And pardon being the first thing we should pray for, it is plain that there is no inconsistency in having a persuasion of the grace of God, and yet proceeding to supplicate his forgiveness. In proof of this, I might refer to the Lord's Prayer, in which we are taught to begin by addressing God as our Father, and yet afterwards to pray for the remission of our sins. God's pardon is full and complete; but our faith cannot take in his overflowing goodness, and it is necessary that it should distil to us drop by drop. It is owing to this infirmity of our faith that we are often found repeating and repeating again the same petition, not with the view surely of gradually softening the heart of God to compassion, but because we advance by slow and difficult steps to the requisite fulness of assurance. — *Commentaries*

97   **APRIL 6**

If I have rewarded evil unto him that was at peace with me; (yea, I have delivered him that without cause is mine enemy:)   Psalm 7:4

He states that he had been a friend, not only to the good, but also to the bad, and had not only restrained himself from all revenge, but had even succored his enemies, by whom he had been deeply and cruelly injured. It would certainly not be very illustrious virtue to love the good and peaceable, unless there were joined to this self-government and gentleness in patiently dealing with the bad. But when a man not only keeps himself from revenging the injuries which he has received, but endeavors to overcome evil by doing good, he manifests one of the graces of a renewed and sanctified nature, and in this way proves himself to be one of the children of God; for such meekness proceeds only from the Spirit of adoption.
—*Commentaries*

*We will not hide them from their children, shewing to
the generation to come the praises of the Lord, and
his strength, and his wonderful works that he hath
done.*   Psalm 78:4

Although your piety, noble lady, is much better known by
certain proofs in the country which you inhabit, you have made
it known to us also, by the pledges you have confided to us.
For in not hesitating to send your children far from you and into
an almost unknown country, that they might better imbibe the
pure doctrine of Christ, you have clearly shown how precious
a virtuous and pious education is in your eyes. Lively indeed
must that zeal be, which forces you to forget and divest yourself for a season of that softness of tender affection which is
naturally implanted in the heart of mothers, till you see your
sons imbued with the uncorrupted faith of Christ, when
you shall welcome their return with a more joyful mind than
if they had never been separated from your embraces and your
sight.

For this holy desire is evangelical, and such as all good men
should study to favor; and the pious discipline which flour-
ishes in your house is no less worthy of praise; and would that
all had at heart to make it a rule for their families, to cherish
as it were a domestic church in their houses. It were also to
be desired, especially while among you the state of affairs is
so unsettled, that there were found not only more ladies, but
men who should spread the light of a similar example.

But because, in the course of our lives, many obstacles occur
which it would not be easy for us to surmount, I will pray the
Lord that he may strengthen you to persevere, enrich you from
day to day with the gifts of his Spirit, and in the meantime
keep you in safety under his hand and protection.

—Correspondence

*Blessed is he that considereth the poor: the Lord will
deliver him in time of trouble.*   Psalm 41:1

Certainly it is an error which is by far too common among
men, to look upon those who are oppressed with afflictions as
condemned and reprobate. As, on the one hand, the most of
men, judging of the favor of God from an uncertain and transitory state of prosperity, applaud the rich, and those upon whom
as they say fortune smiles; so, on the other hand, they act contemptuously towards the wretched and miserable, and foolishly
imagine that God hates them, because he does not exercise so
much forbearance towards them as he does towards the reprobate. The error of which we speak, namely that of judging
wrongly and wickedly, is one which has prevailed in all ages
of the world.

The Scriptures in many places plainly and distinctly declare that God, for various reasons, tries the faithful by adversities, at one time to train them to patience, at another to
subdue the sinful affections of the flesh, at another to cleanse
and as it were purify them from the remaining desires of the
flesh which still dwell within them; sometimes to humble them,
sometimes to make them an example to others, and at other
times to stir them up to the contemplation of the divine life.

For the most part, indeed, we often speak rashly and indis-
criminately concerning others, and, so to speak, plunge even
into the lowest abyss those who labor under affliction. To restrain such a rash and unbridled spirit, David says that they
are blessed who do not suffer themselves, by speaking at random, to judge harshly of their neighbors; but, discerning aright
the afflictions by which they are visited, mitigate, by the wisdom of the Spirit, the severe and unjust judgments to which we
are naturally so prone. As to ourselves, being admonished by
this testimony of the Holy Spirit, let us learn to guard against
a too hasty judgment. We must therefore judge prudently of

our brethren who are in affliction; that is to say, we must hope well of their salvation, lest, if we condemn them unmercifully before the time, this unjust severity in the end shall fall upon our own heads. — *Commentaries*

100 APRIL 9

Speak unto all the congregation of the children of Israel, and say unto them, Ye shall be holy: for I the Lord your God am holy.   Leviticus 19:2

This Scripture plan consists chiefly in these two things — the first, that a love of righteousness, to which we have otherwise no natural inclination, be instilled and introduced into our hearts; the second, that a rule be prescribed to us, to prevent our taking any devious steps in the race of righteousness. Now in the recommendation of righteousness, it uses a great number of very excellent arguments.

With what better foundation can it begin than when it admonishes us that we ought to be holy because *our God is holy?* For when we were dispersed like scattered sheep, and lost in the labyrinth of the world, he gathered us together again, that he might associate us to himself. When we hear any mention of our union with God, we should remember that holiness must be the bond of it; not that we attain communion with him by the merit of holiness (since it is rather necessary for us, in the first place, to adhere to him in order that, being endued with his holiness, we may follow whither he calls), but because it is a peculiar property of his glory not to have any intercourse with iniquity and uncleanness. Wherefore also it teaches, that this is the end of our vocation, which it is requisite for us always to keep in view, if we desire to correspond to the design of God in calling us. For to what purpose was it that we were delivered from the iniquity and pollution of the world, in which we had been immersed, if we permit ourselves to wallow in them as long as we live? — *Institutes*, III, vi, ii

Yet it pleased the Lord to bruise him; he hath put him to grief: when thou shalt make his soul an offering for sin, he shall see his seed, he shall prolong his days, and the pleasure of the Lord shall prosper in his hand.
Isaiah 53:10

But now we are spared. Consider Jesus Christ the only Son of God: he was imprisoned and we are released; he was condemned and we are acquitted; he was exposed to utter disgrace and we are set up in honour; he descended into the depths of hell and to us the kingdom of Heaven is opened. When we hear all these things, should we still stay asleep, pleasing and flattering ourselves in our vices? So let us carefully notice the purpose of the Holy Spirit and always ponder this word — that it was God who wished to afflict him. It is as if he said that we should not think that our Lord Jesus was put by chance into a position where the wicked could torture him as they liked; for they could do nothing outside the counsel of God; just as St. Peter says in the *Acts*: "God has done what his hand and his counsel had determined." So, then, not without cause does the Prophet always lead us back to this, that we must raise our senses to God, and know that, inasmuch as he is the Judge of the world, he wished to take satisfaction of our sins and offences in the person of his only Son that we might be acquitted of them; and that not in vain was Jesus Christ thus harshly smitten that we might walk with uplifted heads. And we must understand that God did not wish to remember all our crimes, which makes us detestable before him. When we have learnt that, we shall have profited greatly, not only for one day, but for the whole of our lives. For, in truth, this is a doctrine to which we must so apply ourselves that, although it seems as if we know it well, we never cease to take pains to conform ourselves to it more and more.

—Sermons

*Then he answered and spake unto me, saying, This is
the word of the Lord unto Zerubbabel, saying, Not by
might, nor by power, but by my spirit, saith the Lord
of hosts.*   Zechariah 4:6

When we now see things in a despairing condition, let this
vision come to our minds — that God is sufficiently able by his
own power to help us, when there is no aid from any other;
for his Spirit will be to us for lamps, for pourers, and for
olive trees, so that experience will at length show that we have
been preserved in a wonderful manner by his hand alone.

Thus we remember that all our confidence ought to be
placed on the favor of God alone; for were it to depend on
human aids, there would be nothing certain or sure. For God,
as I have said, withdraws from us whatever may add courage
according to the judgment of the flesh, in order that he may
invite or rather draw us to himself. Whenever, then, earthly aids
fail us, let us learn to recline on God alone, for it is not by a
host or by might that God raises up his Church, and preserves
it in its proper state; but this he does by his Spirit, that is, by his
own intrinsic and wonderful power, which he does not blend
with human aids; and his object is to draw us away from the
world and to hold us wholly dependent on himself.

—Commentaries

*Are they not all ministering spirits, sent forth to min-
ister for them who shall be heirs of salvation?*
                                          Hebrews 1:14

We shall happily avoid error if we consider why God is
accustomed to provide for the safety of the faithful, and to
communicate the gifts of his generosity by means of angels,
rather than by himself to manifest his own power without their
intervention. He certainly does this not from necessity, as
though he were unable to do without them; for whenever he
pleases, he passes them by, and performs his work with a mere
nod of his power; so far is he from being indebted to their
assistance for relieving him in any difficulty. This, therefore,
conduces to the consolation of our feebleness, that we may
want nothing that can either raise our minds to a good hope, or
confirm them in security. This one thing, indeed, ought to be
more than sufficient for us, that the Lord declares himself to
be our Protector. But while we see ourselves encompassed by
so many dangers, so many annoyances, such various kinds of
enemies — such is our weakness and frailty, that we may sometimes be filled with terror, or fall into despair, unless the Lord
enables us, according to our capacity, to discover the presence
of his grace. For this reason he promises not only that he will
take care of us himself, but also that we shall have innumerable
lifeguards, to whom he has committed the charge of our safety;
and that, as long as we are surrounded by their superintendence
and protection, whatever danger may threaten, we are placed
beyond the utmost reach of evil. I confess, indeed, that it is
wrong for us, after that simple promise of the protection of
God alone, still to be looking around to see from what quarter
our aid may come. But since the Lord, in his infinite clemency
and goodness, is pleased to assist this our weakness, there is
no reason why we should neglect this great favor which he
shows us. — *Institutes,* I, xiv, xi

*And he said unto them, It is not for you to know the
times or the seasons, which the Father hath put in
his own power.*   Acts 1:7

It was too curious of them to desire to know that whereof
their Master would have them ignorant; but this is the true
means to become wise, namely, to go as far forward in learning as our Master Christ goes in teaching, and willingly to
be ignorant of those things which he conceals from us. But
forasmuch as there is naturally aroused in us a certain foolish
and vain curiosity, and also a certain rash kind of boldness, we
must diligently observe this admonition of Christ, by which he
corrects both these vices. But to the end we may know what
his meaning is hereby, we must notice the two things which
he joins together. "It is not for you," he says, "to know those
things which the Father has placed in his own power." He
speaks, indeed, of the times and seasons; but seeing there is
the like reason in other things, we must think this to be a
universal precept, that being contented with the revelation of
God, we think it an heinous crime to inquire any further. This
is the true mean between the two extremes. — *Commentaries*

*Brethren, I count not myself to have apprehended:
but this one thing I do, forgetting those things which
are behind, and reaching forth unto those things which
are before,*   Philippians 3:13

. . . Depravity never ceases in us, but is perpetually producing new fruits — those works of the flesh which we have already described, like the emission of flame and sparks from a
heated furnace, or like the streams of water from an unfailing

spring. For lust never dies, nor is altogether extinguished in men, till by death they are delivered from the body of death, and entirely divested of themselves. Baptism, indeed promises us the submersion of our Pharaoh, and the mortification of sin; yet not so that it no longer exists, or gives us no further trouble; but only that it may never overcome us. For as long as we live immured in this prison of the body, the relics of sin will dwell in us; but if we hold fast by faith the promise which God has given us in baptism, they shall not domineer or reign over us.

But let no man deceive himself, let no one flatter himself in his guilt, when he hears that sin always dwells in us. These things are not said in order that those who are already too prone to do evil may securely sleep in their sins, but only that those who are tempted by their corrupt inclinations may not faint and sink into despondency; but that they may rather reflect that they are yet in the way, and may consider themselves as having made some progress, when they experience their corruptions diminishing from day to day, till they shall attain the mark at which they are aiming, even the final destruction of their depravity, which will be accomplished at the close of this mortal life. In the meantime, let them not cease to fight manfully, to animate themselves to constant advances, and to press forward to complete victory. For it ought to give additional impulse to their exertions, to see that, after they have been striving so long, so much still remains for them to do. We conclude, therefore, that we are baptized into the mortification of the flesh, which commences in us at baptism, which we pursue from day to day, and which will be perfected when we pass out of this life to the Lord. — *Institutes*, IV, xv, xi

*By faith Moses, when he was come to years, refused
to be called the son of Pharaoh's daughter; Choosing
rather to suffer affliction with the people of God,
than to enjoy the pleasures of sin for a season; Esteem-
ing the reproach of Christ greater riches than the
treasures in Egypt: for he had respect unto the recom-
pence of the reward.*   Hebrews 11:24-26

You have already felt, as I think, that the sharpest and
most difficult assault is that of those who under color of
friendship, with insinuating arts, seek to make you swerve from
the right way. Those persons are never unprovided with plausible pretexts and allurements; so much the more then you have
need to put in practice the doctrine of the apostle, to take good
heed and to steel yourself against flatteries as well as fears. It
was the resolution of Moses, who, having it in his power to be
great at the court of Egypt, preferred the reproach of Christ
to all the pomps and perishing delights which would have cost
him too dear, had he allowed himself to be detained. Now
the apostle shows whence he derived this courage; it was in
hardening himself by looking upon God.

Thus, Monseigneur, elevating your thoughts, learn to stop
your ears against all the blasts of Satan, which strive only
to overthrow your salvation, by shaking the constancy of your
faith. Learn to shut your eyes to all distractions that would
tend to turn you aside, aware that they are but so many deceits of our mortal enemy. And by whatever wiles they engage
you to purchase your own safety in breaking the faith pledged
to the Son of God, let this saying be deeply stamped on your
memory, that he will be confessed by you on pain of your being
disavowed and renounced by him. Many, indeed, nowadays,
think they have but to wipe their mouth, after it has denied
the truth; but for all that the confession thereof is too precious
to God to be so lightly esteemed. And though it seems lost
pains to bear witness to the gospel among those who are rebels

to it, or even that such witnessing gives rise but to derision and reproach; yet, since it is a sacrifice well pleasing to God, let us content ourselves with being approved by him. One thing is certain; he will cause our simplicity to bring forth more fruits than we imagine, provided only we observe what he commands. — *Correspondence*

107   April 16

And said, Naked came I out of my mother's womb, and naked shall I return thither: the Lord gave, and the Lord hath taken away; blessed be the name of the Lord.   Job 1:21

The necessary consequences of this knowledge are, gratitude in prosperity, patience in adversity, and a wonderful security respecting the future. Every prosperous and pleasing event, therefore, the pious man will ascribe entirely to God, whether his generosity be received through the ministry of men, or by the assistance of inanimate creatures. For this will be the reflection of his mind, "It is certainly the Lord that has inclined their hearts to favor me, that has united them to me to be the instruments of his kindness towards me." In an abundance of the fruits of the earth, he will consider, that it is the Lord who regards the heaven, that the heaven may regard the earth, that the earth, also, may regard its own productions; in other things he will not doubt that it is the divine benediction alone which is the cause of all prosperity; nor will he bear to be ungrateful after so many admonitions.

If any adversity befall him, in this case also he will immediately lift up his heart to God, whose hand is most capable of impressing us with patience and placid moderation of mind.

                                  —*Institutes*, I, xvii, vii

Thy mercy, O Lord, is in the heavens; and thy faith-
fulness reacheth unto the clouds.   Psalm 36:5

After having spoken of the very great depravity of men, the
prophet, afraid lest he should become infected by it, or be
carried away by the example of the wicked, as by a flood,
quits the subject, and recovers himself by reflecting on a different theme. It usually happens, that in condemning the
wicked, the contagion of their malice insinuates itself into
our minds when we are not conscious of it; and there is scarcely
one in a hundred who, after having complained of the malice
of others, keeps himself in true godliness, pure and unpolluted.
The meaning therefore is: Although we may see among men
a sad and frightful confusion, which, like a great gulf, would
swallow up the minds of the godly, David, nevertheless, maintains that the world is full of the goodness and righteousness
of God, and that he governs heaven and earth on the strictest
principles of equity. And certainly, whenever the corruption
of the world affects our minds, and fills us with amazement,
we must take care not to limit our views to the wickedness of
men, who overturn and confound all things; but in the midst
of this strange confusion it becomes us to elevate our thoughts
in admiration and wonder, to the contemplation of the secret
providence of God. — *Commentaries*

*Arise, O Lord, in thine anger, lift up thyself because
of the rage of mine enemies: and awake for me to the
judgment that thou hast commanded. My defence is
of God, which saveth the upright in heart.*

Psalm 7:6, 10

And, indeed, we can never pray in faith unless we attend,
in the first place, to what God commands, that our minds may
not rashly and at random start aside in desiring more than we
are permitted to desire and pray for. David, therefore, in order
to pray aright, reposes himself on the word and promise of God;
and the import of his exercise is this: Lord, I am not led by
ambition, or foolish headstrong passion, or depraved desire,
inconsiderately to ask from thee whatever is pleasing to my
flesh; but it is the clear light of thy word which directs me,
and upon it I securely depend.

Is it not wonderful that David often mingles meditations with
his prayers, thereby to inspire himself with true confidence?
We may go to God in prayer with great alacrity; but our fervor,
if it does not gather new strength, either immediately fails
or begins to languish. David, therefore, in order to continue
in prayer with the same ardor of devotion and affection with
which he commenced, brings to his recollection some of the
most common truths of religion, and by this means fosters and
invigorates his faith. He declares that as God saves the upright
in heart, he is perfectly safe under his protection. Whence it
follows, that he had the testimony of an approving conscience.
And as he does not simply say the righteous, but the upright
in heart, he appears to have an eye to that inward searching of
the heart and reins mentioned in the preceding verse.

—Commentaries

Now I rejoice, not that ye were made sorry, but that ye sorrowed to repentance: for ye were made sorry after a godly manner, that ye might receive damage by us in nothing. For godly sorrow worketh repentance to salvation not to be repented of: but the sorrow of the world worketh death.   II Corinthians 7:9, 10

Since conversion commences with a dread and hatred of sin, therefore the apostle makes godly sorrow the cause of repentance. He calls it godly sorrow when we not only dread punishment, but hate and abhor sin itself; from a knowledge that it is displeasing to God. Nor ought this to be thought strange; for, unless we felt sharp compunction, our carnal sluggishness could never be corrected, and even these distresses of mind would not be sufficient to arouse it from its stupidity and indolence, if God, by the infliction of his chastisements, did not make a deeper impression.

Besides this, there is a rebellious obstinacy, which requires violent blows, as it were, to overcome it. The severity, therefore, which God uses in his threatenings, is extorted from him by the depravity of our minds; since it would be in vain for him to address kind and alluring invitations to those who are asleep.

The fear of God is called the beginning of repentance also for another reason; because though a man's life were perfect in every virtue, if it be not devoted to the worship of God, it may indeed be commended by the world, but in heaven it will be only an abomination; since the principal branch of righteousness consists in rendering to God the honor due to him, of which he is impiously defrauded, when it is not our end and aim to submit ourselves to his government.

—*Institutes,* III, iii, vii

Jesus answered and said unto her, If thou knewest the gift of God, and who it is that saith to thee, Give me to drink; thou wouldest have asked of him, and he would have given thee living water.   John 4:10

"Jesus answered." Christ, now, availing himself of the opportunity, begins to preach about the grace and power of his Spirit, and that to a woman who did not at all deserve that he should speak a word to her. This is certainly an astonishing instance of his goodness. For what was there in this wretched woman, that, from being a prostitute, she suddenly became a disciple of the Son of God? Though in all of us he has displayed a similar instance of his compassion. All the women, indeed, are not prostitutes, nor are all the men stained by some heinous crime; but what excellence can any of us plead as a reason why he deigned to bestow on us the heavenly doctrine, and the honor of being admitted into his family? Nor was it by accident that the conversation with such a person occurred; for the Lord showed us, as in a model, that those to whom he imparts the doctrine of salvation are not selected on the ground of merit. And it appears at first sight a wonderful arrangement, that he passed by so many great men in Judea, and yet held familiar discourse with this woman. But it was necessary that, in his person, it should be explained how true is that saying of the Prophet, "I was found by them that sought me not; I was made manifest to them that asked not after me. I said to those who sought me not, Behold, here I am" (Isaiah 65:1).— *Commentaries*

Then I said, I have laboured in vain, I have spent my
strength for nought, and in vain: yet surely my judg-
ment is with the Lord, and my work with my God.
Isaiah 49:4

"But my judgment is before Jehovah." Although we do not clearly see the fruit of our labors, yet we are enjoined to be content on this ground, that we serve God, to whom our obedience is acceptable. Christ exhorts and encourages godly teachers to strive earnestly till they rise victorious over this temptation, and, laying aside the malice of the world, to advance cheerfully in the discharge of duty, and not to allow their hearts to languish through weariness. If therefore the Lord be pleased to make trial of our faith and patience to such an extent that it shall seem as if we wearied ourselves to no purpose, yet we ought to rely on this testimony of our conscience. And if we do not enjoy this consolation, at least we are not moved by pure affection, and do not serve God, but the world and our own ambition.

Yet it ought to be observed that here Christ and the Church accuse the whole world of ingratitude. For the Church complains to God in such a manner as to remonstrate with the world, because no good effect is produced in it by the doctrine of the gospel, which in itself is efficacious and powerful. Yet the whole blame rests on the obstinacy and ingratitude of men, who reject the grace of God offered to them, and of their own accord choose to perish. Let those persons now go and accuse Christ, who say that the gospel yields little fruit, and who defame the doctrine of the word by wicked slanders, and who throw ridicule on our labors as vain and unprofitable, and who allege that, on the contrary, they excite men to sedition, and lead them to sin with less control. Let them consider, I say, with whom they have to do, and what advantage they gain by their impudence, since men alone ought to bear the blame, who, as far as lies in their power, render the preaching of the Word unprofitable. — *Commentaries*

Stand in awe, and sin not: commune with your own
heart upon your bed, and be still.   Psalm 4:4

To commune upon one's bed is a form of expression taken
from the common practice and experience of men. We know
that, during our intercourse with men in the daytime, our
thoughts are distracted, and we often judge rashly, being deceived by the external appearance; whereas in solitude, we can
give to any subject a closer attention; and, farther, the sense
of shame does not then hinder a man from thinking without
disguise about his own faults. David, therefore, exhorts his
enemies to withdraw from those who witnessed and judged of
their actions on the public stage of life, and to be alone, that
they may examine themselves more truthfully and honestly.
And this exhortation has a respect to us all; for there is nothing
to which men are more prone than to deceive one another with
empty applause, until each man enter into himself, and commune alone with his own heart. Paul, when quoting this passage in Ephesians 4:26, or, at least, when alluding to the
sentiment of David, follows the Septuagint, "Be ye angry and
sin not." And yet he has skillfully and beautifully applied it
to his purpose. He there teaches us that men, instead of wickedly pouring forth their anger against their neighbors, have
rather just cause to be angry with themselves, in order that,
by this means, they may abstain from sin. And therefore he
commands them rather to fret inwardly and be angry with
themselves; and then to be angry not so much at the persons,
as at the vices of others. — *Commentaries*

*Now Elihu had waited till Job had spoken, because
they were elder than he.*   Job 32:4

So then let God's children be on their guard and see that
they remain modest; this is a beautiful, though unspectacular,
virtue. And although they who seek to advance themselves
despise them because they are not constantly putting themselves forward, let them assure themselves that they are much
rather noticed by God, and that he will bless their honest
behavior and make them to profit more in two years than those
who are too hasty will do in four. We see what happens to
fruit. If fruit is too soon ripe it also fades away quickly.
But the fruit that is slower in maturing also lasts longer. So
it is with those who wish to advance themselves before their
time. Truly they may have some beauty and some taste; but
it will not last. On the other hand, those who are modest and
honest, and not so presumptuous as to put themselves forward
hastily, will surely be slow; but in the meantime the Lord
gives them a more abiding fruit.

It is true that modesty is a virtue proper for all men.
Nevertheless young people ought to note what is said here,
namely that they must yield honor to their elders, acknowledging that they may have excessive passions which need to
be restrained by other men. For they are not sufficiently
established in their own nature, and they lack experience in
self-control.

Furthermore, when a young man has behaved himself thus
modestly, he must at the proper time utter the thing that God
has given him, even though it be among older people. For the
order of nature does not prevent a young man, when older men
do not discharge their duty, to supply what they lack — yes,
even to the shame of those who have lived long, and misspent
the time that God has given them, or rather utterly lost it.
You see, then, the middle position which we have to hold. The
reverence which young folks bear to their elders must not

hinder the maintenance of the truth, that God should be honored and vices suppressed. For it may happen that the older men are destitute of God's Spirit, or else lewd persons shall have in them nothing but craft and unfaithfulness; or perhaps they will be opinionated or headstrong. Now in such cases, should young people be so held under the yoke that they shall by the authority of their elders be turned away from God and his Word and from that which is good and holy? Certainly not. — *Sermons*

115   A<small>PRIL</small> **24**

Greater love hath no man than this, that a man lay down his life for his friends.   John 15:13

"Greater love hath no man than this." Christ sometimes proclaims the greatness of his love to us, that he may more fully confirm our confidence in our salvation; but now he proceeds further, in order to inflame us by his example, to love the brethren. Yet he joins both together; for he means that we should taste by faith how inestimably delightful his goodness is, and next he allures us in this way to cultivate brotherly love. Thus Paul writes, "Walk in love, as Christ also hath loved us, and hath given himself for us an offering and sacrifice to God of a sweet-smelling savor" (Eph. 5:2). God might have redeemed us by a single word, or by a mere act of his will, if he had not thought it better to do otherwise for our own benefit, that, by not sparing his own well-beloved Son, he might testify in his person how much he cares for our salvation. But now our hearts, if they are not softened by the inestimable sweetness of Divine love, must be harder than stone or iron. — *Commentaries*

*For God so loved the world, that he gave his only be-
gotten Son, that whosoever believeth in him should
not perish, but have everlasting life.*   John 3:16

"For God so loved the world." Christ opens up the first
cause, and, as it were, the source of our salvation; and he does
so, that no doubt may remain; for our minds cannot find calm
repose until we arrive at the unmerited grace of God. As the
whole matter of our salvation must not be sought anywhere
else than in Christ, so we must see whence Christ came to us,
and why he was offered to be our Savior. Both points are distinctly stated to us; namely, that faith in Christ brings life to
all, and that Christ brought life, because the Heavenly Father
loves the human race, and wishes that they should not perish.
And this order ought to be carefully observed; for such is the
wicked ambition which belongs to our nature, that when the
question relates to the origin of our salvation, we quickly form
diabolical imaginations about our own merit. Accordingly, we
imagine that God is reconciled to us, because he has reckoned
us worthy that he should look upon us. But Scripture everywhere extols his pure and unmingled mercy, which sets aside
all merits. — *Commentaries*

When I consider thy heavens, the work of thy fingers,
the moon and the stars, which thou hast ordained;
What is man, that thou art mindful of him? and the
son of man, that thou visitest him?   Psalm 8:3, 4

My readers, however, must be careful to note the design
of the Psalmist, which is to enhance by this comparison the
infinite goodness of God; for it is, indeed, a wonderful thing
that the Creator of heaven, whose glory is so surpassingly
great as to ravish us with the highest admiration, condescends
so far as graciously to take upon him the care of the human
race. That the Psalmist makes this contrast may be inferred
from the Hebrew word, which expresses the frailty of man
rather than any strength or power which he possesses. We see
that miserable men, in moving upon the earth, are mingled
with the vilest creatures; and, therefore, God, with very good
reason, might despise them and reckon them of no account
if he were to stand upon the consideration of his own greatness or dignity.

The Psalmist, therefore, speaking interrogatively, abases
their condition, intimating that God's wonderful goodness is
displayed the more brightly in that so glorious a Creator, whose
majesty shines resplendently in the heavens, graciously condescends to adorn a creature so miserable and vile as man is
with the greatest glory, and to enrich him with numberless
blessings. If he had a mind to exercise his liberality towards
any, he was under no necessity of choosing men who are but
dust and clay, in order to prefer them above all other creatures,
seeing he had a sufficient number in heaven towards whom to
show himself liberal. Whoever, therefore, is not astonished and
deeply affected at this miracle, is more than ungrateful and
stupid. — *Commentaries*

*I the Lord have called thee in righteousness, and will
hold thine hand, and will keep thee, and give thee for
a covenant of the people, for a light of the Gentiles;*

Isaiah 42:6

"For a light of the Gentiles." We have here another
clear proof of the calling of the Gentiles, since he expressly
states that Christ was appointed to be "a light" to them. He
calls him *a light*, because the Gentiles were plunged in the
deepest and thickest of darkness, at the time when the Lord
illuminated none but the Jews. Now, then, the blame lies
solely with ourselves, if we do not become partakers of this
salvation; for he calls all men to himself, without a single exception, and gives Christ to all, that we may be illuminated by
him. Let us only open our eyes, he alone will dispel the
darkness, and illuminate our minds by the "light" of truth.

—Commentaries

*My heart was hot within me, while I was musing the
the fire burned: then spake I with my tongue,*

Psalm 39:3

"My heart became hot within me." He now illustrates the
greatness of his grief by the introduction of a simile, telling
us that his sorrow, being internally suppressed, became so
much the more inflamed, until the ardent passion of his soul
continued to increase in strength. From this we may learn the
very profitable lesson that the more strenuously anyone sets
himself to obey God, and employs all his endeavors to attain
the exercise of patience, the more vigorously he is assailed
by temptation; for Satan, while he is not so troublesome to
the indifferent and careless, and seldom looks near them,
displays all his forces in hostile array against that individual.

If, therefore, at any time we feel ardent emotions struggling and raising a commotion in our breasts, we should call to remembrance this conflict of David, that our courage may not fail us, or at least that our infirmity may not drive us headlong to despair.

If the godly who desire to lift up their hearts to God would resign themselves to the vain imaginations which arise in their minds, they might enjoy a sort of unrestrained liberty to indulge in every fancy; but because they endeavor to resist their influence, and seek to devote themselves to God, obstructions which arise from the opposition of the flesh begin to trouble them. Whenever, therefore, the flesh shall put forth its efforts, and shall kindle a fire in our hearts, let us know that we are exercised with the same kind of temptation which occasioned so much pain and trouble to David.—*Commentaries*

These things I have spoken unto you, that in me ye might have peace. In the world ye shall have tribulation: but be of good cheer; I have overcome the world.   John 16:33

"I have overcome the world." As there is always in us much reason for trembling, he shows that we ought to be confident for this reason, that he has obtained a victory over the world, not for himself individually, but for our sake. Thus, though in ourselves almost overwhelmed, if we contemplate that magnificent glory to which our Head has been exalted, we may boldly despise all the evils which hang over us. If, therefore, we desire to be Christians, we must not seek exemption from the cross, but must be satisfied with this single consideration, that, fighting under the banner of Christ, we are beyond all dangers, even in the midst of the combat. — *Commentaries*

Fire, and hail; snow and vapours; stormy wind ful-
filling his word: Psalm 148:8

He then ascends to hail, snows, and storms, which he says
fulfill the word of God; for it is not by an effect of chance
that the heavens are clouded, or that a single drop of rain
falls from the clouds, or that the thunders rage, but one and
all of these changes depend upon the secret will of God,
whether he will show his goodness to the children of men in
irrigating the earth, or punish their sins by tempest, hail, or
other calamities. The passage contains instruction of various
kinds, as, for example, that when dearth impends, however
parched the earth may be by long continued heat, God can
promptly send rain which will remove the drought at his
pleasure. If from incessant rains, on the other hand, the seed
rot in the ground, or the crops do not come to maturity, we
should pray for fair weather. If we are alarmed by thunder, we
are taught to pray to God, for as it is he who sends it in his
anger, so he can still all the troubled elements. And we are
not to take up the narrow view of this truth which irreligious
men advocate, that things in nature merely move according
to the laws impressed upon them from the beginning, while God
stands by idle, but are to hold firmly that God watches over
his creatures, and that nothing can take place without his
present disposal, as we have seen (Psalm 104:4) that "he
maketh the winds his messengers, and his ministers a flaming
fire." — *Commentaries*

*It is a faithful saying: For if we be dead with him, we
shall also live with him:*   II Timothy 2:11

While we live in this world, our life is hidden, even as the
life of trees is hidden in winter. Behold, trees are dry, we see
no strength in them, a man would think it were but dead
wood; but yet their strength shows itself in the springtime.
Even so it is with the faithful. For while they are in this
world, their life is shut up in hope. Now that which we hope
for is not seen, the eye of man cannot attain unto it. It follows,
then, that in dying we must live; not only with one kind of
death, but we must die daily, we must decay, as touching the
outward man; as he says, sickness, poverty, shame, and such
things, serve us to renounce this world and feel that our life
is but a shadow, that it is nothing, yes, and that we receive
so many messages of death when things do not go as we would
have them. And therefore let us note well that Paul meant
here not simply that we must die once, and then live; but
while we live that we are daily buried as it were; that we see
death present as it were; that we are like sheep that have the
knife at their throats. For it is not enough for us to die so,
but we must follow the standard of the Son of God and look
to his resurrection, which is sufficient to make the bitterness of
death sweet to us. — *Sermons*

Therefore my people shall know my name: therefore they shall know in that day that I am he that doth speak: behold, it is I.
          Isaiah 52:6

We ought carefully to observe the word "know"; for to "know the name of the Lord" is to lay aside every false opinion, and to know him from his word, which is his true image, and next from his works. We must not imagine God according to the fancy of men, but must comprehend him as he declares himself to us. The Lord, therefore, concludes that he will actually assist them, and will fulfill all that he has promised, that the people may know that their hope has not been without foundation, and that they may be more and more confirmed in the knowledge of his name. We must keep in remembrance that experiential knowledge confirms the truth of the word.

          —*Commentaries*

I say unto you, Though he will not rise and give him, because he is his friend, yet because of his importunity he will rise and give him as many as he needeth.
          Luke 11:8

In our supplications, let us have a real and permanent sense of our need, and seriously considering our necessity of all that we ask, let us join with the petitions themselves a serious and ardent desire of obtaining them. For multitudes carelessly recite a form of prayer, as though they were discharging a task imposed on them by God; and though they confess that this is a remedy necessary for their calamities, since it would be certain destruction to be destitute of the Divine aid which they implore, yet that they perform this duty merely in compliance with custom, is evident from the coldness of their hearts, and their inattention to the nature of their petitions. They are led to this by some general and confused sense of their necessity, which nevertheless does not excite them to implore a relief for their great need as a case of present urgency.

Now what can we imagine more odious to God than this hypocrisy, when any man prays for the pardon of sins, who at the same time thinks he is not a sinner, or at least does not think that he *is* a sinner? What open mockery of God himself! But such depravity pervades the whole human race, that as a matter of form they frequently implore God for many things which they either expect to receive from some other source independent of his goodness, or imagine themselves already to possess. The crime of some others appears to be smaller, but yet too great to be tolerated; who, having only imbibed this principle, that God must be appeased by devotions, mutter over their prayers without meditation. But believers ought to be exceedingly cautious never to enter into the presence of God to present any petition without being inflamed with a fervent affection of soul, and feeling an ardent desire to obtain it from him.

Moreover, although in those things which we request only for the Divine glory, we do not at the first glance appear to regard our own necessity, yet it is our duty to pray for them with equal fervor and vehemence of desire. As when we pray that his name may be hallowed, or sanctified, we ought (so to speak) ardently to hunger and thirst for that sanctification.

—*Institutes*, III, xx, vi

Seeing many things, but thou observest not; opening the ears, but he heareth not.   Isaiah 42:20

"Seeing many things." The Prophet himself explains what is the nature of this blindness of which he spoke, and shows that it is double; and this shows clearly that he spoke of the Jews, who by wicked contempt had quenched God's light. Our guilt will be double when we shall come to the judgment-seat of God, if we shut our eyes when he exhibits the light, and shut our ears when he teaches by his word. The heathen nations will be indeed without excuse; but the Jews, and others to whom the Lord revealed himself in so many ways, will deserve double condemnation for having refused to see or hear God. We, therefore, who have so many and so illustrious examples set before us at the present day, ought to dread this judgment; for in many persons there will now be found not less blindness and obduracy than formerly existed among the Jews, and not more excusable. — *Commentaries*

Unto Timothy, my own son in the faith: Grace, mercy,
and peace, from God our Father and Jesus Christ our
Lord.　　　　　　　　　　　　　I Timothy 1:2

Let this be well understood, that when God receives us
into his love, there is nothing that moves him to this but our
wretchedness and miserable state; yes, the mercy of God, in
that he pities us and has compassion on us, shows that there
is on our part a wretchedness and misery to be pitied, so that
the one answers to the other. Note well, then, do we want
him to love us? Then we must begin at this end, namely with
a feeling that we are wretched creatures, that we are castaways
and damned. Whoever they would be that would hope for
salvation, and have no taste or feeling of their wretchedness,
are like a man who would try to leap above the clouds. Let
us learn, let us learn the way to come to this grace of God,
which is no other than this, that we shall stand aghast at our
wretchedness and be ashamed and cast down within ourselves,
because there is nothing in us but naughtiness and wickedness. And then let us flee to that infinite mercy and pity
wherewith God is moved to love us. — *Sermons*

And I heard a voice from heaven saying unto me,
Write, Blessed are the dead which die in the Lord
from henceforth: Yea, saith the Spirit, that they may
rest from their labours; and their works do follow
them.　　　　　　　　　　　　Revelation 14:13

But what advantage, you will say, is it to me to have had
a son of so much promise, since he has been torn away from me
in the first flower of his youth? As if, indeed, Christ had
not merited, by his death, the supreme dominion over the

living and the dead! And if we belong to him (as we ought) why may he not exercise over us the power of life and of death? However brief, therefore, either in your opinion or in mine, the life of your son may have been, it ought to satisfy us that he has finished the course which the Lord has marked out for him.

Moreover, we may not reckon him to have perished in the flower of his age who had grown ripe in the sight of the Lord. For I consider all to have arrived at maturity who are summoned away by death; unless, perhaps, one would contend with him, as if he can snatch away any one before his time. This, indeed, holds true of every one; but in regard to Louis, it is yet more certain on another and peculiar ground. For he had arrived at that age when, by true evidences, he could prove himself a member of the body of Christ: having put forth this fruit, he was taken from us and transplanted. Yes, instead of this transient and vanishing shadow of life, he has regained the real immortality of being.

Nor can you consider yourself to have lost him, whom you will recover in the blessed resurrection in the kingdom of God. For they had both so lived and so died, that I cannot doubt but they are now with the Lord; let us, therefore, press forward toward this goal which they have reached. There can be no doubt but that Christ will bind together both them and us in the same inseparable society, in that incomparable participation of his own glory. Beware, therefore, that you do not lament your son as lost, whom you acknowledge to be preserved by the Lord, that he may remain yours for ever who, at the pleasure of his own will, lent him to you only for a season.

Nor will you derive small consolation from this consideration, if you only weigh carefully what is left to you. Charles survives to you, of whom we all entertain this sentiment, that there is not one of us who does not desire that he might have such a son. Do not suppose that these expressions are only intended for your hearing, or that there is exaggeration here, in order to bespeak your favor. This is no more my habit than it is my disposition. — *Correspondence*

*He that descended is the same also that ascended up
far above all heavens, that he might fill all things.*
                                        Ephesians 4:10

Though Christ began to make a more illustrious display of
his glory and power at his resurrection, having now laid aside
the abject and ignoble condition of this mortal life, and the
shame of the cross, yet his ascension into heaven was the real
commencement of his reign. This the apostle shows, when he
informs us that he "ascended that he might fill all things."
Here, in an apparent contradiction, he suggests to us that
there is a beautiful harmony, because Christ departed from us,
that his departure might be more useful to us than that presence,
which, during his continuance on earth, confined itself within
the humble mansion of his body . . . .
The Lord declared to his disciples, "It is expedient for you
that I go away; for if I go not away, the Comforter will not
come unto you." Now, he proposes a consolation for his bodily
absence, that he "will not leave them comfortless, or orphans,
but will come again to them," in a manner invisible, indeed,
but more desirable: because they were then taught by a more
certain experience that the authority which he enjoys, and the
power which he exercises, is sufficient for the faithful, not only
to procure them a blessed life, but to insure them a happy
death.
. . . Being received up into heaven, therefore, he removed
his bodily presence from our view; not that he might no longer
be present with the faithful who were still in a state of
pilgrimage on earth, but that he might govern both heaven and
earth by a more efficacious energy. Moreover, his promise, that
he would be with us till the end of the world, he has performed by his ascension; by which, as his body was elevated
above all heavens, so his power and energy have been diffused
and extended beyond all the limits of heaven and earth.
                                        —*Institutes*, II, xvi, xiv

MAY 8

*And wisdom and knowledge shall be the stability of
thy times, and strength of salvation: the fear of the
Lord is his treasure.* Isaiah 33:6

"The fear of Jehovah is his treasure." This is a very remarkable passage; and it teaches us that our ingratitude shuts
the door against God's blessings, when we disregard the Author
of them, and sink into gross and earthly desires; and that all
the benefits which we can desire or imagine, even though we
actually obtained them, would be of no avail for our salvation if they were not seasoned with the salt of faith and
knowledge. Hence it follows that the Church is not in a
healthy condition unless when all its privileges have been preceded by the light of the knowledge of God, and that it flour-
ishes only when all the gifts which God has bestowed upon it
are ascribed to him as their Author. But when the knowledge
of God has been taken away, and when just views of God
have been extinguished or buried, any kind of prosperity is
worse than all calamities. — *Commentaries*

MAY 9

*The Lord said unto my Lord, Sit thou at my right
hand, until I make thine enemies thy footstool.*
Psalm 110:1

So, in another place, when, speaking in the name of God,
he says, "Sit thou at my right hand, until I make thine
enemies thy footstool," he apprises us that though numerous
and powerful enemies conspire to assault the Church, yet they
are not strong enough to prevail against that immutable decree
of God, by which he has constituted his Son an eternal King.
Whence it follows that it is impossible for the devil, with all
the assistance of the world, ever to destroy the Church, which
is founded on the eternal throne of Christ. Now with respect

to its particular use to each individual, this same eternity ought to encourage our hope of a blessed immortality; for we see that whatever is terrestrial and worldly is temporary and perishable. Therefore, to raise our hope towards heaven, Christ declares that his "kingdom is not of this world." In a word, whenever we hear that the kingdom of Christ is spiritual, excited by this declaration, we ought to penetrate to the hope of a better life, and as we are now protected by the power of Christ, let us expect the full benefit of his grace in the world to come. — *Institutes*, II, xv, iii

131   **MAY 10**

Therefore being justified by faith, we have peace with God through our Lord Jesus Christ: Romans 5:1

The principal hinge on which faith turns is this—that we must not consider the promises of mercy, which the Lord offers, as true only to others, and not to ourselves; but rather make them our own, by embracing them in our hearts. Hence arises that confidence, which the same apostle in another place calls "peace"; unless any one would rather make peace the effect of confidence. It is a security, which makes the conscience calm and serene before the Divine tribunal, and without which it must necessarily be harassed and torn almost asunder with tumultuous trepidation, unless it happens to slumber for a moment in an oblivion of God and itself. And indeed it is but for a moment; for it does not long enjoy that wretched oblivion, but is most dreadfully wounded by the remembrance, which is constantly recurring, of the Divine judgment. In short, no man is truly a believer unless he be firmly persuaded that God is a propitious and benevolent Father to him, and promise himself every thing from his goodness; unless he depend on the promises of the Divine benevolence to him, and feel an undoubted expectation of salvation.

—*Institutes*, III, ii, xvi

*Will a man rob God? Yet ye have robbed me. But
ye say, Wherein have we robbed thee? In tithes and
offerings.*   Malachi 3:8

But we know that other sacrifices are now prescribed to us;
and after prayer and praises he bids us to relieve the poor and
needy. God, then, no doubt, is deprived by us of his right,
when we are unkind to the poor and refuse them aid in their
necessity. We indeed wrong men, and are cruel; but our
crime is still more heinous, inasmuch as we are unfaithful
stewards; for God deals more liberally with us than with others,
for this end — that some portion of our abundance may come
to the poor; and as he consecrates to their use what we abound
in, we become guilty of sacrilege whenever we give not to our
brethren what God commands us; for we know that he engages
to repay, according to what is said in Prov. 19:17, "He who
gives to the poor lends to God." — *Commentaries*

*There is no darkness, nor shadow of death, where the
workers of iniquity may hide themselves.* Job 34:22

So then let us know that it is greatly for our profit that God
today sends us his Word to enlighten us, that we may consider our sins. Though we have not thought of them for a
while, we are reminded of them, so that we may put into
practice what Saint Paul urges, namely to humble ourselves,
to be ashamed before God, and to condemn ourselves by rec-
ognizing the wickedness which is so deeply rooted in us. See,
I say, how God works our salvation, by making us feel such
a power and effectiveness in his Word that we endeavor to

examine our whole life thoroughly, to the end that we may be displeased with ourselves.

But those who are stubborn and despise God, and come like deranged men to fight against him, and cannot endure any warning; he must send them, as unreasonable people, to the day of which Elihu speaks here, where there shall be no darkness or cover so thick, but it shall be laid wide open, in the sight of all creatures. They cannot now endure that God should make them ashamed, that their sins might be buried forever. Nevertheless, in spite of their defiance, angels and devils and men must know their wickedness, and they must be shamed everywhere by this light which discloses all secrets.

Thus you see how we ought to apply this text to our instruction. For surely our Lord's threatening of men with the great day is in order that they should prepare for it; and so the remedy is ready for us. God does not delay to indict us until we appear before him; but executes his jurisdiction daily by the Gospel; as our Lord Jesus Christ says, that when the Holy Spirit comes, he shall judge the world. Therefore, when the Gospel is preached, God exercises a sovereign jurisdiction, not upon men's bodies, as they are today, but upon their souls; and he wills that we should be condemned thereby to our own welfare. And therefore, seeing that God warns us so much and so often that we must in the end come to the great light, let us not persist in shutting our eyes, nor wilfully be blind when he sends us his Word to disclose our filthiness and to show us that we cannot hide ourselves from his sight. So let us profit by the means that are given us today. But if we wish to play the wild beasts and always seek foxholes, yet in the end we shall feel that it is not said in vain that there is no darkness before God. For he will make us to behold those things in his countenance and glorious majesty which we refused to see here in the mirror of his Word. — *Sermons*

*Hear this, all ye people; give ear, all ye inhabitants
of the world:*   Psalm 49:1

As God's providence of the world is not presently apparent,
we must exercise patience, and rise superior to the suggestions
of carnal sense in anticipation of the favorable issue. That
it is our duty to maintain a resolute struggle with our affliction's, however severe these may be, and that it were foolish
to place happiness in the enjoyment of such fleeting possessions as the riches, honors, or pleasures of this world, may be
precepts which even the heathen philosophers have enforced,
but they have uniformly failed in setting before us the true
source of consolation. However admirably they discourse of a
happy life, they confine themselves entirely to commendations
upon virtue, and do not bring prominently forward to our view
that God, who governs the world, and to whom alone we can
repair with confidence in the most desperate circumstances.
But slender comfort can be derived upon this subject from the
teaching of philosophy.

If, therefore, the Holy Ghost in this psalm introduces to
our notice truths which are sufficiently familiar to experience,
it is that he may raise our minds from them to the higher truth
of the Divine government of the world, assuring us of the
fact that God sits supreme even when the wicked are triumph-
ing most in their success, or when the righteous are trampled
under the foot of disgrace, and that a day is coming when he
will dash the cup of pleasure out of the hands of his enemies,
and rejoice the hearts of his friends, by delivering them out
of their severest distresses. This is the only consideration which
can impart solid comfort under our afflictions. Formidable and
terrible in themselves, they would overwhelm our souls, did
not the Lord lift upon us the light of his countenance. Were
we not assured that he watches over our safety, we could find
no remedy from our evils, and no quarter to which we might
resort under them. — *Commentaries*

Took branches of palm trees, and went forth to meet him, and cried, Hosanna: Blessed is the King of Israel that cometh in the name of the Lord.

John 12:13

We ought to derive from this a profitable admonition; for if we are members of the Church, the Lord calls upon us to cherish the same desire which he wished believers to cherish under the Law; that is, that we should wish with our whole heart that the kingdom of Christ should flourish and prosper; and not only so, but that we should demonstrate this by our prayers. In order to give us greater courage in prayer, we ought to observe that he prescribes to us these words. Woe then to our slothfulness, if we extinguish by our coldness or quench by indifference that ardor which God excites. Yet let us know that the prayers which we offer by the direction and authority of God will not be in vain. Provided that we be not indolent or grow weary in praying, he will be a faithful guardian of his kingdom, to defend it by his invincible power and protection.

True, indeed, though we remain drowsy and inactive, the majesty of his kingdom will be firm and sure; but when — as is frequently the case — it is less prosperous than it ought to be at the present day, fearfully scattered and wasted, this unquestionably arises through our fault. And when but a small restoration, or almost none, is to be seen, or when at least it advances slowly, let us ascribe it to our indifference. We daily ask from God that his kingdom may come, but scarcely one man in a hundred earnestly desires it. Justly, therefore, we are deprived of the blessing of God, which we are weary of asking.

—Commentaries

*Blessed is the man whom thou chastenest, O Lord, and
teachest him out of thy law;*   Psalm 94:12

You know, Madame, how we should turn to our profit both
the chastisements we receive from the hand of our merciful
Father and the succor which he sends in time of need. It is
certain that all diseases ought not only to humble us in setting
before our eyes our frailty, but also cause us to look into
ourselves, that having recognized our own poverty we may place
all our trust in his mercy. They should, moreover, serve us
for medicine to purge us from worldly affections, and retrench
what is superfluous in us, and since they are to us the messengers of death, we ought to learn to have one foot raised to take
our departure when it shall please God.

Nevertheless, he lets us taste of his bounty as often as he
delivers us from them, just as it has been a most salutary thing
for you, Madame, to have known the danger in which you
were and from which he has delivered you. It remains for you
to conclude with Saint Paul that when we have been delivered
from many deaths by his hand, he will also withdraw us from
them in time to come. And thus take courage, so much the
more to give yourself up to his service, as you do well to consider that it is to that end he has reserved you.

—Letter to Madame De Coligny

A son honoureth his father, and a servant his master:
if then I be a father, where is mine honour? and if I
be a master, where is my fear? saith the Lord of hosts
unto you, O priests, that despise my name. And ye say,
Wherein have we despised thy name?   Malachi 1:6

It was God's complaint that he was deprived of his own right and in a double sense, for the Jews did not reverence him as their Father, nor fear him as their Lord. He might indeed have called himself Lord and Father by the right of creation; but he preferred to appeal to their adoption; for it was a remarkable favor when the Lord chose some out of all the human race; and we cannot say that the cause of this was to be found in men. Whom then he designs to choose, he binds to himself by a holier bond. But if they disappoint him, their falseness is wholly inexcusable.

This doctrine is not less useful to us at this day than it was to the Jews; for though the adoption is not exactly the same, as it then belonged to one seed and to one family, yet we are not superior to others through our own worthiness, but because God has gratuitously chosen us as a people to himself. Since this has been the case, we are his; for he has redeemed us by the blood of his own Son, and by rendering us partakers, by the gospel, of a favor so ineffably great, he has made us his sons and his servants. Except then we love and reverence him as our Father, and except we fear him as our Lord, there is found in us at this day an ingratitude no less base than in that ancient people. — *Commentaries*

*In whom ye also trusted, after that ye heard the word
of truth, the gospel of your salvation: in whom also
after that ye believed, ye were sealed with that holy
Spirit of promise,*   Ephesians 1:13

Paul asserts that the Ephesians were "sealed with that Holy Spirit of promise." This shows that there is an eternal teacher, by whose agency the promise of our salvation, which otherwise would only strike the air, penetrates into our minds. Similar also is his remark, that the Thessalonians were "chosen by God through sanctification of the Spirit, and belief of truth." By this connection he briefly suggests that faith itself proceeds only from the Spirit. John expresses this in plainer terms: "We know that he abideth in us, by the Spirit which he hath given us." Again, "Hereby know we that we dwell in him, and he in us, because he hath given us of his Spirit." Therefore Christ promised to send to his disciples "the Spirit of truth, whom the world cannot receive," that they might be capable of attaining heavenly wisdom. He ascribes to him the peculiar office of suggesting to their minds all the oral instructions which he had given them. For in vain would the light present itself to the blind, unless the Spirit of understanding would open their mental eyes; so that he may be justly called the key with which the treasures of the kingdom are unlocked to us; and his illumination constitutes our mental eyes to behold them. It is therefore that Paul so highly commends the ministry of the Spirit; because the instructions of preachers would produce no benefit, did not Christ himself, the internal teacher, by his Spirit, draw to him those who were given him by the Father. Therefore, as we have stated, that complete salvation is found in the person of Christ, so, to make us partakers of it, he "baptizes us with the Holy Spirit and with fire," enlightening us unto the faith of his Gospel, regenerating us so that we become new creatures, and purging us from profane impurities, consecrates us as holy temples to God. — *Institutes*, III, i, iv

*It may be the Lord thy God will hear the words of
Rabshakeh, whom the king of Assyria his master hath
sent to reproach the living God, and will reprove the
words which the Lord thy God hath heard: wherefore
lift up thy prayer for the remnant that is left.*

Isaiah 37:4

"Thou wilt therefore lift up a prayer." This is the second
reason why Hezekiah sent messengers to Isaiah; namely, that
he also would pray along with others. Hence we learn that
it is the duty of a prophet, not only to comfort the afflicted
by the word of the Lord, but also to offer his prayers for
their salvation. Let not pastors and ministers of the word,
therefore, think that they have fully discharged their duty,
when they have exhorted and taught, if they do not also add
prayer. This indeed is what all ought to do; but Hezekiah
sent to Isaiah in a particular manner, because he ought to
lead the way to others by his example.

Besides, "to lift up a prayer" is nothing else than "to pray,"
but the mode of expression deserves attention; for it shows how
our feelings ought to be regulated when we pray. Scripture
everywhere enjoins us to "lift up our hearts to heaven," for
otherwise we would have no fear of God. Moreover, our
stupidity is so great that we are immediately seized by gross
imaginations of God; so that if he did not bid us look to heaven,
we would choose rather to seek him at our feet. "To lift up
a prayer," therefore, is to pray in such a manner that our
hearts may not grovel on the earth, or think anything earthly
or gross about God, but may ascribe to him what is suitable to
his majesty, and that our warm and earnest affections may take
a lofty flight. In this sense it is said in the Psalm, "Let my
prayer come up before thee as incense, and as the evening
sacrifice" (Psalm 141:2). — *Commentaries*

*Now when they heard this, they were pricked in their
heart, and said unto Peter and to the rest of the apostles, Men and brethren, what shall we do?*   Acts 2:37

This is the beginning of repentance, this is the entrance
unto godliness, to be sorry for our sins, and to be wounded
with the feeling of our miseries. For so long as men are careless, they cannot take such heed to doctrine as they ought. And
for this cause the word of God is compared to a sword, because it fortifies the flesh, that we may be offered to God
for a sacrifice. But there must be added to this pricking
in heart readiness to obey. Cain and Judas were pricked in
heart, but despair kept them back from submitting themselves
unto God. For the mind oppressed with horror can do nothing
else but flee from God. Therefore we must take a good heart
to us, and lift up our mind with this hope of salvation, that
we may be ready to addict and give ourselves unto God, and
to follow whatever he shall command. — *Commentaries*

And he shall redeem Israel from all his iniquities.
                                    Psalm 130:8

Let us learn from this passage in what way we are to expect
deliverance from all calamities, or the order which it becomes
us to observe seeking it. Remission of sins always goes first,
without which nothing will come to a favorable issue. Those
who only desire to shake off the punishment are like silly in-
valids, who are careless about the disease itself with which
they are afflicted, provided the symptoms which occasion them
trouble for a time are removed. In order, then, that God may
deliver us from our miseries, we must chiefly endeavor to be
brought to a state of favor with him by obtaining the remis-

sion of our sins. If this is not obtained, it will avail us little to
have the temporal punishment remitted; for that often happens
even to the reprobates themselves. This is true and substantial
deliverance, when God, by blotting out our sins, shows himself
merciful towards us. Whence also we gather that having
once obtained forgiveness, we have no reason to be afraid of
our being excluded from free access to, and from enjoying the
ready exercise of, the loving-kindness and mercy of God; for
to redeem from iniquity is equivalent to moderating punish-
ments or chastisements. — *Commentaries*

142   MAY 21

And the servant of the Lord must not strive; but be
gentle unto all men, apt to teach, patient.
II Timothy 2:24

The servant of God must not strive, but be gentle and
patient and fit to teach. Here we will conclude that they who
give themselves to vain questions show plainly that they have
no desire nor zeal to serve God. For though a man be never
so wise, yet notwithstanding we must count him as a desperate devil if we see he does not have this affection in him, to
serve God, if he have not this end and mark before him, to
honor God. And surely it is not without cause that it was
said in an old proverb that learning in a man that does not
rule himself aright is like a sword in a madman's hand.

This is Saint Paul's meaning, to point out all them that
are given to contention, to the end that we may detest them,
and abhor them, as men that seek not in any way to serve God.
And why? For these are things that can no more agree together than fire and water, to serve God and to love contentions
and disputations, which breed nothing but strife and debate.

— *Sermons*

*Can a woman forget her sucking child, that she should
not have compassion on the son of her womb? yea,
they may forget, yet will I not forget thee.* Isaiah 49:15

"Shall a woman forget her child?" In order to correct that
distrust, he adds to the remonstrance an exhortation full of
the sweetest consolation. By an appropriate comparison he
shows how strong is his anxiety about his people, comparing
himself to a mother, whose love toward her offspring is so
strong and ardent as to leave far behind a father's love. Thus
he did not satisfy himself with proposing the example of
a father (which on other occasions he very frequently employs), but in order to express his very strong affection, he
chose to liken himself to a mother, and calls them not merely
"children" but the fruit of the womb, towards which there is
usually a warmer affection. What amazing affection does a
mother feel toward her offspring, which she cherishes in her
bosom, suckles on her breast, and watches over with tender
care, so that she passes sleepless nights, wears herself out by
continual anxiety, and forgets herself! And this carefulness is
manifested, not only among men, but even among savage
beasts, which, though they are by nature cruel, yet in this respect are gentle.

"Even if they shall forget." Since it does sometimes happen
that mothers degenerate into such monsters as to exceed in
cruelty the wild beasts and forget "the fruit of their womb,"
the Lord next declares that, even though this should happen,
still he will never forget his people. The affection which he
bears toward us is far stronger and warmer than the love of
all mothers. We ought also to bear in mind the saying of
Christ, "If ye, being evil, know how to give good things to
your children, how much more your heavenly Father?" (Matt.
7:11). Men, though by nature depraved and addicted to self-
love, are anxious about their children. What shall God do, who
is goodness itself? Will it be possible for him to lay aside a
father's love? Certainly not. Although therefore it should

happen that mothers (which is a monstrous thing) should forsake their own offspring, yet God, whose love toward his people is constant and unremitting, will never forsake them. In a word, the Prophet here describes to us the inconceivable carefulness with which God unceasingly watches over our salvation, that we may be fully convinced that he will never forsake us, though we may be afflicted with great and numerous calamities. — *Commentaries*

144   MAY 23

And let us not be weary in well doing: for in due season we shall reap, if we faint not.   Galatians 6:9

But since no man in this terrestrial and corporeal prison has strength sufficient to press forward in his course with a due degree of alacrity, and the majority are oppressed with such great debility that they stagger and halt, and even creep on the ground, and so make very inconsiderable advances — let us every one proceed according to our small ability, and prosecute the journey we have begun. No man will be so unhappy, but that he may every day make some progress, however small. Therefore let us not cease to strive, that we may be incessantly advancing in the way of the Lord; nor let us despair on account of the smallness of our success; for however our success may not correspond to our wishes, yet our labor is not lost, when this day surpasses the preceding one; provided that, with sincere simplicity, we keep our end in view, and press forward to the goal, not practising self-adulation, nor indulging our own evil propensities, but perpetually exerting our endeavors after increasing degrees of improvement, till we shall have arrived at a perfection of goodness, which, indeed, we seek and pursue as long as we live, and shall then attain, when, divested of all corporeal infirmity, we shall be admitted by God into complete communion with him.

—*Institutes*, III, vi, v

But now he is dead, wherefore should I fast? can I bring him back again? I shall go to him, but he shall not return to me.   II Samuel 12:23

It is God, therefore, who has sought back from you your son, whom he had committed to you to be educated, on the condition that he might always be his own. And, therefore, he took him away, because it was both of advantage to him to leave this world, and by this bereavement to humble you, or to make trial of your patience. If you do not understand the advantage of this, without delay, first of all, setting aside every other object of consideration, ask of God that he may show you. Should it be his will to exercise you still farther, by concealing it from you, submit to that will, that you may become wiser than the weakness of your own understanding can ever attain to. In what regards your son, if you bethink yourself how difficult it is, in this deplorable age, to maintain an upright course through life, you will judge him to be blessed, who, before encountering so many coming dangers which already were hovering over him, and to be encountered in his day and generation, was so early delivered from them all. He is like one who has set sail upon a stormy and tempestuous sea, and before he has been carried out into the deeps, gets in safety to the secure haven. — *Correspondence*

*And he answered me and said, Knowest thou not what
these be? And I said, No, my lord.*   Zechariah 4:13

This is the reason why the angel replies, "Dost thou not
know what these things mean?" For he does not upbraid
Zechariah with ignorance, but rather reminds all the faithful
that they ought to quicken themselves and to exert all their
ardor to learn, lest sloth should close up the way against them.
This reply, then, of the angel no doubt belongs to us all,
"Dost thou not know what these mean?" We ought to remember that the things we esteem as common far exceed our
thoughts. It indeed often happens that one runs over many
parts of Scripture and thinks that he reads nothing but what
is clear and well known, while yet experience teaches us that
we are inflated with too much self-confidence; for we look
down, as it were from on high, on that doctrine which ought, on
the contrary, to be reverently adored by us. Then let every one
of us, being warned by this sentence of the angel, acknowledge that he as yet cleaves to the first principles, or at least does
not comprehend all those things which are necessary to be
known; and that therefore progress is to be made to the very
end of life; for this is our wisdom, to be learners to the end.

—Commentaries

Let nothing be done through strife or vainglory; but in lowliness of mind let each esteem other better than themselves. Look not every man on his own things, but every man also on the things of others.

Philippians 2:3, 4

Let this, then, be our rule for benignity and beneficence — that whatever God has conferred on us, which enables us to assist our neighbor, we are the stewards of it, and must one day render an account of our stewardship; and that the only right dispensation of what has been committed to us, is that which is regulated by the law of love. Thus we shall not only always connect this study to promote the advantage of others with a concern for our own private interests, but shall prefer the good of others to our own.

To teach us that the dispensation of the gifts we receive from heaven ought to be regulated by this law, God anciently enjoined the same even in regard to the smallest bounties of his liberality. For he commanded the people to offer to him the first-fruits of the corn, as a solemn avowal that it was unlawful for them to enjoy any blessings not previously consecrated to him. And if the gifts of God are not sanctified to us till after we have with our own hands dedicated them to their Author, that must evidently be a sinful abuse which is unconnected with such a dedication. — *Institutes,* III, vii, v

Behold, happy is the man whom God correcteth: there-
fore despise not thou the chastening of the Almighty:
For he maketh sore, and bindeth up: he woundeth, and
his hands make whole.   Job 5:17, 18

It would be greatly to be desired that men would come to
God without being spurred, and that they would cling to him
without any warning being given them of their faults, and without any rebukes. This, I say, would be a thing greatly to be
desired, and also that we were without faults, and were as the
angels, desiring nothing but to yield obedience to our Maker
and to honor and love him as our Father. But inasmuch as we
are so perverse as not to cease to offend God; and besides that
play the hypocrites with him, seeking to hide our faults from
him; and inasmuch as there is such great pride in us that we
would have God to let us alone and to uphold us in our lusts,
and finally wish to be his judges rather than that he should be
ours; considering, I say, how we are so perverse, it is necessary
for God to use some violent remedy to draw us to him. For if
he should handle us altogether gently, what would become of
it?

We see this partly even in young children. For if their
fathers and mothers do not chastise them, they send them to the
gallows. It is true that they do not perceive it; but experience shows it, and we have common proverbs to express it, as,
"The more the fathers pamper their children, the more they spoil
them:" and the mothers do it still more, for they are fond of
flattering them, and in the meantime bring them to naught.
Herein God shows us as it were small beams of the thing as
it is in himself. For if he should handle us mildly, we should
be utterly undone and past recovery. Therefore he must show
himself a Father to us, and be rough with us, seeing we are of
so sturdy a nature that if he should deal gently with us we
would take no profit from it.

You see how we may understand the truth of this doctrine,

that the man is happy whom God chastises. That is to say, considering what our nature is, namely how stubborn, how it resists being put in order, and how we would fail to profit if God never chastised us; therefore it is necessary that he should bring us up short and that he would give us so many lashes with his whip that we are forced to take notice of him whether we want to or not. So we shall finally come to the conclusion that that man is happy whom God chastises; especially if he add to this the second grace, namely that he cause his rods and his corrections to be effective. — *Sermons*

149 MAY 28

Judas saith unto him, not Iscariot, Lord, how is it that thou wilt manifest thyself unto us, and not unto the world?   John 14:22

His design was to exhort his disciples to the earnest study of godliness, that they might make greater progress in faith; and therefore he is satisfied with distinguishing them from the world by this mark, that they keep the doctrine of the gospel. Now this mark comes after the commencement of faith, for it is the effect of their calling. In other passages Christ had reminded the disciples of their being called by free grace, and he will afterwards bring it to their recollection. At present, he only enjoins them to observe his doctrine, and to maintain godliness. By these words Christ shows in what manner the gospel is properly obeyed. It is when our services and outward actions proceed from the love of Christ; for in vain do the arms and the feet and the whole body toil, if the love of God do not reign in the heart, to govern the outward members. Now since it is certain that we *keep the commandments* of Christ only in so far as we *love* him, it follows that a perfect *love* of him can nowhere be found in the world, because there is no man who *keeps his commandments* perfectly; yet God is pleased with the obedience of those who sincerely aim at this end. — *Commentaries*

*His ways are always grievous; thy judgments are far
above out of his sight: as for all his enemies, he puffeth
at them. He hath said in his heart, I shall not be
moved: for I shall never be in adversity.*

Psalm 10:5, 6

There is a very great difference between a despiser of God,
who, enjoying prosperity today, is so forgetful of the condition of man in this world, as through a distempered imagination to build his nest above the clouds, and who persuades
himself that he shall always enjoy comfort and repose —
there is a very great difference between him and the godly
man, who, knowing that his life hangs only by a thread, and is
encompassed by a thousand deaths, and who, ready to endure
any kind of afflictions which shall be sent upon him, and living in the world as if he were sailing upon a tempestuous and
dangerous sea, nevertheless bears patiently all his troubles
and sorrows, and comforts himself in his afflictions, because
he leans wholly upon the grace of God, and entirely confides
in it. The ungodly man says, I shall not be moved, or I shall
not shake forever; because he thinks himself sufficiently strong
and powerful to bear up against all the assaults that shall
be made upon him. The faithful man says, What though I may
happen to be moved, yea, even fall and sink into the lowest
depths? My fall will not be fatal, for God will put his hand
under me to sustain me.

By this, in like manner, we are furnished with an explanation of the different effects which an apprehension of danger
has upon the good and the bad. Good men may tremble and
sink into despondency, but this leads them to flee with all
haste to the sanctuary of God's grace; whereas the ungodly,
while they are affrighted even at the noise of a falling leaf,
and live in constant uneasiness, endeavor to harden themselves
in their stupidity, and to bring themselves into such a state of
giddy frenzy, that being, as it were, carried out of themselves,
they may not feel their calamities. — *Commentaries*

For we wrestle not against flesh and blood, but against
principalities, against powers, against the rulers of the
darkness of this world, against spiritual wickedness
in high places.   Ephesians 6:12

But you know the admonition which Saint Paul has given on
that score, that is, that we have not to fight against flesh and
blood, but against the hidden wiles of our spiritual enemy.
Wherefore let us not waste our energies upon men, but rather
let us set ourselves against Satan. Therefore, forgetting and
pardoning the faults of those whom you may conceive to have
been your enemies, apply your whole mind to repel his malice
who thus engaged them to their own destruction in setting
themselves against you to seek your ruin. This magnanimity will
not only be pleasing to God, but it will make you the more
loved among men; and I do not doubt that you have such regard to that as you ought.

However you have also to consider that if God has been
pleased to humble you for a little while, it has not been
without motive. For although you may be innocent in regard
to men, you know that before this great heavenly Judge there
is no one living who is not chargeable. Thus, then, it is
that the saints have honored the rod of God, by yielding their
neck and bowing low their head under his discipline. David
had walked very uprightly, but yet he confessed that it had
been good for him to be humbled by the hand of God.
For which reason, as soon as we feel any chastisement, of
whatsoever kind it may be, the first step should be to retire
into ourselves, and well to examine our own lives, that we may
apprehend those blessings which had been hidden from us;
for sometimes too much prosperity dazzles our eyes, that we
cannot perceive wherefore God chastises us. It is but reasonable that we should do him at least as much honor as we would
a physician, for it is his to heal our inward maladies, which
are unknown to ourselves, and to pursue a course of healing,
not according to our liking, but as he knows and judges to be

fitting. What is more, it must needs happen sometimes that he makes use of preservative remedies, not waiting till we have already fallen into evil, but preventing it before it comes.
—*Letter to Protector Somerset*

152   MAY 31

But of him are ye in Christ Jesus, who of God is made unto us wisdom, and righteousness, and sanctification, and redemption: I Corinthians 1:30

He who imagines that in order to obtain righteousness he must produce any works, however small, can fix no limit or boundary, but renders himself a debtor to the whole law. Avoiding, therefore, all mention of the law, and dismissing all thought of our own works, in reference to justification, we must embrace the Divine mercy alone, and turning our eyes from ourselves, fix them solely on Christ. For the question is not how we can be made righteous, but how, though unrighteous and unworthy, we can be considered as righteous. And the conscience that desires to attain any certainty respecting this must give no admission to the law.

Nor will this authorize any one to conclude that the law is of no use to believers, whom it still continues to instruct and exhort, and stimulate to duty, although it has no place in their consciences before the tribunal of God. For these two things, being very different, require to be properly and carefully distinguished by us. The whole life of Christians ought to be an exercise of piety, since they are called to sanctification. It is the office of the law to remind them of their duty, and thereby to excite them to the pursuit of holiness and integrity. But when their consciences are solicitous how God may be propitiated, what answer they shall make, and on what they shall rest their confidence, if called to his tribunal, there must then be no consideration of the requisitions of the law, but Christ alone must be proposed for righteousness, who exceeds all the perfection of the law. — *Institutes*, III, xix,ii

And he shewed me Joshua the high priest standing before the angel of the Lord, and Satan standing at his right hand to resist him. And the Lord said unto Satan, The Lord rebuke thee, O Satan; even the Lord that hath chosen Jerusalem rebuke thee: is not this a brand plucked out of the fire? Zechariah 3:1, 2

Let us know that Christ never performs the work of the priesthood but that Satan stands at his side, that is, devises all means by which he may remove and withdraw Christ from his office. It hence follows that they are much deceived who think that they can live idly under the dominion of Christ; for we all have a warfare, for which each is to arm and equip himself. Therefore at this day, when we see the world seized with so much madness, that it assails us and would wholly consume us, let not our thoughts be fixed on flesh and blood, for Satan is the chief warrior who assails us, and who employs all the rage of the world to destroy us, if possible, on every side. Satan then ever stands at Christ's right hand, so as not to allow him in peace to exercise his priestly office.

—Commentaries

Woe unto you, scribes and Pharisees, hypocrites!
for ye devour widows' houses, and for a pretence
make long prayer: therefore ye shall receive the greater
damnation.   Matthew 23:14

But this diligence in prayer, although it chiefly respects
the particular and private devotions of each individual, has,
notwithstanding, some reference also to the public prayers of
the Church. But these cannot be unceasing, nor ought they
to be conducted otherwise than according to the polity which
is appointed by the common consent. This, indeed, I confess.
For therefore also certain hours are prescribed and fixed,
though indifferent with God, yet necessary to the customs
of men, that the benefit of all may be regarded, and all the
affairs of the Church administered, according to the direction
of Paul, "decently and in order." But this by no means prevents it from being the duty of every Church often to stimulate
themselves to a greater frequency of prayer, and also to be
inflamed with more ardent devotion on the pressure of any
necessity unusually great.

Moreover these things form no encouragement to those
vain repetitions which Christ has chosen to condemn; for he
does not forbid us to pray long or frequently, or with great
fervor of affection; but he forbids us to confide in our ability
to extort anything from God by stunning his ears with gar-
rulous loquacity, as though he were to be influenced by the
arts of human persuasion. — *Institutes,* III, xx, xxix

*Then was kindled the wrath of Elihu the son of
Barachel the Buzite, of the kindred of Ram: against
Job was his wrath kindled, because he justified him-
self rather than God.*   Job 32:2

If a man be angered by a fleshly passion, he has respect
to himself, and intends to maintain himself. Again, if he
shows special favor to his friends, this is respect of persons,
and he is really seeking his own advancement. We should
rather be angry with ourselves, if we desire God to recognize
our anger and permit it. And how is that done? It is when
a man enters into his own conscience, and searches himself
earnestly, and does not look at others as much as at himself,
to condemn himself, and to fight against his own passions.

You see then how we ought to be angry, and where our
anger ought to begin, if we expect God to permit it. That is,
every man ought to look at himself, and be angry with his own
sins and vices. Let us direct our anger there, seeing that we
have provoked God's wrath against us, and are full of so much
wickedness. Let us be angry and grieved at that; let that
be the point at which our anger begins. And afterwards let us
condemn evil wherever it may be found, in ourselves as well
as in our friends. And let us not be led by personal hatred
to cast our rage at any man just because we are already preoccupied with some evil feeling toward him.

So our anger will be laudable, and we shall show that it
proceeds from a true zeal for God. It is true that we shall
not always be able to control ourselves; for although we were
motivated by a godly zeal, we would still exceed the proper
bounds if God did not restrain us. Therefore in this zealous-
ness it is fitting that we should have discretion and keep a
check upon ourselves. Nevertheless, this anger will be allow-
able, if it springs from the fountain which we have described;
that is to say, if we hate evil wherever it may be found, even if
it be in our own persons. — *Sermons*

*So the angel that communed with me said unto me,
Cry thou, saying, Thus saith the Lord of hosts; I
am jealous for Jerusalem and for Zion with a great
jealousy.*   Zechariah 1:14

When God says that he was moved with great zeal for Jerusalem and Zion it is according to the common language of Scripture. For as God cannot otherwise sufficiently express the ineffable favor which he has towards his elect, he is pleased to adopt this similitude, that he undertakes the defence of his people, according to what is done by a husband who fights with the greatest zeal for his own wife. This is the reason why he says that he was zealous for Jerusalem. And we ought especially to notice this mode of speaking, that we may not think that God is indifferent when he delays and defers his aid; for as we are hasty in our wishes, so we would have God to be hasty in the same manner, and we impute to him indifference when he does not hasten according to our desires. These doubts God checks when he testifies that he is zealous: for he intimates that his slowness did not proceed from neglect, or because he despised or disregarded them; but that there was another reason why he held them in suspense.

We may therefore be fully persuaded that even when God withholds his aid, he is not otherwise affected towards us than the best of fathers towards his own children. And further, that the signs of his love do not appear because it is not always expedient for us to be delivered soon from our troubles. Let this then be our shield against all hasty desires, so that we may not indulge our too ardent wishes, or think that our salvation is neglected by God, when he hides himself for a time and does not immediately stretch forth his hand to help us.

—Commentaries

In meekness instructing those that oppose themselves;
if God peradventure will give them repentance to the
acknowledging of the truth;   II Timothy 2:25

And therefore Saint Paul says precisely, If at any time
God should give them repentance. As if he should say, My
friends, it is a very grievous and hard matter to bear with men
that resist God and set themselves against his grace and cannot
at the first hear the good doctrine that is for their salvation.
Men fret against them, and so they cast them off. But what?
For all that we must be gentle in this behalf and though we
see men lewd for a season, if there be no obstinate malice in
them, if they are not deliberately rebellious against God, so
that they seem past all correction, we must labor to mortify and
tame them; for they are, says he, in God's hand. On the one
hand he says, If at any time; showing that if the conversion
of unbelievers should not come so soon as we would wish, we
must not leave them for all that. For God has them in his
hands. And again he adds, if a man be stubborn today, we
do not know what he will be tomorrow. And why so? For the
conversion of men does not come from themselves nor of their
own strength, nor of their own moving; it is God that reforms
them, that makes them new creatures. And shall we hinder
God to work in a marvelous way and such as passes all our
senses? So then let us wait for more at God's gracious goodness than we can think of. — *Sermons*

*He shall see of the travail of his soul and shall be
satisfied: by his knowledge shall my righteous servant
justify many; for he shall bear their iniquities.*

Isaiah 53:11

Since, then, our Lord Jesus Christ puts his Word in our
hearts, let us pray him that he will be gracious to us, so
that we may have a pure and sincere disposition to seek in
him all that we lack. This is how we shall be justified *by
his knowledge.* For there is question of bringing some satisfaction which will content God; it is not a question of coming
to bargain and saying: "Lord, we deserve to be received by
you;" but "We confess that we are poor sinners, that we are
liable to thy judgment, that it is impossible for us ourselves
to satisfy it, and that only Jesus Christ must be regarded as
sufficient to satisfy it." We shall confess that with all humility;
we shall protest that we are creatures lost and damned until
our Lord Jesus Christ holds out his hand to us to draw us
back from the chasms and depths of hell. Now, have we confessed that? We know also that our Lord Jesus Christ supplies
all that we lack. If we are unclean and full of filth, his blood
is our washing, by which we shall be cleansed; if we are
plunged in debt, not only to God but also to Satan, as our
adversary, the payment has been made in the death and passion
of the Son of God; if we are polluted and detestable, the sacrifice that our Lord Jesus offered has a sweet odour, so that
all the evil in us is destroyed. This, then, is how we are justified by the knowledge of our Lord Jesus Christ. — *Sermons*

*That thou mayest say to the prisoners, Go forth; to
them that are in darkness, Shew yourselves. They shall
feed in the ways, and their pastures shall be in all
high places.*   Isaiah 49:9

If therefore we desire liberty, if we desire the light of
the kingdom of God, let us listen to Christ when he speaks;
otherwise we shall be oppressed by the unceasing tyranny of
Satan. Where then is the liberty of our will? Whosoever
claims for himself light, or reason, or understanding, can have
no share in this deliverance of Christ; for liberty is not promised to any but those who acknowledge that they are captives,
and light and salvation are not promised to any but those
who acknowledge that they are plunged in darkness.

Yet it is probable that indirectly he warns believers not
to desire excessive luxury; because they will never have so
great abundance as not to be attended by many difficulties; and
likewise not to become effeminate, because they will be beset
by dangers; for we know that "the ways" are exposed to the
attacks of enemies and robbers, and that the tops of mountains are for the most part barren. The Church is governed
by Christ in such a manner as not to be free from the attacks
and insults of men, and is fed in such a manner as frequently
to inhabit barren and frightful regions. But though enemies
are at hand, God protects us from their violence and oppression.
If we are thirsty or hungry, he is abundantly able to supply
everything that is necessary for food and maintenance; and
amidst perils and difficulties of this nature we perceive his care
and anxiety more clearly than if we were placed beyond the
reach of all danger. — *Commentaries*

*Wherefore he saith, Awake thou that sleepest, and
arise from the dead, and Christ shall give thee light.*
Ephesians 5:14

As soon as the smallest particle of grace is infused into
our minds, we begin to contemplate the Divine countenance
as now placid, serene, and propitious to us; it is indeed a very
distant prospect, but so clear that we know we are not deceived.
Afterwards, in proportion as we improve — for we ought to be
continually improving by progressive advances — we arrive at
a nearer, and therefore more certain view of him, and by continual habit he becomes more familiar to us. Thus we see that
a mind illuminated by the knowledge of God is at first involved in much ignorance, which is removed by slow degrees.
Yet it is not prevented either by its ignorance of some things,
or by its obscure view of what it beholds, from enjoying a
clear knowledge of the Divine will respecting itself, which is
the first and principal exercise of faith. For, as a man who is
confined in a prison, into which the sun shines only obliquely
and partially through a very small window, is deprived of a
full view of that luminary, yet clearly perceives its splendor
and experiences its beneficial influences — thus we, who are
bound with terrestrial and corporeal fetters, though surrounded
on all sides with great obscurity, are nevertheless illuminated,
sufficiently for all the purposes of real security, by the light
of God shining ever so feebly to discover his mercy.

—*Institutes*, III, ii, xix

And I, if I be lifted up from the earth, will draw all men unto me.   John 12:32

"If I be lifted up." Next follows the method by which the judgment shall be conducted; namely, Christ, being lifted up on the cross, shall gather all men to himself, in order that he may raise them from earth to heaven. The Evangelist says that Christ pointed out the manner of his death; and, therefore, the meaning undoubtedly is, that the cross will be, as it were, a chariot, by which he shall raise all men, along with himself, to his Father. It might have been thought, that at that time he was carried away from the earth, so as no longer to have any interests in common with men; but he declares that he will go in a very different manner, so as to draw upwards to himself those who were fixed on the earth. Now though he alludes to the form of his death, yet he means generally that his death will not be a division to separate him from men, but that it will be an additional means of drawing earth upwards towards heaven.

"I will draw all men to myself." The word *all,* which he employs, must be understood to refer to the children of God, who belong to his flock. Yet I agree with Chrysostom, who says that Christ used the universal term, *all,* because the Church was to be gathered equally from among Gentiles and Jews, according to that saying, "There shall be one shepherd, and one sheepfold." — *Commentaries*

But though he had done so many miracles before
them, yet they believed not on him: John 12:37

"And though he had done so many signs." That no man
may be disturbed or perplexed at seeing that Christ was despised by the Jews, the Evangelist removes this offence by showing that he was supported by clear and undoubted testimonies,
which proved that credit was due to him and to his doctrine;
but that the blind did not behold the glory and power of
God, which were openly displayed in his miracles. First,
therefore, we ought to believe that it was not owing to Christ
that the Jews did not place confidence in him, because by many
miracles he abundantly testified who he was, and that it was
therefore unjust and highly unreasonable that their unbelief
should diminish his authority. But as this very circumstance
might lead many persons to anxious and perplexing inquiry
how the Jews came to be so stupid, that the power of God,
though visible, produced no effect on them, John proceeds
further, and shows that faith does not proceed from the ordinary faculties of men, but is an uncommon and extraordinary gift of God, and that this was anciently predicted concerning Christ, that very few would believe the Gospel.

—Commentaries

When thou passest through the waters, I will be with thee; and through the rivers, they shall not overflow thee: when thou walkest through the fire, thou shalt not be burned; neither shall the flame kindle upon thee.   Isaiah 43:2

"When thou shalt pass through the waters." By *fire* and *water* he means every kind of miseries to which we are liable in this life; for we must contend not with calamities of one kind only, but with infinitely diversified calamities. At one time we must pass through water and at another through fire (Psalm 66:12). In like manner the Apostle James exhorts believers not to faint when they "fall into various temptations" (James 1:2). And, indeed, faith needs to be put to the trial in many ways; for it often happens that he who has been victorious in one combat has been baffled by another kind of temptation. We are therefore tried by afflictions, but are at length delivered; we are baffled by the billows, but are not swallowed up; we are even scorched by the flames, but are not consumed. We have, indeed, the same feeling of pain as other men, but we are supported by the grace of God, and fortified by the spirit of patience, that we may not faint; and at length he will stretch out his hand and lift us up on high. — *Commentaries*

*But they that wait upon the Lord shall renew their
strength; they shall mount up with wings as eagles;
they shall run, and not be weary; and they shall
walk, and not faint.*   Isaiah 40:31

"They shall run and not be weary." It is as if he had said
that the Lord will assist them, so that they shall pursue
their course without any molestation. It is a figurative expression, by which he suggests that believers will always be
ready to perform their duty with cheerfulness. But it will be
said, "There are so many troubles which we must endure in
this life; how then does he say that we shall be free from
weariness?" I reply, believers are indeed distressed and wearied,
but they are at length delivered from their distresses, and feel
that they have been restored by the power of God; for it
happens to them according to the saying of Paul, "While we
are troubled on every side, we are not overwhelmed; we are
perplexed, but not in despair; we suffer persecution, but are
not forsaken; we are cast down, but are not destroyed." Let us
therefore learn to flee to the Lord, who, after we have encountered many storms, will at length conduct us to the harbor; for he who has opened up a path, and has commanded us
to advance in that course in which he has placed us, does
not intend to assist us only for a single day and to forsake us
in the middle of our course, but will conduct us to the goal.

                                        —*Commentaries*

*For who hath despised the day of small things? for
they shall rejoice, and shall see the plummet in the
hand of Zerubbabel with those seven; they are the
eyes of the Lord, which run to and fro through the
whole earth.* Zechariah 4:10

This doctrine may also be applied to us; for God, to ex-
hibit the more his power, begins with small things in building his spiritual temple; nothing grand is seen, which attracts
the eyes and thoughts of men, but everything is almost con-
temptible. God indeed could immediately put forth his power,
and thus rouse the attention of all men and fill them with
wonder; he could indeed do so; but as I have already said,
his purpose is to increase, by doing wonders, the brightness of
his power; which he does when from a small beginning he
brings forth what no one would have thought; and besides,
his purpose is to prove the faith of his people; for it behooves
us ever to hope beyond hope. Now when the beginning
promises something great and sublime, there is no proof and
no trial of faith; but when we hope for that which does not
appear, we give due honor to God, for we depend on his power
and not on the proximate means.

Thus we see that Christ is compared to a shoot which
arises from the stem of Jesse (Isaiah 11:1). God might have
arranged that Christ should have been born when the house
of David was in its splendor, and when the kingdom was in
a flourishing state; yet his will was that he should come forth
from the stem of Jesse, when the royal name was almost cut
off. Again, he might have brought forth Christ as a full-
grown tree; but he was born as an insignificant shoot. So also
he is compared by Daniel to a rough and unpolished stone cut
off from a mountain (Dan. 2:45). The same thing has also
been accomplished in our age, and continues still at this day
to be accomplished. If we consider what is and has been, the
beginning of the growing gospel, we shall find nothing illus-

trious according to the perceptions of the flesh; and on this account the adversaries confidently despise us; they regard us as the offscourings of men, and hope to be able to cast us down and scatter us by a single breath. — *Commentaries*

166 JUNE 14

Submit yourselves therefore to God. Resist the devil, and he will flee from you. James 4:7

Yet, notwithstanding, because of your singular piety, and that good will which you express toward me, you will not, perhaps, be unwilling to recognize in my letter thoughts which have spontaneously occurred to your own mind at some other time. The son whom the Lord had lent you for a season he has taken away. There is no ground, therefore, for those silly and wicked complaints of foolish men; O blind death! O horrid fate! O implacable daughters of destiny! O cruel fortune! The Lord who had lodged him here for a season, at this stage of his career has called him away. What the Lord has done, we must, at the same time, consider has not been done rashly, nor by chance, neither from having been impelled from without; but by that determinate counsel, whereby he not only foresees, decrees, and executes nothing but what is just and upright in itself, but also nothing but what is good and wholesome for us. Where justice and good judgment reign paramount, there it is impious to remonstrate. — *Correspondence*

There was a man of the Pharisees, named Nicode-
mus, a ruler of the Jews . . . . Nicodemus answered
and said unto him, How can these things be?

John 3:1, 9

"Of the Pharisees." This designation was, no doubt, regarded by his countrymen as honorable to Nicodemus. But it
is not for the sake of honor that it is given to him by the
Evangelist, who, on the contrary, draws our attention to it as
having prevented him from coming freely and cheerfully to
Christ. Hence we are reminded that they who occupy a lofty
station in the world are, for the most part, entangled by very
dangerous snares; nay, we see many of them held so firmly
bound that not even the slightest wish or prayer arises from
them towards heaven throughout their whole life.

"How can these things be?" We see what is the chief
obstacle in the way of Nicodemus. Everything that he hears
appears monstrous, because he does not understand the manner of it; so that there is no greater obstacle to us than our
own pride; that is, we always wish to be wise beyond what is
proper, and therefore we reject with diabolical pride everything
that is not explained to our reason; as if it were proper to
limit the infinite power of God to our poor capacity. We are,
indeed, permitted, to a certain extent, to inquire into the
manner and reason of the works of God, provided that we do
so with sobriety and reverence. — *Commentaries*

And he hath cast the lot for them, and his hand hath divided it unto them by line: they shall possess it for ever, from generation to generation shall they dwell therein.   Isaiah 34:17

"And he hath cast the lot for them." Hence we infer that it is vain for men ever to promise themselves a permanent abode, unless so far as every person has obtained his place "by lot," and on the express condition that he shall instantly leave it whenever God calls. We lead a dependent life wherever he supports us; and either on our native soil, or at a distance from our fatherland, we are strangers. If he shall be pleased to give us a peaceable habitation for a long time in one place, it will only be by his special favor that we shall dwell there; and as soon as he thinks proper, he will constrain us to change our abode. Besides, if we acknowledge that a residence in this or that country has been appointed to us by God, we may dwell in it with safety and composure; for if he keeps wild beasts in possession of the place which he has allotted to them, how much more will he preserve men, for whose sake he created heaven, earth, the seas, and all that they contain?

—*Commentaries*

But there is forgiveness with thee, that thou mayest
be feared.   Psalm 130:4

Though all men confess with the mouth that there is no
human being in the world whom God may not justly adjudge
to everlasting death, should it so please him, yet how few are
persuaded of the truth which the Prophet now adds, that the
grace of which they shall stand in need shall not be denied
them! They either sleep in their sins through stupidity, or
fluctuate amidst a variety of doubts, and, at length, are overwhelmed with despair. This maxim, "that no man is free
from sin," is, as I have said, received among all men without
dispute, and yet the majority shut their eyes to their own
faults, and settle securely in hiding places to which, in their
ignorance, they have betaken themselves, if they are not
forcibly roused out of them, and then, when pursued close
by the judgment of God, they are overwhelmed with alarm, or
so greatly tormented as to fall into despair.

The consequence of this want of hope in men, that God
will be favorable to them, is an indifference about coming into
the Divine presence to supplicate for pardon. When a man is
awakened with a lively sense of the judgment of God, he cannot fail to be humbled with shame and fear. Such self-dis-
satisfaction would not however suffice, unless at the same
time there were added faith, whose office it is to raise up the
hearts which were cast down with fear, and to encourage
them to pray for forgiveness.

At the same time let it be understood that he does not
here speak of a confused knowledge of the grace of God, but of
such a knowledge of it as enables the sinner to conclude with
certainty, that as soon as he seeks God he shall find him to
be reconciled to him. — *Commentaries*

*The sacrifices of God are a broken spirit: a broken and
a contrite heart, O God, thou wilt not despise.*

Psalm 51:17

The man of broken spirit is one who has been emptied of
all vainglorious confidence, and brought to acknowledge that
he is nothing. The contrite heart abjures the idea of merit,
and has no dealings with God upon the principle of exchange.
Is it objected that faith is a more excellent sacrifice than
that which is here commended by the Psalmist, and of greater
efficacy in procuring the Divine favor, as it presents to the
view of God that Savior who is the true and only propitiation?
I would observe that faith cannot be separated from the humility of which David speaks. This is such a humility as is
altogether unknown to the wicked. They may tremble in the
presence of God, and the obstinacy and rebellion of their
hearts may be partially restrained, but they still retain some
remainders of inward pride. Where the spirit has been broken,
on the other hand, and the heart has become contrite, through
a felt sense of the anger of the Lord, a man is brought to
genuine fear and self-loathing, with a deep conviction that of
himself he can do or deserve nothing, and must be indebted
unconditionally for salvation to Divine mercy.

That this should be represented by David as constituting
all which God desires in the shape of sacrifice need not excite
our surprise. He does not exclude faith, he does not condescend
upon any nice division of true penitence into its several parts,
but asserts in general that the only way of obtaining the favor
of God is by prostrating ourselves with a wounded heart at the
feet of his Divine mercy, and supplicating his grace with in-
genuous confessions of our own helplessness. — *Commentaries*

*But thou, Israel, art my servant, Jacob whom I have
chosen, the seed of Abraham my friend.*   Isaiah 41:8

"My friend." It was an extraordinary honor which the Lord
bestowed on Abraham when he called him his *friend.* To be
called "the servant of God" is high and honorable; for if it be
reckoned a distinguished favor to be admitted into the family
of a king or a prince, how much more highly should we esteem
it, when God accounts us as his servants and members of his
family? But, not satisfied with that, he bestows on him even
a higher honor and adorns him with the name of "friend."
What is here said about Abraham relates to all believers; and
Christ declared more plainly, "Now I call you not servants,
but ye are my friends; for servants know not their Lord's will,
but to you have been revealed secret and divine mysteries, and
hence you may know my friendly and kind disposition towards
you" (John 15:15). Having therefore obtained from God so
great an honor, we ought to remember our duty, that the more
abundantly he has testified his kindness towards us, we may
the more earnestly and with deeper reverence worship him continually. — *Commentaries*

*Yet if thou warn the wicked, and he turn not from
his wickedness, nor from his wicked way, he shall die
in his iniquity; but thou hast delivered thy soul.*

Ezekiel 3:19

The Prophet is here taught how usefully he will lay out
his labor, although he should appear to fail, for he ought to be
satisfied with this alone, that God approves his efforts. Although, therefore, those who were to be brought back by holy
exhortations remain obstinate, yet God's servants ought not,
through fastidiousness, to throw up their commission as if it
were useless, for they free their own souls. It has been formerly said that a necessity was imposed upon them, but if
they are dumb dogs the destruction of souls will be imputed to
them; but when they have executed their duty and satisfied the
Almighty, ought it not to suffice them to be absolved in his
opinion? We see then that the Prophet was animated by this
consolation, lest he should be weary of admonishing abandoned
and obstinate men, because, if they were not profited by his
teaching, yet its fruit should return to himself. That expression of Christ's is well known, "Into whatsoever house
ye enter, salute it; if the house be unworthy, your blessing
shall return to yourselves." So also when the Prophets anxiously desired to reclaim the wandering sheep and to collect
them within the fold, if they experienced such petulance
that their labor did not profit them, yet their usefulness shall
return to themselves. — *Commentaries*

Arise, O Lord; O God, lift up thine hand: forget not the humble.   Psalm 10:12

"Arise, O Jehovah." It is a disease under which men in general labor, to imagine according to the judgment of the flesh, that when God does not execute his judgments, he is sitting idle, or lying at ease. There is, however, a great difference with respect to this between the faithful and the wicked. The latter cherish the false opinion which is dictated by the weakness of the flesh, and in order to soothe and flatter themselves in their vices, they indulge in slumbering, and render their conscience stupid, until at length, through their wicked obstinacy, they harden themselves into a gross contempt of God. But the former soon shake from their minds that false imagination, and chastise themselves, returning of their own accord to a due consideration of what is the truth on this subject.

Of this we have here set before us a striking example. By speaking of God after the manner of men, the Prophet declares that the same error which he has just now condemned in the despisers of God had gradually stolen in upon his own mind. But he proceeds at once to correct it, and resolutely struggles with himself, and restrains his mind from forming such conceptions of God, as would reflect dishonor upon his righteousness and glory. It is therefore a temptation to which all men are naturally prone, to begin to doubt of the providence of God, when his hand and judgment are not seen. The godly, however, differ widely from the wicked. The former, by means of faith, check this apprehension of the flesh; while the latter indulge themselves in their froward imaginations.

—*Commentaries*

174 JUNE 22

And I said unto the angel that talked with me, What
be these? And he answered me, These are the horns
which have scattered Judah, Israel, and Jerusalem.
Zechariah 1:19

If then we neglect not these helps which God affords
us, and especially if we ask him to guide us by his Spirit,
there will certainly be nothing obscure or intricate in the
prophecies, which he will not, as far as it is necessary, make
known to us. He does not indeed give the Spirit in an equal
degree to all; but we ought to feel assured that though
prophecies may be obscure, there will yet be a sure profit
derived if we be teachable and submissive to God; for we
find that Zechariah was not deprived of his request, as the
angel gave him an immediate answer. — *Commentaries*

175 JUNE 23

Of these things put them in remembrance, charging
them before the Lord that they strive not about words
to no profit, but to the subverting of the hearers.
Study to shew thyself approved unto God, a workman
that needeth not to be ashamed, rightly dividing the
word of truth.   II Timothy 2:14, 15

And therefore when any of us comes to a sermon, let it
not be to hear some pleasant matter and to have our ears tickled
and to have the preacher make flowery discourses; but let
us do it to grow in the fear of God and humbleness, and stir
us up to call upon him and to confirm ourselves in patience.
And so, if we have heard one exhortation today and hear the
same tomorrow again, let us not think it needless, let us not
be grieved at it; for if every one of us will rightly examine

himself, he shall perceive that he is far wide, and has not remembered his lesson well to practise it aright. This it is that we have to note in this place, when Saint Paul says, "Put them in mind of these things." — *Sermons*

176   **JUNE 24**

And I will bring the third part through the fire, and will refine them as silver is refined, and will try them as gold is tried: they shall call on my name, and I will hear them: I will say, It is my people: and they shall say, The Lord is my God.   Zechariah 13:9

After the greater part, both of the world and of the Church (at least such as profess to belong to it) shall be destroyed, we cannot be retained in our position, except God often chastises us. Let us then remember what Paul says, that we are chastened by the Lord that we may not perish with the world; and the metaphors which the Prophet adopts here are to the same purpose; for he says, "I will lead them through the fire." He speaks here of the faithful whom God has chosen unto salvation, and whom he has reserved that they might continue safe; yet he says that they shall be saved through fire, that is, hard trials.

But he sets forth this still more clearly, "He will prove them," he says, "as silver and gold." The stubble and the chaff, as John the Baptist teaches us, are indeed cast into the fire (Matt. 3:12), but without any benefit; for the fire consumes the refuse and the chaff, and whatever is corruptible. But when the gold and the silver are put in the fire and are purified, it is done that greater purity may be produced, and also that what is precious in these metals may become more apparent. For when the silver is drawn out of the mine, it differs not much from what is earthly. The same is the case with gold. But the furnace so purifies the gold and silver from their dross that they attain their value and excellency. Hence Zechariah says that when God casts his faithful people into the fire, he does this according to his paternal purpose in order to burn out their dross and thus they become gold and silver who were before filthy and abominable, and in whom much dross abounded. We see then that the elect of God, even those who may be rightly counted his children, are here distinguished from the reprobate, however they may profess God's name and worship. — *Commentaries*

177 JUNE 25

Ho, every one that thirsteth, come ye to the waters, and he that hath no money; come ye, buy, and eat; yea, come, buy wine and milk without money and without price. Isaiah 55:1

So, because the Apostles have sent us to Jesus Christ, and have declared to us that it is to him we must look, and since he also invites us so sweetly to himself, saying, "Come unto me," let us not hang back or go wandering away; let us approach him boldly. For he did not say that for the prophets alone, or for the apostles and martyrs, or for the virgin Mary; but he wants to keep us all to himself, as also it is very necessary for us. Let us undertake, I say, not to wander here and there when we pray to God, and let us know the good he has done for us when he was pleased to draw us back from the abyss and confusion of the Papacy and to show us the open door to come to him — that is, because Jesus Christ intercedes for us. Let us hold to that, without wandering from one side to the other. For it is certain that, if our prayers are not ruled according to the Word of God, they are trifling and God rejects them. Nor can they be made in faith unless the assurance comes from the same source — that is, from the truth of God. And now, if we want our prayers to be grounded in faith, they must be conformed to the will of God, and we must follow what he commands us — that is, we must have Jesus Christ as our Intercessor, Advocate and Mediator. — *Sermons*

And the Lord make you to increase and abound in love
one toward another, and toward all men, even as we
do toward you: I Thessalonians 3:12

He who forbids the character of our brother to be bespattered
with falsehood wills also that as far as the truth will permit,
it be preserved immaculate. For although he only guards it
against falsehood, he thereby suggests that it is committed to
his charge. But this should be sufficient to induce us to defend the fair character of our neighbor — that God himself is
its protection. Wherefore detraction is without doubt universally condemned.

This commandment also extends so far as to forbid us to
affect a pleasantry tinctured with bitter sarcasms, severely
lashing the faults of another under the appearance of sport;
which is the practice of those who aim at the praise of raillery, to the prejudice of the modesty and feelings of others.
For such wantonness sometimes fixes a lasting stigma on the
characters of our brethren.

Now if we turn our eyes to the Legislator whose proper
right it is to rule our ears and our minds, as much as our
tongues, it will certainly appear that an eagerness to hear detraction, and an unreasonable inclination to unfavorable opin-
ions respecting others, are equally prohibited. For it would
be ridiculous for any one to suppose that God hates slander
in the tongue and does not reprobate malice in the heart.
Wherefore, if we possess the true fear and love of God, let us
make it our study, that as far as is practicable and expedient,
and consistent with charity, we devote neither our tongues nor
our ears to vicious raillery, nor by chance listen to unfavorable suspicions; but that, putting fair constructions on every
man's words and actions, we regulate our hearts, our ears, and
our tongues, with a view to preserve the reputation of all
around us. — *Institutes*, II, viii, xlvii

*Yea doubtless, and I count all things but loss for the
excellency of the knowledge of Christ Jesus my Lord:*
                                              Philippians 3:8

On the other hand, we know not what it is to part with
everything for the love of him, until he has brought us to the
test. True it is, that he who has taken off his affection from
the goods of this world has already sold all, and has made
himself poor, so far as depends on himself; but the fruit and
the proof of this spiritual poverty are, patiently to endure the
loss of worldly goods, and without any regret, when it pleases
our heavenly Father that we should be despoiled of them. I
do not set these things before you as to one who is ignorant,
or who has need of lengthy remonstrances, but for the love
that I bear you, of which God is my witness.

I pray our good Lord that he would so work in you now more
powerfully than ever, to make you despise all that is in the
world, and to make you breathe upwards direct to him with your
whole heart, without being turned aside by anything whatsoever, making you taste what is the worth of the hope which
he reserves for us in heaven; and that it may please him to
lighten your burden as regards the body, in order that you may
be all the better disposed well to meditate upon the favors
he has bestowed on you, and to take delight in them, acknowledging the love which he has shown you.

Whatsoever may happen, if we have the patience to hearken
to our Saviour, he will always give us wherewithal to rejoice
our spirits, and will make us taste and feel, in a lively way,
that it is not in vain that he has promised to make us uncon-
querable in tribulations. Now, then, learn in reality what that
beautiful promise is worth, that we are indeed happy, when
all the world shall speak ill of us, and shall hate us, and shall
persecute us for his name's sake. Therefore it is, that he has prepared you, long before exposing you to danger.—*Correspondence*

There was a man in the land of Uz, whose name was Job; and that man was perfect and upright, and one that feared God, and eschewed evil.   Job 1:1

It is true that we may withhold ourselves from evildoing, and that we may have a fair reputation before men; but that will amount to nothing if we are hypocrites at heart or misrepresent our actions before God, who sees the heart. What must we do then? We must begin with the heart. And then to have perfect soundness, it is proper that our eyes, our hands, our feet, our arms, our legs, be conformed to this standard; so that in our whole life we may show that it is our desire to serve God, and that this is a sincere desire and not a mere pretense. And that is also why Saint Paul exhorts the Galatians to walk by the Spirit if they live in the Spirit; as if he should say, "Verily it behooves us to have the Spirit of God living in us." For it is to no purpose to have a gay life that pleases men and is held in high estimation, unless we are renewed by the grace of God. But what then? We must walk, that is to say, we must show in fact, and by our works, that the Spirit of God reigns in our souls. For if our hands are stained with robbery, with cruelty, or with any other vices; if the eyes are carried away with lewd and unchaste looks, with coveting other men's goods, with pride or with vanity; or if the feet, as the Scripture says, are swift to do evil; thereby we will declare that our heart is full of wickedness and corruption. For there are neither feet, nor hands, nor eyes, which are led by themselves; the leading comes from the Spirit and the heart.

Therefore let us endeavor to have the consistency which the Scripture shows us, when it is said that Job, having this soundness and integrity, also lived uprightly, that is to say, conversed with his neighbors without injury, without annoying them, without seeking his own profit, but kept equity with all the world. — *Sermons*

*To whom then will ye liken God? or what likeness will
ye compare unto him?* Isaiah 40:18

"To whom then have ye likened God?" The Prophet, as
we formerly suggested, does not address merely the men of
his own age, but posterity; who would have a still severer contest with the mockeries of the nations whose captives they were,
and likewise with bad examples and customs; for when, in consequence of being mingled with heathen nations, they daily
beheld many corruptions of piety, it was more difficult for
them steadily to persevere. That they might not entertain
any foolish notion that high prosperity attended the worshippers of false gods, the Prophet meets this error, and reminds
them that God, whom they and their fathers worshipped, ought
not to be compared with the gods of the Gentiles; for these
were made by men, and were composed of gold or sliver, wood
or stone; but God created all things; and therefore that the
highest injury is done to God, not only by comparing his
majesty with things of no value, but even by not placing him
far above the angels and everything that is reckoned divine.

—*Commentaries*

*Charge them that are rich in this world, that they be
not highminded, nor trust in uncertain riches, but in
the living God, who giveth us richly all things to enjoy;*
I Timothy 6:17

And seeing this fault reign in us, they have need of this
correction that Saint Paul gives here. For he speaks not of an
exhortation that is common to all, but that must precisely
serve as a medicine to them that presume under color of their
riches, and set themselves aloft, and make no more account
of the kingdom of God, being too much given to fleeting and
fading things.

Therefore Paul says here not to Timothy, that he should
command all men without exception to walk humbly and
not to put their confidence in fleeting things of this world, but
he will have him exhort the rich man in this matter. And why
so? Because they have need.

True it is that it is a great irritation to them to be so restrained, for they think they should be spared more than other
men; because they stand looking upon their feathers like
peacocks, they would have all men to stoop to them, and not
to be so bold as to look upon them, not between the eyes and
under the brows. Such is the pride of rich men. But Saint
Paul on the other hand, to beat down this pride, says that
they that are rich have but a vain appearance and show that
passes and vanishes away very quickly. They must not therefore presume because they abound in gold and silver, and have
great possessions, for these things shall soon be taken away
from them. And that this is so, what is the life of men, but
a very swift race? Is there any such matter then, to give occasion of pride and make them haughty that have riches? For
after that Saint Paul has warned that they are rich but for
a short time, and that their great wealth shall pass away very
quickly, he sets this down beside, that they should behave
themselves humbly. — *Sermons*

For after that in the wisdom of God the world by wisdom knew not God, it pleased God by the foolishness of preaching to save them that believe.

I Corinthians 1:21

Philosophy is, consequently, the noble gift of God, and those learned men who have striven hard after it in all ages have been incited thereto by God himself, that they might enlighten the world in the knowledge of the truth. But there is a wide difference between the writings of these men and those truths which God, of his own pleasure, delivered to guilty men for their sanctification. In the former, you may fall in with a small particle of truth, of which you can get only a taste, sufficient to make you feel how pleasant and sweet it is; but in the latter, you may obtain in rich abundance that which can refresh the soul to the full.

In the one, a shadow and an image is placed before the eyes which can only excite in you a love of the object, without admitting you to a familiar intercourse with it; in the other, the solid substance stands before you, with which you may not only become intimately acquainted, but may also, in some measure, handle it. In the one, the seed is in a manner choked; in the other, you may possess the fruit in its very maturity. There, in short, only a few small sparks break forth, which so point out the path that they fail in the middle of the journey — and can only restrain the traveller from going further astray; but here, the Spirit of God, like a brilliant torch, or rather like the sun itself, shines in full splendor, not only to guide the course of your life, even to its final goal, but also to conduct you to a blessed immortality. Draw then from this source, wherever you may wander, and as soon as he finds you a settled abode, you ought to make that your place of rest. — *Letter to Martin Bucer*

*Thy kingdom come. Thy will be done in earth, as
it is in heaven.*   Matthew 6:10

"Thy will be done." We are therefore commanded to desire
that, as in heaven nothing is done but according to the Divine
will, and the angels are placidly conformed to everything that
is right, so the earth, all obstinacy and depravity being anni-
hilated, may be subject to the same government. And in praying for this, we renounce our own carnal desires; because, unless we resign all our affections to God, we are guilty of all the
opposition in our power to his will, for nothing proceeds from
us but what is sinful. And we are likewise habituated by
this petition to a renunciation of ourselves, that God may
rule us according to his own pleasure, and not only so, but
that he may also create in us new minds and new hearts,
annihilating our own, that we may experience no emotion of
desire within us, but a mere consent to his will; in a word,
that we may have no will of our own, but that our hearts may
be governed by his Spirit, by whose internal teachings we may
learn to love those things which please him, and to hate
those which he disapproves; consequently, that he may render
abortive all those desires which are repugnant to his will.

                                        —*Institutes*, III, xx, xlii

And he said unto me, Son of man, I send thee to
the children fo Israel, to a rebellious nation that hath
rebelled against me . . .   Ezekiel 2:3a

He threatens them, therefore, and that not only once, because such was the hardheartedness of the people that it was
not enough to utter the threatenings of God three or four
times, unless he should continually impress them. But, at the
same time, he shows the causes why God determined to treat
his people so severely; namely, because they were contam-
inated with many superstitions, because they were perfidious,
greedy, cruel, and full of rapine, given up to luxury and depraved by lust; all these things are united by our Prophet, that
he may show that the vengeance of God is not too severe,
since the people had arrived at the very last pitch of impiety
and all wickedness.

At the same time, he gives them, here and there, some taste
of the mercy of God. For all threats are vain, unless some
promise of favor is held out. Nay, the vengeance of God, as
soon as it is displayed, drives men to despair, and despair
casts them headlong into madness; for as soon as any one
apprehends the anger of God, he is necessarily agitated, and
then, like a raging beast, he wages war with God himself. For
this reason I said that all threats are vain without a taste of
the mercy of God. The prophets always argue with men with
no other intention than that of stirring them up to penitence,
which they could never effect unless God could be reconciled
to those who had been alienated from him. This then is the
reason why our prophet, as well as Jeremiah, when they reprove
the people, temper their sharpness by the interposition of
promises. — *Commentaries*

For, brethren, ye have been called unto liberty;
only use not liberty for an occasion to the flesh, but
by love serve one another.   Galatians 5:13

Ivory and gold, and riches of all kinds, are certainly blessings of Divine Providence; not only permitted, but expressly
designed for the use of men; nor are we anywhere prohibited
to laugh, or to be satiated with food, or to annex new possessions to those already enjoyed by ourselves or by our an-
cestors, or to be delighted with musical harmony, or to drink
wine. This indeed is true; but amidst an abundance of all
things, to be immersed in sensual delights, to inebriate the heart
and mind with present pleasures, and perpetually to grasp at
new ones — these things are very remote from a legitimate use
of Divine blessings.

Let them banish, therefore, immoderate desire, excessive
profusion, vanity, and arrogance; that with a pure conscience
they may make a proper use of the gifts of God. When their
hearts shall be formed to this sobriety, they will have a rule
for the legitimate enjoyment of them. On the contrary, without this moderation, even common and ordinary pleasures are
chargeable with excess. For it is truly observed that a proud
heart frequently dwells under coarse and ragged garments,
and that simplicity and humility are sometimes concealed under
purple and fine linen. Let all men, in their respective stations,
whether of poverty, of competence, or of splendor, live in
the remembrance of Christian liberty, that they may learn the
lesson which Paul had learned, when he said, "I have learned
in whatsoever state I am, therewith to be content. I know both
how to be abased, and I know how to abound; everywhere and
in all things I am instructed, both to be full and to be hungry,
both to abound and to suffer need." — *Institutes*, III, xix, ix

He delighteth not in the strength of the horse: he taketh not pleasure in the legs of a man. Psalm 147:10

"Not in the strength of the horse." After the Psalmist has shown that there is proof of the divine goodness in every part of the world, he takes particular notice that men have no strength but what is given them from above, and this he adds with the express purpose of checking the pride by which almost all men are inflamed, and which leads them to trust in their own strength. The meaning of the passage is, that let man come in the preparation of his own strength, and with all the assistances that seem to him most prevalent, this will only issue in smoke and vanity; nay, that in arrogating the very least to himself, this will only be a hindrance in the way of the mercy of God, by which alone we stand. The strength of the horse is mentioned to denote any kind of protection. Not that God is displeased with those things in themselves considered which he has given us as helps, but it is necessary that we be withdrawn from a false confidence in them, for very commonly when any resource is at hand, we are foolishly intoxicated and lifted up with pride. He opposes the fear of God therefore to the strength of both men and of horses, and places his hope in his mercy, intimating that it is highly incumbent upon us to show our moderation in worshipping God with reverence and holiness, and depending on his grace. Hence we learn that he only condemns that strength which would take from God the honor due to him. — *Commentaries*

*Will he reprove thee for fear of thee? will he enter
with thee into judgment?*   Job 22:4

It is true that men make great noise when they conspire together. And especially if kings and princes conspire together
against the living God, and the people also agree with them,
they make much ado. And yet all this takes place here beneath,
and they are like grasshoppers. Grasshoppers have such long legs
that they can leap; but they must fall down again after a while.
So then they may make a great stir here, but can they leap
above the clouds? Certainly not.

However he that dwells in the high places will laugh them
to scorn. This serves to show us where God's throne is,
namely above the clouds, so that men can never reach unto him.
He shall, from his resting place above, laugh them to scorn,
while they make great noise here on earth.

And so let us learn, when God summons us, and lays
something to our charge, it is not that we shall be able to
hurt him, or for any respect that he has for himself that
he checks us, lest we should take the initiative away from him
and do him harm. Certainly that is not the reason. What
then? It is to make us feel the evil that is in us, that we may be
led to seek some remedy, and be stirred up to come to him with
true repentance, and be governed by his will. God, then, in
punishing men, procures their salvation; in condemning them,
he wishes to absolve them; or better, when they are chastised,
he intends to ratify and confirm his justice, to show that no
evil shall remain unpunished. And at the same time he wishes
to abate men's pride, which leads them to delight and glory
in their sins. God will bring down all those things when he
brings them to judgment.

And so let us learn to cease flattering ourselves; whenever
we shall have some remorse within, and are condemned by the
Word of God, and men show us our faults, and rub salt in our
wounds, it is for our good. Let us learn, I say, no longer to

use excuses, for we shall do nothing else than increase our guilt. And let us know that God is not afraid of us, lest we should do him some damage; but he invites us to be aware of our faults so that we may be displeased with them; and by this means he extends his hand to us to lead us to salvation.

—*Sermons*

189   JULY 7

In that day, saith the Lord, I will smite every horse with astonishment, and his rider with madness: and I will open mine eyes upon the house of Judah, and will smite every horse of the people with blindness.

Zechariah 12:4

There is nothing better for us than to be gathered under the shadow of God's protection, however destitute of any fortress the Church may be, yea, were she to have innumerable enemies hostile to her, and to be without any strength to resist them. Though then the Church were thus grievously tried, and be in the midst of many dangers, and exposed even to death, let us learn from this passage that those are miserable indeed who through fear or cowardice separate themselves from her, and that they who call on God, and cast on him the care of their safety, shall be made blessed, though the whole world were mad against them, though the weapons of all nations were prepared for their ruin, and horses and horsemen were assembled to overwhelm them; for the defence of God is a sufficient protection to his Church. This is one thing. Then let us learn to exercise our faith, when God seems to cast us as it were between the teeth of wolves; for though he may not afford any visible aid, yet he knows how to deliver us, and possesses hidden means of support which we do not perceive, because his purpose is to try our faith and our patience.

—*Commentaries*

He that overcometh, the same shall be clothed in white raiment; and I will not blot out his name out of the book of life, but I will confess his name before my Father, and before his angels.   Revelation 3:5

Therefore we have need to be armed and equipped at every point. But you need not be daunted, seeing that God has promised to equip his own according as they are assaulted by Satan. Only commit yourself to him, distrusting all in yourself, and hope that he only will suffice to sustain you. Further you have to take heed chiefly to two things; first, what the side is you defend, and next, what crown is promised to those who continue steadfast in the Gospel. The service of God, the boundless grace which he has manifested to us in his Son, and all the glory of his kingdom, are such precious things, that no mortal man ought to think it hard to spend his life in fighting against the base corruptions, whose reign throughout the world tends to bring to naught those blessings. And then, we know what will be the end of our warfare, and that he who has bought us will never suffer so dear a price as his blood to be lost, if we be but signed with it.

Now we know how he owns as his own, and declares solemnly that he will own at the last day, all those who have confessed him here below. We do not know as yet what he has determined to do concerning you, but there is nothing better for you than to sacrifice your life to him, being ready to part with it whenever he wills, and yet hoping that he will preserve it, in so far as he knows it to be profitable for your salvation. And although this be difficult to the flesh, yet it is the true happiness of his faithful ones; and you must pray that it may please this gracious God so to imprint it upon your heart that it may never be effaced therefrom. For our part, we also shall pray that he would make you feel his power, and vouchsafe you the full assurance that you are under his keeping; that he bridles the rage of your enemies, and in every way manifests himself as your God and Father. — *Correspondence*

And he saith unto them, Why are ye fearful, O ye of little faith? Then he arose, and rebuked the winds and the sea; and there was a great calm.
Matthew 8:26

To sustain these attacks, faith arms and defends itself with the word of the Lord. And when such a temptation as this assails us — that God is our enemy, because he is angry with us — faith, on the contrary, objects, that he is merciful even when he afflicts, because chastisement proceeds rather from love than from wrath. When it is pressed with this thought, that God is an avenger of iniquities, it opposes the pardon provided for all offenses, whenever the sinner makes application to the Divine clemency. Thus the pious mind, however strangely it may be agitated and harassed, rises at length superior to all difficulties, nor ever suffers its confidence in the Divine mercy to be shaken. The various disputes which exercise and fatigue it terminate rather in the confirmation of that confidence.

It is a proof of this, that when the saints conceive themselves to feel most the vengeance of God, they still confide their complaints to him, and when there is no appearance of his hearing them, they continue to call upon him. For what end would be answered by addressing complaint to him from whom they expected no consolation? And they would never be disposed to call upon him unless they believed him to be ready to assist them. Thus the disciples, whom Christ reprehends for the weakness of their faith, complained indeed that they were perishing, but still they implored his assistance. Nor, when he chides them for their weak faith, does he reject them from the number of his children, or class them with unbelievers; but he excites them to correct that fault. Therefore we repeat the assertion already made, that faith is never eradicated from a pious heart, but continues firmly fixed, however it may be shaken, and seem to bend this way or that; that its light is never so extinguished or smothered, but that it lies at least concealed under embers; and that this is an evident proof that the word, which is an incorruptible seed, produces fruit similar to itself, whose germ never entirely perishes.

—Institutes, III, ii, xxi

192   JULY 10

If I have lifted up my hand against the fatherless, when I saw my help in the gate: Then let mine arm fall from my shoulder blade, and mine arm be broken from the bone.   Job 31:21, 22

Let us bear well in mind that if the poor pass before us, and we see their need, and keep our purses shut, so as not to help them, it is a sure sign that we are like wild beasts, and that there is not one spark of pity in us. We ourselves shall some day feel the same lack of mercy when God sends us afflictions; and although we shall be miserable, no man will be moved by it, but men shall look on us with disdain, and we shall be pushed aside and left utterly destitute. For it is the measure and wages which God is accustomed to give to all who are hardhearted toward their neighbors; according as it is said, that he who is merciless shall have judgment without mercy.

God thinks it is not enough that we should merely abstain from evildoing and from hurting our neighbors, and from taking away other men's substance and goods. It is true that it is already a kind of virtue if we can protest that we have clean hands, and are not given to thievery, deceit, and extortion. But yet for all that let us not think that we are completely acquitted. For if God has given us means to help such as have need, and we do not do it, we are blameworthy. And why? Because we have taken away God's goods and put them to another use than he intended.

God gives us his goods to the intent that we should relieve our poor brothers with them. Now if on the contrary we are so straight-laced that not a penny goes out of our purses, nor a morsel of bread from our tables, what shall become of us?

Is this not defrauding them whom God has ordained to have part of our substance, and robbing God in the thing that he has put into our hands? So let us learn to be more merciful. And although no man can give us a definite assignment, as if to say, "You should give so much," yet let every man exert himself, and consider his own ability, knowing well that when we have done all that can do, yet we are not discharged.

—*Sermons*

193   **JULY 11**

Against thee, thee only, have I sinned, and done this evil in thy sight: that thou mightest be justified when thou speakest, and be clear when thou judgest.

Psalm 51:4

"Against thee, thee only have I sinned." Though all the world should pardon him, he felt that God was the Judge with whom he had to do, that conscience hailed him to his bar, and that the voice of man could administer no relief to him, however much he might be disposed to forgive, or to excuse, or to flatter. His eyes and his whole soul were directed to God, regardless of what man might think or say concerning him. To one who is thus overwhelmed with a sense of the dreadfulness of being obnoxious to God, there need be no other accuser. God is to him instead of a thousand. There is every reason to believe that David, in order to prevent his mind from being soothed into a false peace by the flatteries of his court, realized the judgment of God upon his offense, and felt that this was in itself an intolerable burden, even supposing that he should escape all trouble from the hands of his fellow creatures. This will be the exercise of every true penitent. It matters little to obtain our acquittal at the bar of human judgment, or to escape punishment through the connivance of others, provided we suffer from an accusing conscience and an offended God. And there is, perhaps, no better remedy against deception in the matter of our sins than to turn our thoughts inward upon ourselves, to concentrate them on God, and lose every self-complacent imagination in a sharp sense of his displeasure.

—*Commentaries*

194   JULY 12

I speak not of you all: I know whom I have chosen:
but that the scripture may be fulfilled, He that eateth
bread with me hath lifted up his heel against me.

John 13:18

"I know whom I have chosen." This very circumstance, that they will persevere, he ascribes to their *election;* for the virtue of men, being frail, would tremble at every breeze, and would be laid down by the feeblest stroke, if the Lord did not uphold it by his hand. But as he governs those whom he has *elected,* all the engines which Satan can employ will not prevent them from persevering to the end with unshaken firmness. And not only does he ascribe to election their perseverance, but likewise the commencement of their piety. Whence does it arise that one man, rather than another, devotes himself to the word of God? It is because he was elected. Again, whence does it arise that this man makes progress, and continues to lead a good and holy life, but because the purpose of God is unchangeable, to complete the work which was begun by his hand? In short, this is the source of the distinction between the children of God and unbelievers, that the former are drawn to salvation by the Spirit of adoption, while the latter are hurried to destruction by their flesh, which is under no restraint. Otherwise Christ might have said, "I know what kind of person each of you will be." But that they may not claim anything for themselves, but on the contrary may acknowledge that by the grace of God alone, and not by their own virtue, they differ from Judas, he places before them that election by free grace on which they are founded. Let us, therefore, learn that every part of our salvation depends on election. — *Commentaries*

JULY 13

Rivers of waters run down mine eyes, because they keep not thy law.   Psalm 119:136

Wherever the Spirit of God reigns, he excites this ardent zeal, which burns the hearts of the godly when they see the commandment of the Most High accounted as a thing of nought. It is not enough that each of us endeavor to please God. We must also desire that his law may be held in estimation by all men. In this way holy Lot, as the Apostle Peter testifies, vexed his soul when he beheld Sodom a sink of all kinds of wickedness. If, in former times, the ungodliness of the world extorted from the children of God such bitter grief, so great is the corruption into which we at this day are fallen, that those who can look upon the present state of things unconcerned and without tears are thrice, yea four times insensible. How great in our day is the frenzy of the world in despising God and neglecting his doctrine! A few, no doubt, are to be found who with the mouth profess their willingness to receive it, but scarcely one in ten proves the sincerity of his profession by his life. Meanwhile countless multitudes are hurried away to the impostures of Satan and to the Pope; others are as thoughtless and indifferent about their salvation as the lower animals; and many Epicureans openly mock at all religion. If there is, then, the smallest portion of piety remaining in us, full rivers of tears, and not merely small drops, will flow from our eyes. But if we would give evidence of pure and uncorrupted zeal, let our grief begin at ourselves — at our seeing that we are yet far from having attained to a perfect observance of the law, yea, that the depraved lusts of our carnal nature are often rising up against the righteousness of God.

—Commentaries

*And lead us not into temptation, but deliver us from
evil: For thine is the kingdom, and the power, and the
glory, for ever. Amen.*   Matthew 6:13

Because our obedience to God is not without continual warfare, and severe and arduous conflicts, we here pray for arms
and assistance to enable us to gain the victory. Now the forms
of temptations are many and various. For the corrupt conceptions of the mind, provoking us to transgressions of the law,
whether suggested by our own lust or excited by the devil, are
temptations; and things not evil in themselves, nevertheless
become temptations through the subtlety of the devil, when
they are obtruded on our eyes in such a manner that their
intervention occasions our seduction or declension from God.
And these temptations are either from prosperous or from
adverse events. From prosperous ones, as riches, power, honors;
which generally dazzle men's eyes by their glitter and external
appearance of goodness, and ensnare them with their blandish-
ments that, caught with such delusions and intoxicated with
such delights, they forget their God. From unpropitious
ones, as poverty, reproaches, contempt, afflictions, and other
things of this kind; overcome with the bitterness and difficulty
of which, they fall into despondency, cast away faith and
hope, and at length become altogether alienated from God. To
both these kinds of temptations which assail us, whether
kindled within us by our lust or presented to us by the craft
of Satan, we pray our heavenly Father not to permit us to
yield, but rather to sustain and raise us up with his hand,
that, strong in his might, we may be able to stand firm against
all the assaults of our malignant enemy, whatever imaginations
he may inject into our minds; and also, that whatever is presented to us on either quarter, we may convert it to our benefit; that is, by not being elated with prosperity or dejected
with adversity. — *Institutes*, III, xx, xlvi

*Fight the good fight of faith, lay hold on eternal life,
whereunto thou art also called, and hast professed a
good profession before many witnesses.*

I Timothy 6:12

We say that faith is never without fighting. And why so?
For if a man dispose himself to do well, and to submit himself
to God, the devil will cast many blocks in his way to turn him
aside; the world is full of deceits, we are not able to set one
foot forwards, but we shall meet with a shrew; we walk here
among thorns, they that should help us forward draw us back;
for the devil uses their malice that live with us, to fight against
us. And when any man does us harm, he gives us occasion
to answer him in kind; or else we become disheartened, we are
angry, we are so spoiled that the wool is eaten from our backs,
when we walk simply and seek nothing but to do our duty.

And again, though a Christian do not go out of himself,
he must fight to stand steadfast in the faith. That is so, there
is nothing more contrary to our nature than to forego these
earthly things and not to be given to them, and to seek that
with all our heart and with all our soul which we do not see,
and which is completely hidden from our eyes, and such as
our senses can in no way attain unto. A Christian and faithful
man must look higher than himself, when there is any question of thinking upon the kingdom of God and everlasting life.
And yet we know how our minds are bent to the things we
have in our hands. How then is it possible for us to stand
fast in the faith, unless we mightily resist and strive stoutly
against all our nature? And therefore, when we meet with
these temptations and are stirred up to fight, let us make this
doctrine of Saint Paul our buckler, namely that faith is never
without struggle, that we can never serve God, but we must
be soldiers. And why so? Because we have enemies before us,
we are compassed about on every side. And therefore it is
requisite for us to be used to fighting, or else we must be fain
to yield.

Seeing it is so that no man can serve God, but he must exercise himself in patience, and that in the midst of afflictions wherewith the children of God are tormented, let us beware that we do not renounce our faith, but march on still. I would to God I could employ myself wholly to praise God joyfully, and to be at rest and contentment, that I were not troubled by men, but all my senses were given to do well; this were to be wished, but yet God will try me and my chiefest battle must be against my own affections; and then when the devil moves many combats against me, I must beware that I be not overcome, when temptations come on all sides; I must stand fast, I must be strong and constant. — *Commentaries*

198   **JULY 16**

Fear thou not; for I am with thee: be not dismayed; for I am thy God: I will strengthen thee; yea, I will help thee; yea, I will uphold thee with the right hand of my righteousness.   Isaiah 41:10

"For I am with thee." This is a solid foundation of confidence, and if it be fixed in our minds, we shall be able to stand firm and unshaken against temptations of every kind. In like manner, when we think that God is absent, or doubt whether or not he will be willing to assist us, we are agitated by fear, and tossed about amidst many storms of distrust. But if we stand firm on this foundation, we shall not be overwhelmed by any assaults or tempests. And yet the Prophet does not mean that believers stand so boldly as to be altogether free and void of fear; but though they are distressed in mind, and in various ways are tempted to distrust, they resist with such steadfastness as to secure the victory. By nature we are timid and full of distrust, but we must correct that vice by this reflection, "God is present with us, and takes care of our salvation." — *Commentaries*

These words spake Jesus, and lifted up his eyes to heaven, and said, Father, the hour is come; glorify thy Son, that thy Son also may glorify thee: John 17:1

"And lifted up his eyes to heaven." Yet if we desire actually to imitate Christ, we must take care that outward gestures do not express more than is in our mind, but that the inward feelings shall direct the eyes, the hands, the tongue, and everything about us. We are told, indeed, that the publican, with downcast eyes, prayed aright to God (Luke 18:13) but that is not inconsistent with what has now been stated; for, though he was confused and humbled on account of his sins, still this self-abasement did not prevent him from seeking pardon with full confidence. But it was proper that Christ should pray in a different manner, for he had nothing about him of which he ought to be ashamed; and it is certain that David himself prayed sometimes in one attitude and sometimes in another, according to the circumstances in which he was placed. — *Commentaries*

For they are impudent children and stiffhearted. I do send thee unto them; and thou shalt say unto them, Thus saith the Lord God. And they, whether they will hear, or whether they will forbear, (for they are a rebellious house,) yet shall know that there hath been a prophet among them.   Ezekiel 2:4, 5

We may learn from this place, that although the impious furiously endeavor to reject the doctrine of God, yet they obtain no other end than the more complete manifestation of their own wickedness. Hence also we may learn that God's doctrine is precious to himself, and that he cannot bear us to despise it. The wicked then can never escape punishment when they treat with contempt the divine teaching, for it is as if they trampled upon inestimable treasure. Those who are left without the law and the prophets shall not escape God's hand, because their conscience is sufficient to take away all excuse (Rom. 2:12). But when God invites men to himself, and approaches near them, and offers himself to them in a peculiar manner as their Father and Teacher, if they reject so remarkable a benefit, truly their ingratitude is worthy of the utmost severity. For as often as God raises up prophets for us and faithful ministers of his doctrine, let this which has just been said come into our minds; unless we embrace such a benefit, we at length shall know that a prophet has been among us, because God will exact fearful vengeance for the contempt of his great loving-kindness. — *Commentaries*

201 JULY 19

For it is God which worketh in you both to will and to do of his good pleasure. Philippians 2:13

But I have heard that God, of his infinite goodness, has touched your heart, so that you desire to be a Christian, not in name only but in reality. If I may express myself thus, it is because the word Christian passes glibly indeed from the lips of all, but when it is required of us to humble ourselves beneath the gospel, which is the sceptre by which Jesus Christ wills to reign over us, almost all shrink back; in which fact we see that it is but too common a thing from hypocrisy to wear like a mask the title of Christian, and by so doing profane it. And it is not a small nor a vulgar virtue to approve by deeds that we desire to be the disciples of the Son of God, to the end that he also may avow us for his disciples. For that reason you are so much the more bound to recognize the mercy of God in advancing you thus far. For it is not of our own impulse that we come thitherward, but only inasmuch as he has been pleased to draw us. And that this goodness may have greater lustre by being better known, he has chosen us out and set us apart from among those to whom we are otherwise alike. — *Correspondence*

*Then the angel of the Lord answered and said, O Lord
of hosts, how long wilt thou not have mercy on Jerusalem and on the cities of Judah, against which thou
hast had indignation these threescore and ten years?*
                                    Zechariah 1:12

Why does Scripture testify that angels supplicate God for
us? Is it that each of us may flee to them? By no means; but
that being assured of God's paternal love, we may entertain
more hope and confidence; yea, that we may courageously fight,
being certain of victory, since celestial hosts contend for us,
according to what appears from many examples. For when the
servant of Elisha saw not the chariots flying in the air, he
became almost lost in despair; but his despair was instantly
removed when he saw so many angels ready at hand for help;
so whenever God declares that angels are ministers for our
safety, he means to animate our faith; at the same time he does
not send us to angels; but this one thing is sufficient for us,
that when God is propitious to us, all the angels have a care
for our salvation.

And we must further notice what is said by Christ, "hereafter
ye shall see angels ascending and descending" (John 1:51),
which means that when we are joined to the head, there will
thence proceed a sacred union between us and angels; for
Christ, we know, is equally Lord over all. When therefore
we are united to the body of Christ, it is certain that angels
are united to us, but only through Christ. All this favor then
depends on the one true Mediator. Far then is it from being
the case that Scripture represents angels as patrons to whom
we may pray. The meaning then is this, when Zechariah
says that the angels thus prayed, "O Jehovah of hosts, how
long wilt thou not have mercy on Jerusalem and the cities of
Judah?" — *Commentaries*

*For the love of money is the root of all evil: which
while some coveted after, they have erred from the
faith, and pierced themselves through with many sorrows.*   I Timothy 6:10

We shall find a restraint laid upon us, to keep us from
being inflamed with an inordinate desire of growing rich, and
from ambitiously aspiring after honors. For with what face can
any man confide in the assistance of God, towards obtaining
things which he desires in opposition to the Divine word? Far
be it from God to follow with the aid of his blessing what
he curses with his mouth. Lastly, if our success be not equal
with our wishes and hopes, yet we shall be restrained from im-
patience and from speaking evil of our condition, whatever it
may be; because we shall know, that this would be murmuring
against God, at whose pleasure are dispensed riches and poverty,
honor and contempt. In short, he who shall repose himself on
the Divine blessing will neither hunt after the object violently
coveted by men in general, by evil methods, from which he will
expect no advantage; nor will he impute any prosperous event
to himself, and to his own diligence, industry, or good fortune;
but will acknowledge God to be the author of it.

—*Institutes*, III, vii, ix

*Blessed are ye, when men shall revile you, and per-
secute you, and shall say all manner of evil against
you falsely, for my sake.*   Matthew 5:11

If we are not satisfied with that, he shows us that as
much as our faith is more precious than gold or silver, so it is
the more reasonable that it should be tried. Also it is by
this means that we are mortified, in order not to be rooted in
our love for this world, and more evil affections than we can
imagine are thus corrected, were it but to teach us humility

and bring down that pride which is always greater in us than it ought to be. By it he also wishes to put us in mind of the esteem in which we ought to hold his word; for if it cost us nothing we should not know its worth. He permits us then to be afflicted for it, in order to show us how very precious he considers it. But above all by sufferings he wishes us to be conformed to the image of his Son, as it is fitting that there should be conformity between the head and the members. Let us not then suppose that we are forsaken of God when we suffer persecution for his truth, but rather he so disposes matters for our greater good. If that is repugnant to our senses, it is so because we are always more inclined to seek for our rest here below than in the kingdom of heaven. Now since our triumph is in heaven, we must be prepared for the combat while we live here upon earth. — *Correspondence*

205   **JULY 23**

When I say unto the wicked, Thou shalt surely die;
and thou givest him not warning, nor speakest to warn
the wicked from his wicked way, to save his life; the
same wicked man shall die in his iniquity; but his
blood will I require at thine hand.   Ezekiel 3:18

Meanwhile those fanatics are to be rejected who, under pretext of this place, wish to give license to sin, and assert that there is no difference between good and evil, because it is not our duty to condemn. For, properly speaking, we do not assume anything to ourselves when we recite what has proceeded from the mouth of God. God condemns adulterers, thieves, drunkards, murderers, enviers, slanderers, oppressors; if one inveigh against an adulterer, another a thief, a third a drunkard, shall we say that they take upon themselves more than they ought? By no means, because they do not pronounce of themselves, as we have said, but God has said it, and they are but witnesses and messengers of his sentence. Yet this moderation must be maintained, not to condemn anyone through moroseness, since many immediately abominate whatever displeases them, and cannot be induced to use diligent inquiry. Inquiry, therefore, should precede our sentences; but when God has spoken, then we must follow the rule which was given to the Prophet, if thou hast not admonished him, and spoken for his admonition. — *Commentaries*

206   JULY **24**

Quench not the Spirit.   I Thessalonians 5:19

But to come to the point, make a right use of the knowledge which he has for a long time past vouchsafed to you; and do not allow the zeal which he has at one time imprinted by the Holy Spirit upon your heart to die away; and do not knowingly quench the holy desire which has burned within you in bygone times. Behold how God allows those to slip away who grow careless little by little, and how easily he permits them to be so utterly depraved that they go to perdition; and it is just that the Lord should thus avenge himself upon those who have preferred the vanities of the world to the treasure of his gospel. Now, while many allow themselves to be seduced by such examples, let this serve as a warning to you, to keep all the more closely fenced about in fear and solicitude. Finally, let the adversity which you have passed through, during a part of your life, make you ponder all the more seriously that true happiness and perfect glory which is prepared for us in heaven, that we may not beguile ourselves with worldly repose, which can only be fleeting and highly seasoned with never-ceasing care and troubles, and, worse than all, which makes us unmindful of that soul-rest which alone is blessed.

—*Correspondence*

*Jesus saith unto him, I am the way, the truth, and the
life: no man cometh unto the Father, but by me.*
                                                  John 14:6

"I am the way." Though Christ does not give a direct reply
to the question put to him, yet he passes by nothing that is
useful to be known. It was proper that Thomas' curiosity
should be checked; and, therefore, Christ does not explain
what would be his condition when he should have departed
out of this world to go to the Father, but dwells on a subject
far more necessary. Thomas would gladly have heard what
Christ intended to do in heaven, as we never become weary
of those intricate speculations; but it is of greater importance to
us to employ our study and labor on another inquiry, how we
may become partakers of the blessed resurrection. The statement amounts to this, that whoever obtains Christ is in want
of nothing; and therefore that whoever is not satisfied with
Christ alone strives after something beyond absolute perfection.
"The way, the truth, and the life." He lays down three
degrees, as if he had said that he is the beginning and the
middle and the end; and hence it follows that we ought to
begin with him, to continue in him, and to end in him. We
certainly ought not to seek for higher wisdom than that which
leads us to eternal *life,* and he testifies that this *life* is to be
found in him. Now the method of obtaining life is to become
new creatures. He declares that we ought not to seek it anywhere else and at the same time reminds us that *he is the way*
by which alone we can arrive at it. That he may not fail
us in any respect, he stretches out the hand to those who are
going astray, and stoops so low as to guide sucking infants.
Presenting himself as a leader, he does not leave his people in
the middle of the course, but makes them partakers of *the
truth.* At length he makes them enjoy the fruit of it, which
is the most excellent and delightful thing that can be imagined.
                                                  —*Commentaries*

Owe no man any thing, but to love one another: for he that loveth another hath fulfilled the law.

Romans 13:8

The third use of the law, which is the principal one, and which is more nearly connected with the proper end of it, relates to the faithful, in whose hearts the Spirit of God already lives and reigns. For although the law is inscribed and engraven on their hearts by the finger of God — that is, although they are so excited and animated in the direction of the Spirit that they desire to obey God — yet they derive a twofold advantage from the law. For they find it an excellent instrument to give them, from day to day, a better and more certain understanding of the Divine will to which they aspire, and to confirm them in the knowledge of it. As, though a servant be already influenced by the strongest desire of gaining the approbation of his master, yet it is necessary for him carefully to inquire and observe the orders of his master, in order to conform to them. Nor let any one of us exempt himself from this necessity; for no man has already acquired so much wisdom, that he could not by the daily instruction of the law make new advances into a purer knowledge of the Divine will.

In the next place, as we need not only instruction, but also exhortation, the servant of God will derive this further advantage from the law; by frequent meditation on it he will be excited to obedience, he will be confirmed in it, and restrained from the slippery path of transgression. For in this manner should the saints stimulate themselves, because with whatever alacrity they labor for the righteousness of God according to the Spirit, yet they are always burdened with the indolence of the flesh, which prevents their proceeding with due promptitude. To this flesh the law serves as a whip, urging it, like a dull and tardy animal, forward to its work; and even to the spiritual man, who is not yet delivered from the burden of the flesh, it will be a perpetual spur, that will not permit him to loiter.

—*Institutes*, II, vii, xii

Then came the word of the Lord to Isaiah, saying,
Isaiah 38:4, 5

"Then came the word of Jehovah." What interval of time elapsed between the Prophet's departure and return we know not, but it is certain that the glad tidings of life were not brought until, after long and severe struggles, he perceived that he was utterly ruined; for it was a severe trial of faith that he should be kept plunged in darkness by the hiding of God's face. We have said that, while the doctrine of consolation was taken away, still the faith of the good king was not extinguished so as not to emit some sparks, because, by the secret influence of the Spirit, "groans that could not be uttered" (Rom. 8:26) arose to God out of the gulf of sorrow. Hence also we conclude that, while "in the day of trouble" (Psalm 50:15) God heareth believers, yet the favor of God does not all at once shine on them, but is purposely delayed till they are sincerely humbled. And if a king so eminent in piety needed almost to suffer anguish, that he might be more powerfully excited to seek the favor of God, and, being almost wasted by grief, might groan from hell to God; let us not wonder if he sometimes permits us for a time to be agitated by fears and perplexities, and delays longer to bestow consolation in answer to our prayers. — *Commentaries*

*Is not thy wickedness great? and thine iniquities in-
finite?*   Job 22:5

We are shown here that men must not confess their sins
before God lightly, and as it were out of mere form, as they
do when they say, "Oh, I do not deny that there are some
faults in me." No, we must not do this; but we must make
the burden so heavy that we can no longer bear it. For this
is how God will be glorified; not when men say that they have
some small infirmities and imperfections in them; but when
with David they speak of the greatness of their sins and the
multitude of their iniquities. And as Daniel — who was as an
angel compared with other men — speaks in his confession; "I
have confessed my sins and the sins of my people." He does
not speak of some small fault, but he says, "Our sins are great
and enormous, O Lord." And so let us confess what we are,
and that in such a way that God may be truly glorified.

And what hope may we have that God will receive us, and
be merciful and favorably inclined toward us, if we are not
overwhelmed with the sins which we have committed? Our
Lord Jesus Christ does not say to us, "Come unto me, all ye
that say, I am a sinner, there are infirmities in me." No, he
says, "All ye that are laden and weary, whose shoulders stoop
under the weight of your sins." These are they that are called
by Jesus Christ, to the end that they may find mercy in him;
and not such as mock at God and make a light confession, without ever being touched in their hearts. — *Sermons*

*Blessed is the man that walketh not in the counsel of
the ungodly, nor standeth in the way of sinners, nor
sitteth in the seat of the scornful.*   Psalm 1:1

The sum of the whole is that the servants of God must endeavor utterly to abhor the life of ungodly men. But as it is the policy of Satan to insinuate his deceits in a very crafty way, the Prophet, in order that none may be insensibly deceived, shows how by little and little men are ordinarily induced to turn aside from the right path. They do not, at the first step, advance so far as a proud contempt of God; but having once begun to give ear to evil counsel, Satan leads them, step by step, farther astray, till they rush headlong into open transgression. The Prophet, therefore, begins with *counsel*, by which term I understand the wickedness which does not as yet show itself openly. Then he speaks of the *way*, which is to be understood of the customary mode or manner of living. And he places at the top of the climax the *seat*, by which metaphorical expression he designates the obduracy produced by the habit of a sinful life. In the same way, also, ought the three phrases, *to walk*, *to stand*, and *to sit*, to be understood. When a person willingly *walks* after the gratification of his corrupt lust, the practice of sinning so infatuates him that, forgetful of himself, he grows hardened in wickedness; and this the Prophet terms standing in the way of sinners. Then at length follows a desperate obstinacy, which he expresses by the figure of sitting. — *Commentaries*

*And now why tarriest thou? arise, and be baptized,
and wash away thy sins, calling on the name of the
Lord.*   Acts 22:16

For as baptism is given for the support, consolation, and confirmation of our faith, it requires to be received as from the hand of the Author himself; we ought to consider it as beyond all doubt, that it is he who speaks to us by this sign; that it is he who purifies and cleanses us, and obliterates the remembrance of our sins; that it is he who makes us partakers of his death, who demolishes the kingdom of Satan, who weakens the power of our corrupt propensities, who even makes us one with himself, that, being clothed with him, we may be reckoned children of God; and that he as truly and certainly performs these things internally on our souls, as we see that our bodies are externally washed, immersed, and enclosed in water.

—*Institutes*, IV, xv, xiv

213 JULY 31

And they were all amazed, and were in doubt, saying one to another, What meaneth this? Acts 2:12

If God should openly and visibly descend from heaven, his majesty could scarcely appear more manifestly than in this miracle. Whoever has any drop of sound understanding in him must be stricken with only hearing of it. How beastly, then, are those men who see it with their eyes, and yet scoff, and go about with their jests to mock the power of God? But the matter is so. There is nothing so wonderful which those men do not turn to a jest who are touched with no care of God; because they do, even purposely, harden themselves in their ignorance of things most plain. And it is a just punishment of God, which he brings upon such pride, to deliver them to Satan, to be driven headlong into blind fury. Wherefore there is no cause that we should marvel that there be so many at this day so blind in so great light, if they be so deaf when such manifest doctrine is declared, yea, if they wantonly refuse salvation when it is offered unto them. For if the wonderful and strange works of God, wherein he wonderfully sets forth his power, be subject to the mockery of men, what shall become of doctrine, which they think tastes of nothing but of that which is common? — *Commentaries*

But thou, when thou prayest, enter into thy closet, and when thou hast shut thy door, pray to thy Father which is in secret; and thy Father which seeth in secret shall reward thee openly.   Matthew 6:6

He immediately adds a better direction, which is to enter into our closet, and there to pray with the door shut. In which words, as I understand them, he has taught us to seek retirement, that we may be enabled to descend into our own hearts with all our powers of reflection, and promised us that God, whose temples our bodies ought to be, will accede to the desires of our souls. For he did not intend to deny the expediency of praying also in other places; but shows that prayer is a kind of secret thing, which lies principally in the heart, and requires a tranquillity of mind undisturbed by all cares. It was not without reason therefore that the Lord himself, when he would engage in an unusual vehemence of devotion, retired to some solitary place, far from the tumult of men. And so it is to be concluded that whoever refuses to pray in the solemn assembly of the saints knows nothing of private prayer, either solitary or domestic. And again, that he who neglects solitary and private prayer, no matter how regularly he may frequent the public assemblies, only forms there such as are mere wind, because he pays more deference to the opinion of men than to the secret judgment of God. — *Institutes*, III, xx, xxix

215   AUGUST 2

*And they shall know that I am the Lord, and that I
have not said in vain that I would do this evil unto
them.*   Ezekiel 6:10

God therefore says, "They shall then know that I have not
spoken in vain, when I bring upon them this evil." This knowledge, which is produced by real dissatisfaction with self, is
very useful. I have said that it is the fruit of repentance, but
at the same time it profits the miserable, to humble themselves
seriously before God, and to call to memory their own ingratitude; then they perceive what they have never admitted before, that God is trustworthy as well in his threats as in his
promises. Hence it happens that they reverently embrace his
word which they had formerly despised.

He pronounced the same thing previously concerning the
reprobate, who as we have already said, feel God's hand without producing fruit. But because he now speaks of those very
few whose conversion he had previously praised, he doubtless
comprehends the fear of God under recognition or perception
of him. For if all God's threats had been buried, the people
could not be thought to have returned to the right way, nor
could their conversion have any existence before God. That the
sinner may submit himself sincerely to God, he ought to consider how he had formerly repudiated or neglected the word
of God. — *Commentaries*

216   AUGUST 3

*When the poor and needy seek water, and there is
none, and their tongue faileth for thirst, I the Lord will
hear them, I the God of Israel will not forsake them.*
                                      Isaiah 41:17

"I Jehovah will listen to them." God declares that he will
relieve them, when they are brought to this needy condition;
and hence we ought to learn to whom this promise belongs,

namely, to those who, having been reduced to extremity, are as it were parched with thirst and almost fainting. Hence also we see that the Church does not always possess an abundance of blessings, but sometimes feels the pressure of great poverty, that she may be driven by these spurs to call upon God. For we commonly fall into slothfulness, when everything moves on according to our wish. It is therefore advantageous to us to thirst and hunger, that we may learn to flee to the Lord with our whole heart. In a word, we need to be deeply affected with a conviction of our poverty, that we may feel the Lord's assistance. The Prophet unquestionably intended, by this circumstance, partly to illustrate the greatness of the favor, and partly to advise the people not to lose heart on account of their poverty. — *Commentaries*

217   ## AUGUST 4

I, even I, am he that comforteth you: who art thou,
that thou shouldest be afraid of a man that shall die,
and of the son of man which shall be made as grass;
Isaiah 51:12

"I, I am . . ." Here the Lord not only promises grace and salvation to the Jews, but remonstrates with them for refusing to believe him, and for valuing his power less than they ought. It is exceedingly base to tremble at the threatenings of men to such a degree as to care nothing about God's assistance; for he displays his power for this purpose, that he may at least fortify us against every attack. Accordingly, by an excessive fear of men we betray contempt of God.

Hence it is evident how sinful it is to be agitated by the terrors of men, when God calls us to repose. And indeed it is amazing ingratitude of men who, when they hear that God is on their side, derive no hope from his magnificent promises, so as to venture boldly to exclaim, "If God be for us, who can be against us?" (Rom. 8:31). The consequence is that when dangers arise, they are terrified and confounded, and attribute far more to the power of mortal man in attacking them than to the power of God in defending. Justly, therefore, does he upbraid the Jews with not fortifying themselves by these promises, and with not rendering themselves invincible against every danger; for God is treated with the highest dishonor when we doubt his truth, that is, when we are so completely overcome by human terrors that we cannot rest on his promises.

—Commentaries

218 **AUGUST 5**

I pray not that thou shouldest take them out of the world, but that thou shouldest keep them from the evil. John 17:15

"I ask not that thou shouldest take them out of the world." He shows in what the safety of believers consists, not that they are free from annoyance, and live in luxury and at their ease, but that in the midst of dangers they continue to be safe through the assistance of God. For he does not admonish the Father of what is proper to be done, but rather makes provision for their weakness, that, by the method which he prescribes, they may restrain their desires, which are apt to go beyond all bounds. In short, he promises to his disciples the grace of the Father; not to relieve them from all anxiety and toil, but to furnish them with invincible strength against their enemies, and not to suffer them to be overwhelmed by the heavy burden of contests which they will have to endure. If, therefore, we wish to be kept according to the rule which Christ has laid down, we must not desire exemption from evils, or pray to God to convey us immediately into a state of blessed rest, but must rest satisfied with the certain assurance of victory, and in the meantime, resist courageously all the evils from which Christ prayed to his Father that we might be set free. In short, God does not take his people out of the world, because he does not wish them to be effeminate and slothful; but he delivers them from evil, that they may not be overwhelmed; for he wishes them to fight, but does not suffer them to be mortally wounded.

—Commentaries

He withdraweth not his eyes from the righteous . . . .
He openeth also their ear to discipline . . . . If they
obey and serve him, they shall spend their days in
prosperity . . . . But if they obey not, they shall perish
by the sword . . .   Job 36:7a, 10a, 11a, 12a

So then let us not murmur any longer when we see God
sending such troubles into the world, neither let us be offended
as though he had his eyes shut. For he well knows what he
is doing, and he has an infinite wisdom which is not immediately
apparent to us. In the end we shall see that he has disposed
all things in good order and measure. Let us learn not to be
too greatly grieved when we are so afflicted, assuring ourselves
that God by that means is furthering our salvation.

Besides, do we wish to be healed when we are in torment
and pain? Do we want these things to have a favorable out-
come? Then let us follow the way that is showed to us here,
namely to hear and obey. How shall we hear? By being taught
when God sends us to school, so that our afflictions may be like
so many lessons to make us flee to him. Then let us hear these
things, and let them not go in one ear and out the other. And
let us obey, that is to say, let us yield to God the obedience
that we owe him; and let us not seek anything else than to be
conformed to him.

What follows? We must not marvel when men linger in
pain and are daily plunged deeper and deeper into misery;
for which of them listens to God when he speaks? It is apparent how many are afflicted and tormented, and it is evident
that God's whips are occupied everywhere nowadays. But how
few are there that reflect upon them! You see a whole people
oppressed with wars until they can endure no more; and yet
we can hardly find a dozen men among a hundred thousand
that hear God speak. Behold, the snapping of his whips do
sound and echo in the air; there is horrible weeping and wailing
everywhere; men cry out, "Alas, and woe is me!" And yet all
the while they do not look at the hand that smites them.

So then is it any wonder that God sends incurable wounds and does what is said in the Prophet Isaiah; namely, that from the sole of the foot to the crown of the head there is not a drop of soundness in the people, but there is leprosy, so that they are all rotten and infected, and their sores are incurable? Is this any wonder, seeing men are so thankless toward God that they shut him out of doors and will not listen to him, that they might obey him? — *Sermons*

220 AUGUST 7

And if any man hear my words, and believe not, I judge him not: for I came not to judge the world, but to save the world. John 12:47

"If any man hear my words." After having spoken concerning his grace, and exhorted his disciples to steady faith, he now begins to strike the rebellious, though even here he mitigates the severity due to the wickedness of those who deliberately — as it were — reject God; for he delays to pronounce judgment on them, because, on the contrary, he has come for the salvation of all. In the first place, we ought to understand that he does not speak here of all unbelievers without distinction, but of those who, knowingly and wittingly, reject the doctrine of the gospel which has been exhibited to them. Why then does Christ not choose to condemn them? It is because he lays aside for a time the office of a judge, and offers salvation to all without reserve, and stretches out his arms to embrace all, that all may be the more encouraged to repent. And yet there is a circumstance of no small moment, by which he points out the aggravation of the crime, if they reject an invitation so kind and gracious, for it is as if·he had said, "Lo, I am here to invite all, and, forgetting the character of a judge, I have this as my single object, to persuade all, and to rescue from destruction those who are already twice ruined." No man, therefore, is condemned on account of having despised the gospel, except he who, disdaining the lovely message of salvation, has chosen of his own accord to draw down destruction on himself. — *Commentaries*

*On the next day much people that were come to the
feast, when they heard that Jesus was coming to Jerusalem,*   John 12:12

This entrance of Christ is more copiously related by the
other Evangelists; but John here embraces the leading points.
In the first place, we ought to remember Christ's design, which
was that he came to Jerusalem of his own accord, to offer himself to die; for it was necessary that his death should be
voluntary, because the wrath of God could be appeased only by
a sacrifice of obedience. And, indeed, he well knew what would
be the result; but before he is dragged to the cross, he wishes
to be solemnly acknowledged by the people as their King;
nay, he openly declares that he commences his reign by advancing to death. But though his approach was celebrated by a vast
crowd of people, still he remained unknown to his enemies
until, by the fulfillment of prophecies, which we shall afterwards see in their own place, he proved that he was the true
Messiah; for he wished to omit nothing that would con-
tribute to the full confirmation of our faith.

Thus strangers were more ready to discharge the duty of
paying respect to the Son of God than the citizens of Jerusalem, who ought rather to have been an example to all others.
For they had sacrifices daily; the temple was always before
their eyes, which ought to have kindled in their hearts the desire of seeking God; these too were the highest teachers of the
Church, and *there* was the sanctuary of Divine light. It is
therefore a manifestation of excessively base ingratitude in them
that, after they have been trained to such exercise from their
earliest years, they reject or despise the Redeemer who had been
promised to them. But this fault has prevailed in almost every
age, that the more nearly and the more familiarly God ap-
proached to men, the more daringly did men despise God.

—Commentaries

Ye have heard that it was said by them of old time,
Thou shalt not kill; and whosoever shall kill shall be
in danger of the judgment: but I say unto you, That
whosoever is angry with his brother without a cause
shall be in danger of the judgment: and . . . whosoever
shall say, Thou fool, shall be in danger of hell fire.
Matthew 5:21, 22

The end of this precept is that since God has connected mankind together in a kind of unity, every man ought to consider himself as charged with the safety of all. In short, then, all violence and injustice, and every kind of mischief, which may injure the body of our neighbor, are forbidden to us. And therefore we are enjoined, if it be in our power, to assist in protecting the lives of our neighbors; to exert ourselves with fidelity for this purpose; to procure those things which conduce to their tranquillity; to be vigilant in shielding them from injuries; and in cases of danger to afford them our assistance. If we remember that this is the language of the Divine Legislator, we should consider at the same time that he intends this rule to govern the soul. For it were ridiculous that he who beholds the thoughts of the heart and principally insists on them, should content himself with forming only the body to true righteousness. Mental homicide, therefore, is likewise prohibited, and an internal disposition to preserve the life of our brother is commanded in this law.

Now the Scripture states two reasons on which this precept is founded; the first, that man is the image of God; the second, that he is our own flesh. Wherefore unless we would violate the image of God, we ought to hold the personal safety of our neighbor inviolably sacred; and unless we would divest ourselves of humanity, we ought to cherish him as our own flesh. These two characters, which are inseparable from the nature of man, God requires us to consider as motives to our exertions for his security; so that we may reverence his image impressed on him, and show an affectionate regard for our own flesh.

—*Commentaries*

Doth not he see my ways, and count all my steps?
　　　　　　　　　　　　　　　　　Job 31:4

Let us note the style that Job uses; which is that God marks his ways and steps and keeps a reckoning of them. This serves to indicate that God does not see them from a distance, nor does he see these things alone which are evident on the surface; but he looks closely at all our works and carefully notes every one of them. His sight is not dim, nor does he look at random, but he counts and numbers all things, so that nothing escapes him or is forgotten by him. Now then, I ask you, have we not good cause to consider our own ways and count our own steps when we see that all of them come forth before God?

Why is it that men scarcely know the hundredth part of their sins? Some even commit the same sin a hundred times a day, and yet hardly think about it once. Why is this? It is because we do not think that God watches us, nor that we are so observed by him that nothing escapes his vision and nothing is forgotten by him. Therefore let us weigh well what is said here, that God knows our ways and counts our steps, that is to say, that the number of them is set down before him, and that every deed, from the first to the last, must come to account. You can see how much they will gain who have hidden their evil deeds with lying and flattery; for all must come to light.

What remains, then? To watch ourselves more closely than we have been accustomed to do, and to be continually careful lest we be taken unawares by the snares that are laid for us on all sides. And seeing we are in danger from so many vices with which our nature is filled, let us examine them well, that we may be sorry for them and plead guilty before God; and while we mourn for them, let us still confess with David that it is impossible for us to know all our faults. And therefore let us pray the good God that when he has looked upon the faults and sins which we ourselves cannot see, it may please him to blot them out; that thereby we may come to repose our trust for our welfare and salvation in nothing else than in his receiving us in mercy for Jesus Christ's sake; and also in our having the washing with which he has cleansed us, that is to say, the blood which he has shed for our redemption. — *Sermons*

224   **AUGUST 11**

It is vain for you to rise up early, to sit up late, to eat the bread of sorrows: for so he giveth his beloved sleep.

Psalm 127:2

It is not surprising to find those growing rich in a short time who spare no exertion, but consume night and day in plying their occupations and allow themselves only scanty fare from the product of their labor. Solomon, however, affirms that neither living at small expense, nor diligence in business will by themselves profit anything at all. Not that he forbids us to practise temperance in our diet and to rise early to engage in our worldly business; but to stir us up to prayer, and to calling upon God, and also to recommend gratitude for the divine blessings, he brings to nought whatever would obscure the grace of God.

Consequently, we shall then enter upon our worldly avocations in a right way when our hope depends exclusively upon God, and our success in that case will correspond to our wishes. But if a man, taking no account of God, eagerly makes haste, he will bring ruin upon himself by his too precipitate course. It is not, therefore, the design of the Prophet to encourage men to give way to sloth, so that they should think upon nothing all their life long, but fall asleep and abandon themselves to idleness; but his meaning is rather that in executing what God has enjoined upon them, they should always begin with prayer and calling upon his name, offering to him their labors that he may bless them. — *Commentaries*

225 AUGUST 12

And looking upon Jesus as he walked, he saith, Behold the Lamb of God!   John 1:36

"Behold the Lamb of God." The principal office of Christ is briefly but clearly stated; that he "takes away the sins of the world" by the sacrifice of his death, and reconciles men to God. There are other favors, indeed, which Christ bestows upon us, but this is the chief favor, and the rest depend on it; that, by appeasing the wrath of God, he makes us to be reckoned holy and righteous. For from this source flow all the streams of blessings, that, by not imputing our sins, he receives us into favor. Accordingly, John, in order to conduct us to Christ, commences with the gratuitous forgiveness of sins which we obtain through him. — *Commentaries*

226 AUGUST 13

I will praise thee, O Lord, with my whole heart; I will shew forth all thy marvelous works.   Psalm 9:1

Even irreligious men, I admit, when they have obtained some memorable victory, are ashamed to defraud God of the praise which is due to him; but we see that as soon as they have uttered a single expression in acknowledgment of the assistance God has afforded them, they immediately begin to boast loudly, and to sing triumphs in honor of their own valor, as if they were under no obligations whatsoever to God. In short, it is a piece of pure mockery when they profess that their exploits have been done by the help of God; for, after having made oblation to him, they sacrifice to their own counsels, skill, courage, and resources. Observe how the prophet Habakkuk, under the person of one presumptuous king, wisely reproves the ambition which is common to all (Hab. 1:16).

David, therefore, with good reason, affirms that he is unlike the children of this world, whose hypocrisy or fraud is discovered by the wicked and dishonest distribution which they make between God and themselves, arrogating to themselves the greater part of the praise which they pretended to ascribe to God. He praised God with his whole heart, which they did not; for certainly it is not praising God with the whole heart when mortal man dares to appropriate the smallest portion of the glory which God claims for himself. God cannot bear with seeing his glory appropriated by the creature in even the smallest degree, so intolerable to him is the sacrilegious arrogance of those who, by praising themselves, obscure his glory as far as they can. — *Commentaries*

227   AUGUST 14

Therefore will I divide him a portion with the great, and he shall divide the spoil with the strong; because he hath poured out his soul unto death: and he was numbered with the transgressors; and he bare the sin of many, and made intercession for the transgressors.
Isaiah 53:12

So then, to be submissive to our Lord Jesus Christ, let us confess him as our King and do it sincerely. There is no doubt we obtain from him liberty in the first place; and after that, the blessings we need and which we lack unless we receive them at his hand. See how wretched we should be if Satan had not been plundered; for he possesses us, he enjoys us at his ease, just as our Lord Jesus declares. In a word, we are like his own possession and property.

So we have need that the death and passion of our Lord Jesus Christ brings forth its fruit in us, and that our enemies may be not only overcome but also put to flight; that Jesus Christ may, as it were, keep his foot on their throats, so that they may be powerless, though they scheme to do us harm. — *Sermons*

And enter not into judgment with thy servant: for in thy sight shall no man living be justified.

Psalm 143:2

To this point our eyes ought to have been raised, that we might learn rather to tremble through fear than to indulge in vain exultation. It is easy indeed, while the comparison is made only between men, for every man to imagine himself to be possessed of something which others ought not to despise; but when we ascend to the contemplation of God, that confidence is immediately lost. And the case of our soul with respect to God is similar to that of our body with respect to the visible heavens; for the eye, as long as it is employed in beholding adjacent objects, receives proofs of its own perspicacity; but if it be directed towards the sun, dazzled and confounded with his overpowering brightness, it feels no less debility in beholding him, than strength in the view of inferior objects.

Let us not, then, deceive ourselves with a vain confidence, although we consider ourselves equal or superior to other men. That is nothing to God, to whose decision this cause must be submitted. But if our insolence cannot be restrained by these admonitions, he will reply to us in the language which he addressed to the Pharisees, "Ye are they which justify yourselves before men; but that which is highly esteemed among men is abomination in the sight of God." Go now, and among men proudly glory in your righteousness, while the God of heaven abominates it. But what is the language of the servants of God, who are truly taught by his Spirit? One says, "Enter not into judgment with thy servant; for in thy sight shall no man living be justified." And another, though in a sense somewhat different, "How shall man be just with God? If he will contend with him, he cannot answer him one of a thousand." Here we are plainly informed respecting the righteousness of God, that it is such as no human works can satisfy; and such as renders it impossible for us, if accused of a thousand crimes, to exculpate ourselves from one of them.

—*Institutes,* III, xii, ii

*Offer unto God thanksgiving; and pay thy vows unto
the most High: And call upon me in the day of
trouble: I will deliver thee, and thou shalt glorify me.*
                                        Psalm 50:14, 15

There is in all men by nature a strong and ineffaceable
conviction that they ought to worship God. Indisposed to worship him in a pure and spiritual manner, it becomes necessary
that they should invent some specious appearance as a sub-
stitute; and however clearly they may be persuaded of the
vanity of such conduct, they persist in it to the last, because
they shrink from a total renunciation of the service of God.
Men have always, accordingly, been found addicted to ceremonies until they have been brought to the knowledge of
that which constitutes true and acceptable religion.

Praise and prayer are here to be considered as representing
the whole of the worship of God, according to a figure of
speech. The Psalmist specifies only one part of Divine worship,
when he enjoins us to acknowledge God as the Author of all
our mercies, and to ascribe to him the praise which is justly
due unto his name; and adds, that we should betake ourselves
to his goodness, cast all our cares into his bosom, and seek
by prayer that deliverance which he alone can give, and
thanks for which must afterwards be rendered to him. Faith,
self-denial, a holy life, and patient endurance of the cross,
are all sacrifices which please God. But as prayer is the offspring of faith, and uniformly accompanied with patience and
mortification of sin, while praise, where it is genuine, indicates holiness of heart, we need not wonder that these two
points of worship should here be employed to represent the
whole. Praise and prayer are set in opposition to ceremonies
and mere external observances of religion, to teach us that the
worship of God is spiritual. — *Commentaries*

Jesus saith unto her, Go, call thy husband, and come hither.   John 4:16

"Call thy husband." Such too is the obstinacy of many, that they will never listen to Christ until they have been subdued by violence. Whenever then we perceive that the oil of Christ has no flavor, it ought to be mixed with wine, that its taste may begin to be felt. Nay more, this is necessary for all of us; for we are not seriously affected by Christ speaking unless we have been aroused to repentance. So then, in order that any one may profit in the school of Christ, his hardness must be subdued by the demonstration of his misery, as the earth, in order that it may become fruitful, is prepared and softened by the plowshare. For this knowledge alone shakes off all our flatteries, so that we no longer dare to mock God. Whenever, therefore, a neglect of the word of God steals upon us, no remedy will be more appropriate than that each of us should arouse himself to the consideration of his sins, that he may be ashamed of himself, and, trembling before the judgment seat of God, may be humbled to obey him whom he had wantonly disobeyed. — *Commentaries*

A bruised reed shall he not break, and the smoking flax shall he not quench: he shall bring forth judgment unto truth. Isaiah 42:3

"Nor will he quench the smoking flax." Isaiah ascribes to Christ that forbearance by which he bears with our weakness, which we find to be actually fulfilled in him; for wherever any spark of piety is seen, he strengthens and kindles it, and if he were to act towards us with the utmost rigor, we should be reduced to nothing. Although men therefore totter and stumble, although they are even shaken out of joint, yet he does not at once cast them off as utterly useless, but bears long, till he makes them stronger and more steadfast.

Not only did he act in this manner when he was manifested to the world, but this is what he daily shows himself to be by the gospel. Following this example, the ministers of the gospel, who are his deputies, ought to show themselves to be meek, and to support the weak, and gently to lead them in the way, so as not to extinguish in them the feeblest spark of piety, but, on the contrary, to kindle them with all their might.

—Commentaries

Therefore let no man glory in men. For all things are yours; Whether Paul, or Apollos, or Cephas, or the world, or life, or death, or things present, or things to come; all are yours; I Corinthians 3:21, 22

But believers should accustom themselves to such a contempt of the present life as may not generate either hatred of life, or ingratitude towards God. For this life, though it is replete with innumerable miseries, is yet deservedly reckoned among the Divine blessings which must not be despised. Wherefore, if we discover nothing of the Divine beneficence in it, we are already guilty of no small ingratitude towards God himself. But to believers especially, it should be a testimony of the Divine benevolence, since the whole of it is destined to the advancement of their salvation. For before he openly discovers to them the inheritance of eternal glory, he intends to reveal himself as our Father in inferior instances; and those are the benefits which he daily confers on us. Since this life, then, is subservient to a knowledge of the Divine goodness, shall we fastidiously scorn it, as though it contained no particle of goodness in it? We must therefore have this sense and affection, to class it among the bounties of the Divine benignity which are not to be rejected. For if Scripture testimones were wanting, which are very numerous and clear, even nature itself exhorts us to give thanks to the Lord for having introduced us to the light of life, for granting us the use of it, and giving us all the helps necessary to its preservation.

And it is a far superior reason for gratitude, if we consider that here we are in some measure prepared for the glory of the heavenly kingdom. For the Lord has ordained that they who are to be hereafter crowned in heaven must first engage in conflicts on earth, that they may not triumph without having surmounted the difficulties of warfare and obtained the victory. Another reason is that here we begin in various blessings to taste the sweetness of the Divine benignity, that our hope and desire may be excited after the full revelation of it. When we have come to this conclusion, that our life in this world is a gift of the Divine clemency, which, as we owe to him, we ought to remember with gratitude, it will then be time for us to descend to a consideration of its most miserable condition, that we may be delivered from excessive love of it, to which, as has been observed, we are naturally inclined. — *Institutes,* III, ix, iii

*And of his fulness have all we received and grace
for grace.*   John 1:16

"And of his fulness." True indeed, the fountain of life,
righteousness, virtue, and wisdom, is with God, but to us it is
a hidden and inaccessible fountain. But an abundance of
those things is exhibited to us in Christ, that we may be permitted to have recourse to him; for he is ready to flow to us,
provided that we open up a channel by faith. He declares in
general that out of Christ we ought not to seek anything good,
though this sentence consists of several clauses. First, he shows
that we are all utterly destitute and empty of spiritual blessings; for the abundance which exists in Christ is intended to
supply our deficiency, to relieve our poverty, to satisfy our
hunger and thirst. Secondly, he warns us that, as soon as we
have departed from Christ, it is in vain for us to seek a single
drop of happiness, because God has determined that whatever
is good shall reside in him alone. Accordingly, we shall find
angels and men to be dry, heaven to be empty, the earth to be
unproductive, and in short all things to be of no value, if we
wish to be partakers of the gifts of God in any other way than
through Christ. Thirdly, he assures us that we shall have no
reason to fear the want of any thing, provided that we draw
from the fulness of Christ, which is in every respect so complete, that we shall experience it to be a truly inexhaustible
fountain; and John classes himself with the rest, not for the
sake of modesty, but to make it more evident that no man
whatever is excepted. — *Commentaries*

*For I will defend this city to save it for mine own sake,
and for my servant David's sake.*   Isaiah 37:35

"For my own sake." When he says that he will do this "for his own sake," he calls on Hezekiah and all believers to remember his gracious covenant. In order to prevent them from despairing, he shows that God will be their defender, not because he finds any cause in them, but rather because he looks to himself; first that he may adhere firmly to his purpose, not to cast away the posterity of Abraham which he adopted, not to abolish religious worship, not to blot out the remembrance of his name on the earth by destroying his sanctuary; and, secondly, not to expose his name to the jeers and blasphemies of the nations. And these words contain an implied reproof which that nation ought to have felt to be severe, and justly; because the good king had more difficulty in pacifying them than in repelling the enemy; for they distrusted and stormed and thought that no hope of safety was left for them. The Lord, therefore, did not look at the merits of the people or of any other person, but only had regard to his own glory; for the contrast which is expressed by Ezekiel must be here understood, "Not for your sakes, O house of Israel, will I do this, but for my own sake" (Ezek. 36:22).

Now, since we have the same argument to plead in the present day, let us not hesitate to make use of this shield against our sins, "Though we most highly deserve a thousand deaths, yet it is enough for God to look to his goodness and faithfulness, that he may fulfill what he has promised." Though it is of no advantage to hypocrites that God is the continual protector of his Church, yet the elect will always have this as a very safe refuge, that although they bring nothing of their own to appease the wrath of God, yet since God, moved by nothing else than his infinite goodness, built his Church and determined to defend it, he will never suffer it to perish. — *Commentaries*

*But ye have not so learned Christ; If so be that ye
have heard him, and have been taught by him, as
the truth is in Jesus: That ye put off concerning the
former conversation the old man, which is corrupt
according to the deceitful lusts;*   Ephesians 4:20-22

This is a proper place to address those who have nothing
but the name and the symbol of Christ, and yet would be
called Christians. But with what face do they glory in his
sacred name? For none have any intercourse with Christ but
those who have received the true knowledge of him from the
word of the gospel. Now the apostle denies that any have
rightly learned Christ, who have not been taught that they
must put off the old man, which is corrupt according to the
deceitful lusts, and put on Christ. Their knowledge of Christ,
then, is proved to be a false and injurious pretense, with
whatever eloquence and volubility they may talk concerning
the gospel. But it is a doctrine, not of the tongue, but of the
life; and is not apprehended merely with the understanding and
memory, like other sciences, but is then only received, when
it possesses the whole soul, and finds a seat and residence in
the inmost affection of the heart. Let them, therefore, either
cease to insult God by boasting themselves to be what they are
not, or show themselves disciples not unworthy of Christ, their
Master. We have allotted the first place to the doctrine which
contains our religion, because it is the origin of our salvation;
but that it may not be unprofitable to us, it must be transfused
into our breast, pervade our manners, and thus transform us
into itself. — *Institutes*, III, vi, iv

Paul, an apostle of Jesus Christ by the commandment
of God our Saviour, and Lord Jesus Christ, which is
our hope;   I Timothy 1:1

No man ought to be heard in the Church of Christ unless
he be sent; for our faith must not hang upon mortal man,
neither upon creatures. None has sovereignty and rule over our
souls, but God only, and as for the doctrine of our salvation,
we may receive it of none, but of him only. Notwithstanding,
he does not come down from heaven in visible shape to speak
to us, nor does he send his angels unto us; but he wills that
we be taught by means of men. And therefore, if we will
show our obedience to God, we must receive his word, which
is preached unto us by them to whom he has given this charge
and office. — *Sermons*

Herein is love, not that we loved God, but that he
loved us, and sent his Son to be the propitiation for
our sins.   I John 4:10

Thus, by a pure and gratuitous love towards us, he is
excited to receive us into favor. But if there is a perpetual
and irreconcilable opposition between righteousness and iniquity, he cannot receive us entirely, as long as we remain sinners. Therefore, to remove all occasion of enmity, and to reconcile us completely to himself, he abolishes all our guilt, by
the expiation exhibited in the death of Christ, that we, who
before were polluted and impure, may appear righteous and
holy in his sight. The love of God the Father therefore pre-
cedes our reconciliation in Christ; or rather it is because he
first loves, that he afterwards reconciles us to himself. But

because, till Christ relieves us by his death, we are not freed from that iniquity which deserves the indignation of God, and is accursed and condemned in his sight; we have not a complete and solid union with God, before we are united to him by Christ. And therefore if we would assure ourselves that God is pacified and propitious to us, we must fix our eyes and hearts on Christ alone, since it is by him only that we really obtain the non-imputation of sins, the imputation of which is connected with the Divine wrath. — *Institutes* II, xvi, iii

AUGUST 25

If I have walked with vanity, or if my foot hath hasted to deceit; Let me be weighed in an even balance, that God may know mine integrity. Job 31:5, 6

Let us learn also to humble ourselves, seeing that the devil is trying to put us to sleep by hypocrisy in order that we may not recognize our faults, and that they may grow worse and worse. Let us then look within ourselves, and after we have examined our imperfections, let us cry out before God, "Alas, Lord! thou hast given me thy grace to go forward in thy service; I do my best, I strive, I resist all my passions, and I fight against myself; and yet I am not righteous before thee, but there is much wrong with me still." That is how the faithful, after striving to the limit of their strength, ought always to retain this opinion when there remains any sinfulness mingled with the good which God enables them to do; they must learn to plead guilty before him and to humble themselves, that they may receive grace.

But although we have many fantasies running in our heads from day to day, and thereby perceive that there is terrible corruption in our nature, yet we must not lose heart, but march on still, praying God that he who has begun to give us progress will continue to set us forward and increase in us the strength of his Holy Spirit. And when the devil comes to incite us to evil, let him not succeed against us, but let us look for help from above; and let us pray that God's Spirit may so reign in our hearts that though there be wicked affections there, they may be so bridled and fettered that they should not toss us hither and thither, but that we may stand steadfast, and be always ready to say, "It is good that God should govern us, and that we should follow his holy will." — *Sermons*

239   AUGUST 26

Neither give heed to fables and endless genealogies, which minister questions, rather than godly edifying which is in faith: so do.   I Timothy 1:4

So then God has not given us his word to feed us only without profit, as the world would that we should tickle their ears, and that there were nothing in us but only to delight their mind and make them merry. God does not mean to dally here with us, but his mind is that we receive some good instruction, that is to say, that we receive profit by his word. Therefore all they that do not apply the word of God to good profit and use, are contemners and falsifiers of good and wholesome doctrine. In short, the word of God is as it were profaned and made vile, unless we apply it thus profitably that we receive good instruction to our salvation by it.

Therefore let us learn that God will not have temples here to sport and laugh in as if there were plays played here; but there must be majesty in his word, by which we may be moved and touched; and moreover a profitable instruction to salvation, and we must be nourished with this spiritual food, so that we may feel that it is not in vain that God speaks to us. — *Sermons*

*But there is a spirit in man: and the inspiration of the
Almighty giveth them understanding.*   Job 32:8

If it is God that gives special understanding to men to
understand the things that pertain to this fleeting life, what
is to be said of the Gospel and of true religion? Have we
these by nature? Can we purchase them by our own labor?
Alas, we must fall far short. If a man should be a good school-
master to teach children, or a good lawyer or physician, or a good
merchant in a city or a good laborer in the country; it is the
Spirit of God that accomplishes all these things. One man
needs to be sharp-witted in one thing more than in another;
as sometimes mechanical arts require greater skill than mer-
chandising.

Now then, when we come to the doctrine of the Gospel, there
is a wisdom which surmounts all of man's understanding, and is
wonderful even to the angels. The very secrets of heaven are
contained in the Gospel, for it concerns the knowledge of
God in the person of his Son. And although our Lord Jesus
Christ descended here below, yet we must comprehend his
godly majesty, or else we cannot establish our faith in him. This
is a matter, I say, which is incomprehensible to human nature.

Now then, if God with respect to mechanical arts, with
respect to human sciences which concern this transitory life,
must distribute to us his Holy Spirit, much more ought we to
realize that our wisdom is not sufficient to know the things
of God and the secrets of his kingdom, and that it is necessary
that we be taught by him. In the meantime we must become
fools in ourselves that we may be taught by him, as Saint
Paul says (I Corinthians 3:18). . . . And this ought to be carefully noted; for we are often dazzled when we see that there
are so few who acknowledge the things of God, and indeed,
that many aged people who have lived a long time in the
world are lost in their superstitions, and fight stubbornly
against the doctrine of the Gospel. — *Sermons*

I have been young, and now am old; yet have I not seen the righteous forsaken, nor his seed begging bread.   Psalm 37:25

We must bear in mind that with respect to the temporal blessings which God confers upon his people, no certain or uniform rule can be established. There are various reasons why God does not manifest his favor equally to all the godly in this world. He chastises some, while he spares others; he heals the secret maladies of some, and passes by others, because they have no need of a like remedy; he exercises the patience of some, according as he has given them the spirit of fortitude; and, finally, he sets forth others by way of example. But in general he humbles all of them by the tokens of his anger, that by secret warnings they may be brought to repentance. Besides, he leads them, by a variety of afflictions, to fix their thoughts in meditation upon the heavenly life; and yet it is not a vain or imaginary thing that, as is set forth in the Law, God vouchsafes earthly blessings to his servants as proofs of his favor toward them. I confess, I say, that it is not in vain, or for nought, that an abundance of earthly blessings sufficient for the supply of all their wants, is promised to the godly. This, however, is always to be understood with this limitation, that God will bestow these blessings only in so far as he shall consider it expedient; and, accordingly, it may happen that the blessing of God may be manifested in the life of men in general, and yet some of the godly be pinched with poverty, because it is for their good. — *Commentaries*

And God blessed them, and God said unto them, Be fruitful, and multiply, and replenish the earth, and subdue it: and have dominion over the fish of the sea, and over the fowl of the air, and over every living thing that moveth upon the earth.   Genesis 1:28

Now, as I have just before suggested, God himself has demonstrated, by the very order of creation, that he made all things for the sake of man. For it was not without reason that he distributed the making of the world into six days; though it would have been no more difficult for him to complete the whole work, in all its parts, at once, in a single moment, than to arrive at its completion by such progressive advances. But in this he has been pleased to display his providence and paternal solicitude towards us, since, before he would make man, he prepared everything which he foresaw would be useful or beneficial to him. How great would be now the ingratitude to doubt whether we are regarded by this best of fathers, whom we perceive to have been solicitous on our account before we existed! How impious would it be to tremble with diffidence, lest at any time his kindness should desert us in our necessities, which we see was displayed in the greatest affluence of all blessings provided for us while we were yet unborn! Besides, we are told by Moses that this liberality has subjected to us all that is contained in the whole world. He certainly has not made this declaration in order to tantalize us with the empty name of such a donation. Therefore we never shall be destitute of anything which will conduce to our welfare. Finally, to conclude, whenever we call God the Creator of heaven and earth, let us at the same time reflect, that the dispensation of all those things which he has made is in his own power, and that we are his children, whom he has received into his charge and custody, to be supported and educated; so that we may expect every blessing from him alone, and cherish a certain hope that he will never suffer us to want those things which are necessary to our well-being, that our hope may depend on no other; that, whatever we need or desire, our prayers may be directed to him, and that, from whatever quarter we receive any advantage, we may acknowledge it to be his benefit, and confess it with thanksgiving; that, being allured with such great sweetness of goodness and beneficence, we may study to love and worship him with all our hearts. — *Institutes*, I, xiv, xxii

243   **AUGUST 30**

*O Lord, rebuke me not in thy wrath: neither chasten
me in thy hot displeasure.*   Psalm 38:1

"O Jehovah! rebuke me not in thy wrath." David does not expressly ask that his afflictions should be removed, but only that God would moderate the severity of his chastisements. Hence we may infer that David did not give loose rein to the desires of the flesh, but offered up his earnest prayer in a duly chastened spirit of devotion. All men would naturally desire that permission should be granted them to sin with impunity. But David lays a restraint upon his desires, and does not wish the favor and indulgence of God to be extended beyond measure, but is content with a softening of his affliction; as if he had said, Lord, I am not unwilling to be chastised by thee, but I entreat thee, meanwhile, not to afflict me beyond what I am able to bear, but to temper the fierceness of thy indignation according to the measure of my infirmity, lest the severity of the affliction should entirely overwhelm me. This prayer, as I have said, was framed according to the rule of godliness; for it contains nothing but what God promises to all his children. It should also be noticed that David does not secretly indulge a fretful and repining spirit, but spreads his complaint before God; and this he does, not in the way of sinful complaining, but of humble prayer and unfeigned confession, accompanied with the hope of obtaining forgiveness. He has used *anger* and *wrath* as denoting extreme rigor, and has contrasted them with fatherly chastisement. — *Commentaries*

Thy kingdom come. Thy will be done in earth, as it is in heaven.   Matthew 6:10

Now since the Divine word resembles a royal sceptre, we are commanded to pray that he will subdue the hearts and minds of all men to a voluntary obedience to it. This is accomplished when by the secret inspiration of the Spirit he displays the efficacy of his word and causes it to obtain the honor it deserves. Afterwards it is our duty to descend to the impious, by whom his authority is resisted with the perseverance of obstinacy and the fury of despair. God therefore erects his kingdom on the humiliation of the whole world, though his methods of humiliation are various; for he restrains the passions of some, and breaks the unsubdued arrogance of others. It ought to be the object of our daily wishes, that God would collect churches for himself from all the countries of the earth, that he would enlarge their numbers, enrich them with gifts, and establish a legitimate order among them; that on the contrary he would overthrow all the enemies of the pure doctrine and religion, that he would confound their counsels and defeat their attempts. — *Institutes,* III, xx, xlii

*Now them that are such we command and exhort by
our Lord Jesus Christ, that with quietness they work,
and eat their own bread.*   II Thessalonians 3:12

The Lord commands every one of us, in all the actions of
life, to regard his vocation. For he knows with what great un-
rest the human mind is inflamed, with what desultory levity
it is hurried hither and thither, and how insatiable is its ambition to grasp different things at once. Therefore, to prevent
universal confusion being produced by our folly and temerity,
he has appointed to all their particular duties in different
spheres of life. And that no one might rashly transgress the
limits prescribed, he has styled such spheres of life *vocations*
or *callings*. Every individual's line of life, therefore, is, as it
were, a post assigned him by the Lord, that he may not wander about in uncertainty all his days. And so necessary is this
distinction, that in his sight all our actions are estimated according to it, and often very differently from the sentence
of human reason and philosophy. There is no exploit esteemed
more honorable, even among philosophers, than to deliver our
country from tyranny; but the voice of the celestial Judge
openly condemns the private man who lays violent hands on a
tyrant. It is not my design, however, to pause to list examples.
It is sufficient if we know that the principle and foundation of
right conduct in every case is the vocation of the Lord, and that
he who disregards it will never keep the right way in the
duties of his station.

He that is in obscurity will lead a private life without dis-
content, so as not to desert the station in which God has
placed him. It will also be no small alleviation of his cares,
labors, troubles, and other burdens, when a man owns that in
all these things he has God for his guide. The magistrate will
execute his office with greater pleasure, the father of a family
will confine himself to his duty with more satisfaction, and
all, in their respective spheres of life, will bear and surmount

the inconveniences, cares, disappointments, and anxieties which befall them, when they shall be persuaded that every individual has his burden laid upon him by God. Hence also will arise peculiar consolation, since there will be no employment so mean and sordid (provided we follow our vocation) as not to appear truly respectable, and be deemed highly important in the sight of God. — *Institutes*, III, x, vi

Thus saith the Lord, In an acceptable time have I heard thee, and in a day of salvation have I helped thee: and I will preserve thee, and give thee for a covenant of the people, to establish the earth, to cause to inherit the desolate heritages;   Isaiah 49:8

How shall we reconcile these statements? By considering that Christ is not so much his own as ours; for he neither came, nor died, nor rose again, for himself. He was sent for the salvation of the Church, and seeks nothing as his own; for he has no want of anything. Accordingly, God makes promises to the whole body of the Church. Christ, who occupies the place of Mediator, receives these promises, and does not plead on behalf of himself as an individual, but the whole Church, for whose salvation he was sent. On this account he does not address Christ separately, but so far as he is joined and continually united to his body. It is an inconceivable honor which our heavenly Father bestows upon us, when he listens to his Son on our account, and when he even directs the discourse to the Son, while the matter relates to our salvation. Hence we see how close is the connection between us and Christ. He stands in our room, and has nothing separate from us. And the Father listens to our cause. — *Commentaries*

And thou shalt teach them diligently unto thy chil-
dren, and shalt talk of them when thou sittest in thine
house, and when thou walkest by the way, and when
thou liest down, and when thou risest up.

Deuteronomy 6:7

If we desire to be exalted to the glory of our Lord Jesus
Christ, we must bear the reproach of his cross. Thus I entreat
you, according as necessity may remind you, to shake off your
sloth and bestir yourself to do battle valiantly against Satan
and the world, desiring to be dead unto yourself so as to be
fully renewed in God. And because we must know before we
can love, I entreat you also to exercise yourself in reading the
holy exhortations that may be helps to this end. For the coldness we observe in certain persons arises from that careless-
ness which disposes them to fancy that it is enough to have
briefly relished some passage of the Scriptures, without laying down as a rule to profit by it as need should require. On
the contrary, we have to practise what is said by St. Paul, that
by contemplating the face of Jesus Christ in the mirror of the
gospel, we may conform ourselves to him from glory to glory.
Whereby the apostle means that in proportion as we draw nearer
to Jesus Christ, and know him more intimately, the grace and
virtue of his Spirit will at the same time grow and be multi-
plied in us. So then be it your constant care to profit more and
more.

And besides all that, you have to think of your children,
whom God has confided to your charge for this end, that they
should be dedicated to him, and that he should be the supreme
Father of them as of you. It is true that many persons are
prevented from discharging their duties toward their children,
because their single desire is to further the advancement of their
offspring in the world. But this is a pitiful and perverse consideration. I entreat you then since God has bestowed on you
a race of children gifted with good dispositions, and as you
value this inestimable treasure, to take measures for having

them brought up betimes in his fear, and preserved from the corruptions and pollutions by which we have been surrounded. I am aware that you have not waited for my exhortations to begin this happy work, but that you have provided for them a man endowed with knowledge to instruct them and zealous in the discharge of his functions; but because both father and children should be entirely devoted to God, and because the obstacles which Satan lays in the way of so good an end are almost insurmountable, it is highly necessary that you should train them up for the possession of a heavenly inheritance, rather than that of perishable wealth and honors here below.

—*Correspondence*

248   SEPTEMBER 4

Kings of the earth, and all people; princes, and all judges of the earth: Both young men, and maidens; old men, and children: Let them praise the name of the Lord: Psalm 148:11-13a

"Kings of earth." He now turns his address to men, with a respect to whom it was that he called for a declaration of God's praises from creatures, both above and from beneath. As kings and princes are blinded by the dazzling influence of their station, so as to think the world was made for them, and to despise God in the pride of their hearts, he particularly calls them to this duty; and, by mentioning them first, he reproves their ingratitude in withholding their tribute of praise when they are under greater obligations than others. As all men originally stand upon a level as to condition, the higher persons have risen, and the nearer they have been brought to God, the more sacredly are they bound to proclaim his goodness. The more intolerable is the wickedness of kings and princes who claim exemption from the common rule, when they ought rather to inculcate it upon others and lead the way. He could have addressed his exhortation at once summarily to all men, as indeed he mentions peoples in general terms; but by thrice specifying princes he suggests that they are slow to discharge the duty, and need to be urged to it.

Then follows a division according to age and sex, to show that all without exception are created for this end, and should unitedly devote their energies to it. As to old men, the more God has lengthened their lives the more should they be exercised in singing his praises; but he joins the young men with them, for though they have less experience from continued habit, it will be inexcusable for them if they do not acknowledge the great mercy of God in the vigor of their lives. Even the young women who are not so liberally educated as the male sex, being considered born for domestic offices, will omit their duty if they do not join with the rest of the Church in praising God. It follows that all from the least to the greatest are bound by this common rule. — *Commentaries*

249   **SEPTEMBER 5**

It is a fearful thing to fall into the hands of the living God.   Hebrews 10:31

Let us note, then, this sentence of the Apostle, that it is a dreadful thing to fall into the hands of the living God; and therefore as often as there is any punishment, let us be moved by it. And thereby we shall be taught to pity those who are in distress, and say, "Alas, this poor creature; if it were some mortal man that afflicted him, a man might give him some relief. But God is against him, and ought we not to have pity as we see this?" Someone may say, "Are we not resisting God when we are sorry for those who are punished for their sins? Is this not a striving against God's justice?" No; for we may recognize God's justice and praise and glorify him for what he does; and yet nevertheless be sorry for those who are punished, because we ourselves may have deserved as much or more, and ought to seek the welfare of all men, especially those who are nearest to us. And when God has established any bond between them and us, we must pity them also. In like manner we recognize civil justice, which is a little mirror of

God's justice, and yet do not cease to have pity on the offender. When a criminal is punished, men do not say that he has been wronged, or that the judge is cruel. But they say that those who are in the place of justice do their duty and render an acceptable sacrifice to God, when they put an offender to death. But yet in the meanwhile we do not cease to pity the poor creature that shall suffer for his evil deeds. If we are not touched by this, there is no humanity in us. If we grant this with respect to earthly justice, which is as a little spark of God's justice, I pray you when we come to the sovereign seat of justice on high, ought we not first to glorify God for all that he does, assuring ourselves that he is just and upright in all respects? And yet this shall not hinder us from pitying those who suffer punishment, to comfort them and aid them; and when we are unable to do them any good, to wish for their salvation, praying God to make their corrections profitable, in drawing them home, and not to allow them to become hardhearted, and to strive against his hand. — *Sermons*

250   **SEPTEMBER 6**

The night is far spent, the day is at hand: let us there-
fore cast off the works of darkness, and let us put on
the armour of light.   Romans 13:12

Although it may be difficult to the weakness of our flesh to continue steadfast when we see no end to our warfare; nay more, see that things grow worse; yet when girt about with the armor which God bestows upon us, we must not fear but that we shall overcome all the devices of Satan. I call "the armor of God" not merely the promises and holy exhortations by which he strengthens us, but the prayers which are to obtain the strength we need. And therefore, sir, according to your necessity, get by heart what Scripture sets before us, both as to the present condition of Christians, and the miseries to which they must needs be subject, and also as to the happy and desirable issue promised them; and how, moreover, they shall never be forsaken in the time of their need. I know —

long continued maladies being the most harassing — that it is extremely hard for you to languish for such a length of time. But if the enemies of the truth are thus obstinate in their fury, we ought to be ashamed of not being at least equally steadfast in well-doing; and most of all when it concerns the glory of our God and Redeemer, which, of his infinite goodness, he has bound up with our salvation. And I have no doubt that you put in practice what the Apostle tells you about strengthening the feeble knees and lifting up the hands which hang down. For it cannot be but that the first blows dismay, unless we rouse our virtue to resist temptation.

—*Correspondence*

251   **SEPTEMBER 7**

For we are saved by hope: but hope that is seen is not hope: for what a man seeth, why doth he yet hope for?   Romans 8:24

Now wherever this living faith shall be found, it must necessarily be attended with the hope of eternal salvation as its inescapable counterpart. For if faith be, as has been stated, a certain persuasion of the truth of God, that it can neither lie, nor deceive us, nor be frustrated — they who have felt this assurance, likewise expect a period to arrive when God will accomplish his promises, which according to their persuasion, cannot but be true; so that, in short, hope is no other than an expectation of those things which faith has believed to be truly promised by God. Thus faith believes the veracity of God, hope expects the manifestation of it in due time; faith believes him to be our Father, hope expects him always to act towards us in this character; faith believes that eternal life is given to us, hope expects it one day to be revealed; faith is the foundation on which hope rests, hope nourishes and sustains faith. For as no man can have any expectations from God, but he who has first believed his promises, so also the weakness of our faith must be sustained and cherished by patient hope and expectation, lest it grow weary and faint. For which reason, Paul rightly places our salvation in hope. For hope, while it is silently expecting the Lord, restrains faith, that it may not waver in the Divine promises, or begin to doubt the truth of them; it refreshes it, that it may not grow weary; it extends it to the farthest goal, that it may not fail in the midst of the course, or even at the entrance of it. Finally, hope, by continually renewing and restoring faith, causes it frequently to persevere with more vigor than hope itself.

—*Institutes*, III, ii, xlii

252 SEPTEMBER 8

And said, Remember now, O Lord, I beseech thee, how I have walked before thee in truth and with a perfect heart, and have done that which is good in thy sight. And Hezekiah wept sore. Isaiah 38:3

"Remember now that I have walked before thee in truth." He does not plead his merits against God, or remonstrate with him in any respect, as if he were unjustly punished, but fortifies himself against a sore temptation, that he may not think that God is angry with him for correcting the vices and removing the corruptions which prevailed throughout the whole of his kingdom, and especially in regard to religion. Yet the Lord permits his people even to glory, in some degree, on account of their good actions, not that they may boast of their merits before him, but that they may acknowledge his benefits, and . may be affected by the remembrance of them in such a manner as to be prepared for enduring everything patiently. But sometimes the unreasonable conduct of their enemies constrains them to holy boasting, that they may commend their good cause to their judge and avenger; as David boldly meets the wicked slanders of enemies by pleading his innocence before the judgment seat of God (Ps. 7:8; 17:2). But here Hezekiah intended to meet the craftiness of Satan, which believers feel, when, under the pretence of humility, he overwhelms them with despair; and therefore we ought earnestly to beware lest our hearts be swallowed up by grief. — *Commentaries*

253   SEPTEMBER 9

*The morning is come unto thee, O thou that dwellest
in the land: the time is come, the day of trouble is
near, and not the sounding again of the mountains.*
         Ezekiel 7:7

We know that hypocrites commit all their sins as if no eye
were upon them; as long as God is silent and at rest they revel
without shame or fear. But the chosen remain faithful even in
secret; but God's word always shines before them, as Peter
says — ye do well when ye attend to the Prophetic word, as a
lamp shining in darkness. Although the faithful may be surrounded by darkness, yet they direct their eye to the light of
celestial doctrine, so that they are watchful, and are not children of the night and of darkness as Paul says (I Thess. 5:4, 5).
But the impious are, as it were, immersed in darkness, and think
they shall enjoy perpetual night. As the rising morning dispels
the darkness of night, so also God's judgment, on its sudden
appearance, strikes the reprobate with unexpected terror, but
too late. — *Commentaries*

254   SEPTEMBER 10

*Who hath believed our report? and to whom is the
arm of the Lord revealed?*   Isaiah 53:1

Let us reckon with this fact, that the world will never be
so entirely converted to God that there will not be a majority
possessed by Satan and remaining stupidly in his power, who
would not rather perish than accept the blessing that is offered
to us. And there are different sorts of men: some will be
stupid, others will be so arrogant as to mock God and so madly
presumptuous as to condemn everything in the Gospel; others
will be wrapped up in the cares of this world, preoccupied with
their refinements and delusions so that they have no taste at
all for heavenly things; others will be so besotted that one

cannot reach their minds so as to give them any teaching. So when we see this, let us reckon with the fact that, although the Gospel is preached and the voice of God resounds and echoes everywhere, many men will stay just as they were, quite unchanged, and all teaching will be, as it were, dead to them.

And thus let us take note that the number of believers is small. But yet we must not be led astray by that. Rather we ought to realize that God is bringing to pass what he declared with his mouth. And meanwhile we ought to be so much the more careful to gather ourselves, as it were, under the wings of God, seeing that the world today is full of malice and rebellion. . . . When we see the whole world trampling the Word of God under foot, let us devote ourselves to it. And not only that, but we must be all the more careful to cleave to our God when we see that scandals and bad examples might succeed in turning us from him; for we must remain in the integrity to which God calls us. — *Sermons*

255   **SEPTEMBER 11**

. . . ye shall be sorrowful, but your sorrow shall be turned into joy.   John 16:20b

"Your sorrow will be turned into joy." He means the *joy* which they felt after having received the Spirit; not that they were afterwards free from all *sorrow*, but that all the sorrow which they would endure was swallowed up by spiritual joy. We know that the apostles, so long as they lived, sustained a severe warfare, that they endured base reproaches, that they had many reasons for weeping and lamenting; but renewed by the Spirit, they had laid aside their former consciousness of weakness, so that, with lofty heroism, they nobly trampled under foot all the evils that they had endured. Here then is a comparison between their present weakness and the power of the Spirit, which would soon be given to them; for, though they were nearly overwhelmed for a time, yet afterwards they not only fought bravely, but obtained a glorious triumph in the midst of their struggles. Yet it ought also to be observed, that he points out not only the interval that elapsed between the resurrection of Christ and the death of the apostles, but also the period which followed afterwards; as if Christ had said, "You will lie prostrate, as it were, for a short time; but when the Holy Spirit shall have raised you up again, then will begin a new joy, which will continue to increase, until, having been received into the heavenly glory, you shall have perfect joy."

—Commentaries

256   **SEPTEMBER 12**

But we have this treasure in earthen vessels, that the excellency of the power may be of God, and not of us.
                                        • II Corinthians 4:7

In the next place, I have something about which I wish to admonish yourself. For I understand the length of your discourses has furnished the ground of complaint to many. You have frequently confessed to us that you were aware of this defect, and that you were endeavoring to correct it. But if private grumblings are disregarded because they do not in the meanwhile give trouble, they may, nevertheless, one day break forth into seditious clamors. I beg and beseech of you to strive to restrain yourself, that you may not afford Satan an opportunity, which we see he is so earnestly desiring. You know that while we are not called upon to show too much indulgence to the foolish, we are nevertheless bound to give them something to allure them. And you are well enough aware that you have to do with the morose and choleric; and in truth their aversion arises simply from too much pride on their part. Yet, since the Lord commands us to ascend the pulpit, not for our own edification, but for that of the people, you should so regulate the matter of your teaching, that the word may not be brought into contempt by your tediousness. It is more appropriate also for us to lengthen our prayers in private, than when we offer them in the name of the whole Church. You are mistaken if you expect from all an ardor equal to your own. — *Letter to Farel*

*Therefore being justified by faith, we have peace with
God through our Lord Jesus Christ:*   Romans 5:1

The following observation of Bernard is worthy of recital;
"that the name of Jesus is not only light, but also food; that
it is likewise oil, without which all the food of the soul is dry;
that it is salt, unseasoned by which, whatever is presented
to us is insipid; finally, that it is honey in the mouth, melody
in the ear, joy in the heart, and medicine to the soul; and
that there are no charms in any discourse where his name is
not heard." But here we ought diligently to examine how
he has procured salvation for us; that we may not only know
him to be the author of it, but, embracing those things which
are sufficient for the establishment of our faith, may reject
everything capable of drawing us aside to the right hand or to
the left. For since no man can descend into himself and seriously consider his own character, without perceiving that God
is angry with him and hostile to him, and consequently he
must find himself under a necessity of anxiously seeking some
way to appease him, which can never be done without a satisfaction — this is a case in which the strongest assurance is required. For sinners, till they be delivered from guilt, are
always subject to the wrath and malediction of God, who,
being a righteous Judge, never suffers his law to be violated
with impunity, but stands prepared to avenge it.

—*Institutes,* II, xvi, i

The righteousness of thy testimonies is everlasting:
give me understanding, and I shall live.

Psalm 119:144

Farther, he here teaches that men cannot, properly speaking, be said to live when they are destitute of the light of heavenly wisdom; and as the end for which men are created is not that, like swine or asses, they may stuff their bellies, but that they may exercise themselves in the knowledge and service of God, when they turn away from such employment, their life is worse than a thousand deaths. David therefore protests that for him to live was not merely to be fed with meat and drink, and to enjoy earthly comforts, but to aspire after a better life, which he could not do save under the guidance of faith. This is a very necessary warning; for although it is universally acknowledged that man is born with this distinction, that he excels the lower animals in intelligence, yet the great bulk of mankind, as if with deliberate purpose, stifle whatever light God pours into their understandings. I indeed admit that all men desire to be sharp-witted; but how few aspire to heaven, and consider that the fear of God is the beginning of wisdom. Since then meditation upon the celestial life is buried by earthly cares, men do nothing else than plunge into the grave, so that while living to the world, they die to God. — *Commentaries*

*These all continued with one accord in prayer and sup-
plication, with the women, and Mary the mother of
Jesus, and with his brethren.*   Acts 1:14

Luke expresses two things which are proper to true prayer,
namely that they persisted and that they were all of one mind.
This was an exercise of their patience, in that Christ made them
wait a while, when he could have immediately sent the Holy
Spirit; as God often delays, and as it were suffers us to languish,
that he may accustom us to persevere. The hastiness of our
petition is a corrupt, yea hurtful plague. Wherefore it is no
marvel if God sometimes corrects it. In the meantime he
exercises us to be constant in prayer. Therefore if we would
not pray in vain, let us not be wearied with the delay of time.

As touching the unity of their minds, it is set against that
scattering abroad which fear had caused before. Yet, notwithstanding, we may easily gather, even by this, how needful
a thing it is to pray generally, in that Christ commands every
one to pray for the whole body, and generally for all men,
as it were, in the person of all men: Our Father, Give us this
day, etc. Whence comes this unity of their tongues but from
one Spirit? Wherefore when Paul would prescribe to Jews and
Gentiles a right form of prayer, he removes far away all division and dissension. That we may, says he, being all of one
mind, glorify God (Rom. 15:6). And truly it is needful that
we be brethren and agree together like brethren, that we may
rightly call God Father. — *Commentaries*

But he shall say, I am no prophet, I am an husband-
man; for man taught me to keep cattle from my
youth.   Zechariah 13:5

Zechariah mentions these two particulars — the false prophets
will give up their office and that they will then spend their
labor in doing what is right and just, supporting themselves
in a lawful and innocent manner, and affording aid to their
brethren. It is the first thing in repentance when they who
had been previously the servants of Satan in the work of
deception cease to deal in falsehoods, and thus put an end to
their errors.

Now follows the progress — that they who lived before in
idleness and in pleasures under the pretext of sanctity, willingly
devote themselves to labor. A half reformation might probably
succeed with many at this day. But the second part of
reformation is very hard, which requires toil and labor; in this
case the stomach has no ears, according to the old proverb.
And yet we see what the prophet says, that those are they who
truly and from the heart repent who not only abstain from
impostures, but who are also ready to get their own living,
acknowledging that they had before defrauded the poor, and
procured their support by rapine and fraud. — *Commentaries*

Teach me to do thy will; for thou art my God: thy spirit is good; lead me into the land of uprightness.

Psalm 143:10

"Teach me that I may do thy will." He now rises to something higher, praying not merely for deliverance from outward troubles, but, what is of still greater importance, for the guidance of God's Spirit, that he might not decline to the right hand or to the left, but be kept in the path of rectitude. This is a request which should never be forgotten when temptations assail us with great severity, as it is peculiarly difficult to submit to God without resorting to unwarrantable methods of relief. As anxiety, fear, disease, languor, or pain, often tempt persons to particular steps, David's example should lead us to pray for divine restraint, and that we may not be hurried, through impulses of feeling, into unjustifiable courses. We are to mark carefully his way of expressing himself, for what he asks is not simply to be taught what the will of God is, but to be taught and brought to the observance and doing of it. The former kind of teaching is of less avail, as upon God's showing us our duty we by no means necessarily follow it, and it is necessary that he should draw out our affections to himself. God therefore must be master and teacher to us not only in the dead letter, but by the inward motions of his Spirit; indeed, there are three ways in which he acts the part of our teacher, instructing us by his word, enlightening our minds by the Spirit, and engraving instruction upon our hearts, so as to bring us to observe it with a true and cordial consent. The mere hearing of the word would serve no purpose, nor is it enough that we understand it; there must be besides the willing obedience of the heart. — *Commentaries*

He was oppressed, and he was afflicted, yet he opened
not his mouth: he is brought as a lamb to the slaughter,
and as a sheep before her shearers is dumb, so he
openeth not his mouth.   Isaiah 53:7

Moreover, we are also exhorted to conform to his example;
not that we shall be able to humiliate ourselves perfectly before
God, but yet we must force ourselves towards it. I say, that
when God is pleased to chastise us and we feel great roughness
at his hand, so that it seems as if we are overwhelmed, we
must nevertheless keep silence, confessing that God is righteous
and fair, and not letting one murmur be heard from our
mouths. Let us glorify God by our silence; even as if we were
poor sinners convicted of their crimes and without an excuse.
St. Peter applies the passage like this: when we are afflicted
by the hand of God, even persecuted by the hand of men,
we must not cease to bear patiently all the injuries done to us:
knowing that God wishes to test us, or even to punish us for
our faults. And let us take care not to make frivolous excuses,
like many do, who bring forward their infirmity and say that
they are too weak and cannot stay quiet while God presses them
so straitly. We must therefore be conformed to the Son of God,
for he is our mirror and pattern — not, as I have said, that we
can have goodness equal to his; but although we cannot come
near it, we must strive towards it. — *Sermons*

*For ye are bought with a price: therefore glorify God
in your body, and in your spirit, which are God's.*

I Corinthians 6:20

This is a very important consideration, that we are consecrated and dedicated to God; that we may not hereafter think,
speak, meditate, or do anything but with a view to his glory.
For that which is sacred cannot, without great injustice towards
him, be applied to unholy uses. If we are not our own, but
the Lord's, it is manifest both what error we must avoid, and
to what end all the actions of our lives are to be directed. We
are not our own; therefore neither our reason nor our will
should predominate in our deliberations and actions. We are
not our own; therefore let us not propose it as our end, to
seek what may be expedient for us according to the flesh. We
are not our own; therefore let us, as far as possible forget
ourselves and all things that are ours. On the contrary, we
are God's; to him, therefore, let us live and die. We are God's;
therefore let his wisdom and will preside in all our actions. We
are God's; towards him, therefore, as our only legitimate end,
let every part of our lives be directed. Oh, how great a pro-
ficiency has that man made, who, having been taught that he
is not his own, has taken the sovereignty and government of
himself from his own reason, to surrender it to God! For as
compliance with their own inclinations leads men most effectually to ruin, so to place no dependence on our own knowledge or will, but merely to follow the guidance of the Lord,
is the only way of safety. Let this, then, be the first step, to
depart from ourselves, that we may apply all the vigor of our
faculties to the service of the Lord. — *Institutes*, III, vii, i

Neither give heed to fables and endless genealogies,
which minister questions, rather than godly edifying
which is in faith: so do.   I Timothy 1:4

These are the two causes for which many forsake the pure
doctrine of salvation; namely, because they are moved with
their pride to seek out new matters, and God will have his
students to be humble. Do we wish to profit in his school?
Let us have this humility, not to presume to know too much,
but only to be taught by him as he pleases. And again, there
are others so shallow that they have no desire to master what
is contained in the gospel, and wish often to change their pasture, and think that their ears are being abused if anyone
repeat often to them a thing which is to their profit; as when
we preach of the virtue of our Lord Jesus Christ, and of his
grace, it seems to them that they already know this too well
and that they are too much accustomed to it. Inasmuch as
this curiosity tickles many brains, God allows them to feed
themselves with wind; for indeed they are not worthy to be
nourished with good pasturage. Therefore if we wish God to
hold us in the purity of his Word, let us first of all be humble
and modest, and then let us be sober and not desire by vain
curiosity to know more than is lawful for us. — *Sermons*

265   SEPTEMBER 21

And they gave forth their lots; and the lot fell upon
Matthias; and he was numbered with the eleven apos-
tles.   Acts 1:26

It came to pass as no man would have looked for; for we may
gather by that which goes before that there was not so great
account made of Matthias as of the other; for, besides that
Luke gave him the former place, the two surnames which Barsabas had show that he was in great estimation. He was called

Barsabas, as if he were some mirror, either of faithfulness and innocency, or of a quiet and modest nature. The other name indicated singular honesty. This man, therefore, in men's judgment, was superior; but God preferred Matthias before him. Whereby we are taught that we must not glory if we be extolled unto the skies in the opinion of men, and if by their voices and consents we be judged to be most excellent men; but we must rather have regard of this, to approve ourselves unto God, who alone is the most lawful and just judge, by whose sentence and judgment we stand or fall. And we may oftentimes mark this also that God passes over him who is the chiefest in the sight of men, that he may throw down all pride which is in men. — *Commentaries*

266 SEPTEMBER 22

For God so loved the world, that he gave his only be-gotten Son, that whosoever believeth in him should not perish, but have everlasting life. John 3:16

"He gave his only-begotten Son, that whosoever believeth on him may not perish." This, he says, is the proper look of faith, to be fixed on Christ, in whom it beholds the breast of God filled with love; this is a firm and enduring support, to rely on the death of Christ as the only pledge of that love. The word "only-begotten" is emphatic, to magnify the fervor of the love of God towards us. For as men are not easily convinced that God loves them, in order to remove all doubt, he has expressly stated that we are so very dear to God that, on our account, he did not even spare his only-begotten Son. Since, therefore, God has most abundantly testified his love towards us, whoever is not satisfied with this testimony, and still remains in doubt, offers a high insult to Christ, as if he had been an ordinary man given up at random to death. But we ought rather to consider that, in proportion to the estimation in which God holds his only-begotten Son, so much the more precious did our salvation appear to him, for the ransom of which he chose that his only-begotten Son should die.—*Comm.*

*Depart from evil, and do good; and dwell for ever-
more.*   Psalm 37:27

If the meek possess the earth, then every one, as he
regards his own happiness and peace, should also endeavor to
walk uprightly, and to apply himself to works of beneficence.
It should also be observed, that he connects these two things:
first, that the faithful should strictly do good; and, secondly,
that they should restrain themselves from doing evil; and this
he does not without good reason; for as is shown in the
thirty-fourth Psalm, it often happens that the same person who
not only acts kindly towards certain persons, but even with a
bountiful hand deals out largely of his own, is yet all the while
plundering others, and amassing by extortion the resources by
means of which he displays his liberality.

Whoever, therefore, is desirous to have his good offices
approved by God, let him endeavor to relieve his brethren who
have need of his help, but let him not injure one in order to
help another, or afflict and grieve one in order to make another
glad. Now David, under these two expressions, has briefly
comprised the duties of the second table of the law; first, that
the godly should keep their hands free from all mischief, and
give no occasion of complaint to any man; and, secondly, that
they should not live to themselves, and to the promotion merely
of their own private interests, but should endeavor to promote
the common good of all according to their opportunities, and
as far as they are able. — *Commentaries*

*I poured out my complaint before him; I shewed before
him my trouble.*   Psalm 142:2

He tells us still more clearly in the next verse that he
disburdened his cares unto God. To pour out one's thoughts
and tell over his afflictions implies the reverse of those perplexing anxieties which men brood over inwardly to their
own distress, and by which they torture themselves, and are
chafed by their afflictions rather than led to God; or it implies
the reverse of those frantic exclamations to which others give
utterance who find no comfort in the superintending providence of God. In short, we are left to infer that while he
did not give way before men to loud and senseless lamentations, neither did he suffer himself to be tormented with
inward and suppressed cares, but made known his griefs with
unsuspecting confidence to the Lord. — *Commentaries*

*One thing have I desired of the Lord, that will I seek
after; that I may dwell in the house of the Lord all
the days of my life, to behold the beauty of the Lord,
and to enquire in his temple.*   Psalm 27:4

Call to mind, I beseech you, the continual sighs you have
been heaving for so long a time. Although you had many kinds
of grief, I doubt not that your chief regret was that of not
being permitted to devote yourself entirely to the service of
God. Consider well, whether you have not vowed daily before
God, that you wished for nothing but the means of getting rid
of the servitude in which you were held. Now that your wish
is granted, rely upon it that God holds you to your promise. It
is for you to anticipate him, even as your conscience prompts
you, without incitements from without. And yet further,
call to remembrance that Saint Paul, in saying that married per-

sons are as it were divided, but that widows have nothing to do but to apply themselves entirely to God, takes away from you the excuse which you have hitherto alleged. It is certain that nothing whatever ought to hinder us from the discharge of what is due our heavenly Father, and to that kind Redeemer whom he has sent to us; but the better the opportunity of each, so much the more guilty does he become if he does not the more readily discharge his duty. I am well aware that you have regard to your children, and I do not say but that this is right, provided that the sovereign Father of both you and them is not left out. But consider that the greatest benefit which you can confer on them is to show them the way to follow God.

—*Letter to Madame De Pons*

270   SEPTEMBER 26

And the God of peace shall bruise Satan under your feet shortly. The grace of our Lord Jesus Christ be with you. Amen.   Romans 16:20

But, as the promise respecting breaking the head of Satan belongs to Christ and his members in common, I therefore deny that the faithful can ever be conquered or overwhelmed by him. They are frequently filled with consternation, but recover themselves again; they fall by the violence of his blows, but are raised up again; they are wounded, but not mortally; finally, they labor through their whole lives in such a manner as at last to obtain the victory. This, however, is not to be restricted to each single action. For we know that, by the righteous vengeance of God, David was for a time delivered to Satan, that by his instigation he might number the people; nor is it without reason that Paul admits a hope of pardon even for those who may have been entangled in the snares of the devil. Therefore the same Apostle shows, in another place, that the promise before cited is begun in this life, where we must engage in the conflict; and that after the termination of the conflict it will be completed. "And the God of peace," he says, "shall bruise Satan under your feet shortly." In our Head this victory, indeed, has always been complete, because the prince of this world had nothing in him; in us, who are his members, it yet appears only in part, but will be completed when we shall have put off our flesh, which makes us still subject to infirmities. — *Institutes*, I, xiv, xviii

271   SEPTEMBER 27

Incline thine ear, O Lord, and hear; open thine eyes,
O Lord, and see: and hear all the words of Sennach-
erib, which hath sent to reproach the living God.
                                        Isaiah 37:17

"Incline thine ear, O Jehovah." From these words we conclude how great was the perplexity of Hezekiah; for the earnestness that pervades the prayer breathes an amazing power of anguish, so that it is easily seen that he had a struggle attended by uncommon difficulty to escape from the temptation. Though his warmth in prayer shows the strength and eminence of his faith, yet at the same time it exhibits, as in a mirror, the stormy passions. Whenever we shall be called to sustain such contests, let us learn by the example of the pious king to combat our passions by everything that is fitted to strengthen our faith, so that the very disturbance may conduct us to safety and peace, and that we may not be terrified by a conviction of our weakness, if at any time we shall be powerfully assailed by fear and perplexity. It is, indeed, the will of the Lord that we shall toil hard, and sweat and shiver; for we must not expect to gain the victory while we repose in indolence, but after diversified contests he promises us a prosperous issue, which he will undoubtedly grant. — *Commentaries*

Son of man, I have made thee a watchman unto the house of Israel: therefore hear the word at my mouth, and give them warning from me.   Ezekiel 3:17

It is now added, "Thou shalt hear words from my mouth, and shalt announce them to the people from me." Here a general rule is prescribed to all prophets and pastors of the Church, namely that they should hear the word from the mouth of God; by which God wishes to exclude whatever men fabricate or invent for themselves. For it is evident when God claimed to himself the right of speaking that he orders all men to be silent and not to offer anything of their own, and then, when he orders them to hear the word from his mouth, that he puts a bridle upon them that they should neither invent anything, nor hanker after their own devices, nor dare to conceive either more or less than the word; and, lastly, we see that whatever men offer of their own selves is here abolished, when God alone wishes to be heard, for he does not mingle himself here with others as in a crowd, as if he wished to be heard only in part. He assumes to himself, therefore, what we ought to attribute to his supreme command over all things, namely that we should hang upon his lips. — *Commentaries*

And you, that were sometime alienated and enemies in your mind by wicked works, yet now hath he reconciled.   Colossians 1:21

For if it were not clearly expressed that we are obnoxious to the wrath and vengeance of God, and to eternal death, we should not so fully discover how miserable we must be without the Divine mercy, nor should we so highly estimate the blessing of deliverance. For example, let any man be addressed in the following manner: "If, while you remained a sinner, God had hated you, and rejected you according to your demerits, horrible destruction would have befallen you; but because he has voluntarily, and of his own gratuitous kindness, retained you in his favor, and not permitted you to be alienated from him, he has thus delivered you from that danger;" he will be affected, and will in some measure perceive how much he is indebted to Divine mercy. But if, on the contrary, he be told what the Scripture teaches, "that he was alienated from God by sin, an heir of wrath, obnoxious to the punishment of eternal death, excluded from all hope of salvation, a total stranger to the Divine blessing, a slave to Satan, a captive under the yoke of sin, and, in a word, condemned to, and already involved in, a horrible destruction; that in this situation Christ interposed as an intercessor; that he has taken upon himself and suffered the punishment which by the righteous judgment of God hung over all sinners; that by his blood he has expiated those crimes which render them odious to God; that by this expiation God the Father has been appeased; that this is the foundation of peace between God and men; that this is the bond of his benevolence towards them;" will he not be the more affected by these things in proportion to the more correct and lively representation of the depth of calamity from which he has been delivered? In short, since it is impossible for the life which is presented by the mercy of God to be embraced by our hearts with sufficient ardor, or received with becoming gratitude, unless we have been previously terrified and distressed with the fear of the Divine wrath, and the horror of eternal death, we are instructed by the sacred doctrine that irrespective of Christ we may contemplate God as in some measure incensed against us, and his hand armed for our destruction, and that we may embrace his benevolence and paternal love only in Christ. — *Institutes*, II, xvi, ii

*Be careful for nothing; but in every thing by prayer
and supplication with thanksgiving let your requests
be made known unto God.*   Philippians 4:6

Wherefore, although we are stupid and insensible to our
own miseries, he vigilantly watches and guards us, and sometimes affords us unsolicited help, yet it highly concerns us
faithfully to pray to him, that our heart may be always inflamed with a serious and ardent desire of seeking, loving,
and worshipping him, while we accustom ourselves in all our
necessities to resort to him as our sheet anchor. Further, that
no desire or wish, which we should be ashamed for him to
know, may enter our minds; when we learn to present our
wishes, and so to pour out our whole heart in his presence.
Next, that we may be prepared to receive his blessings with
true gratitude of soul, and even with grateful acknowledg-
ments; being reminded by our praying that they have come
from his hand. Moreover, that when we have obtained what we
sought, the persuasion that he has answered our requests may
excite us to more ardent meditations on his goodness, and produce a more joyful welcome of those things which we acknowledge to be the fruits of our prayers. Lastly, that use and experience itself may yield our minds a confirmation of his
providence in proportion to our weakness, while we realize
that he not only promises never to forsake us, and freely opens
a way of access for our addressing him in the very moment of
necessity; but that his hand is always extended to assist his
people, whom he does not feed with mere words, but supports
with present aid. On these accounts our most merciful Father,
though liable to no sleep or languor, yet frequently appears as if
he were sleepy or tired, in order to exercise us, who are otherwise slothful and inactive, in approaching, supplicating, and
earnestly beseeching him to our own advantage. It is extremely
absurd, therefore, in them who, with a view to divert the minds
of men from praying to God, pretend that it is useless for us by
our interruptions to weary the Divine Providence, which is

engaged in the conservation of all things; whereas the Lord declares, on the contrary, that he "is nigh to all that call upon him in truth." — *Institutes*, III, xx, iii

275 OCTOBER 1

Therefore say thou unto them, Thus saith the Lord of hosts; Turn ye unto me, saith the Lord of hosts, and I will turn unto you, saith the Lord of hosts.

Zechariah 1:3

"Return unto me and I will return unto you." It must be noticed that we cannot enjoy the favor of God even when he kindly offers to be reconciled to us, except we from the heart repent. However graciously, then, God may invite us to himself, and be ready to remit our sins, we yet cannot embrace his offered favor except our sins become hateful to us; for God ceases not to be our judge, except we anticipate him, and condemn ourselves, and deprecate the punishment of our sins. Hence we then pacify God when real grief wounds us, and we thus really turn to God, without falsehood. Now the experience of God's wrath ought to lead us to this; for extremely heedless are they who, having found God to be a judge, do carelessly disregard his wrath, which ought to have filled their hearts with fear. "Let no one deceive you with vain words," says Paul, "for on account of these things comes the wrath of God on the children of unbelief," or on all the unbelieving. Paul bids us to consider all the evidences which God gives of his wrath in the world, that they may instruct us as to the fear of God; how much more then should domestic examples be noticed by us? For the prophet speaks not here of foreign nations; but he says, "God has been angry with anger against your fathers." Since, then, it appeared evident that God had not spared even his chosen people, they ought, unless they were extremely stubborn, to have carefully continued in obedience to the law. Hence the prophet here condemns their tardiness, inasmuch as they had made so little progress under the chastisements of God. — *Commentaries*

*Can a man be profitable unto God, as he that is wise
may be profitable unto himself?*	Job 22:2

We see that he compares himself to a husbandman who has
a vineyard which, when he has tended it, yields wine to him;
or who has a field and reaps corn from it. God in using such
figures of speech, declares that he so accounts of our works
that they are like pleasant and sweet sacrifices to him. And
he says also that when we do good to the poor, it is as if we
did it to him, and he accepts it as done to himself. Jesus
Christ speaks thus of it, saying, "Whatsoever you shall do to
one of the least of my members, I accept it as if it had been
done to my own person."

Seeing, then, that our Lord descends so far that he subjects
himself to the condition of a sinful and mortal man, and says
that he receives whatever we do to our brethren, although we
can bring him nothing; and willingly binds himself to us when
he is not in debt to us; on our part, when we see all this,
must we not be ravished with admiration for such great gentleness as our God shows toward us? So then, let us note well
what is said in this passage, that when man will have taken
pains to live in holiness and in uprightness according to the
commandments of God, it cannot be said that in all his life he
has profited God at all; he has been profitable only to himself.
But yet our Lord to give us courage to do well surely wishes to
accept that which in itself is of no profit; he requires it as
if he were improved by it, and he declares to us that our
efforts will be neither lost nor useless. — *Sermons*

Then saith the damsel that kept the door unto Peter,
Art not thou also one of this man's disciples? He saith,
I am not.   John 18:17

"Then the maid that kept the door said to Peter . . ."
Peter is introduced into the high priest's hall; but it cost him
very dear, for as soon as he sets his foot within it, he is constrained to deny Christ. When he stumbles so shamefully at
the first step, the foolishness of his boasting is exposed. He
had boasted that he would prove to be a valiant champion,
and able to meet death with firmness; and now at the voice of a
single maid, and that voice without threatening, he is confounded and throws down his arms. Such is a demonstration of
the power of man.

Certainly all the strength that appears to be in men is
smoke, which a breath immediately drives away. When we
are out of the battle, we are too courageous; but experience
shows that our lofty talk is foolish and groundless; and even
when Satan makes no attacks, we contrive for ourselves idle
alarms which disturb us before the time. The voice of a feeble
woman terrified Peter; and what is the case with us? Do we
not continually tremble at the rustling of a falling leaf? A
false appearance of danger, which was still distant, made
Peter tremble; and are we not every day led away from Christ
by childish absurdities? In short, our courage is of such a
nature that of its own accord it gives way where there is no
enemy; and thus does God revenge the arrogance of men by
reducing fierce minds to a state of weakness. A man filled not
with fortitude but with wind, promises that he will obtain an
easy victory over the whole world; and yet no sooner does he
see the shadow of a thistle than he immediately trembles. Let
us therefore learn not to be brave in any other than the Lord.
                                              —*Commentaries*

For there shall arise false Christs, and false prophets, and shall shew great signs and wonders; insomuch that, if it were possible, they shall deceive the very elect. Behold, I have told you before.

Matthew 24:24, 25

But you know how the Son of God forewarns us, so that nothing should trouble us, seeing that we have been prepared for it beforehand. Think rather that this is not the end, but that God is trying you very gently, supporting your weakness, until you have more strength to sustain blows. But be this as it may, beware of letting yourself be cast down by indifference or despair. Many are overcome, because they allow their zeal to grow cold, and run off in self-flattery. Others, on the contrary, become so alarmed when they do not find in themselves the strength they wish, that they get confused, and give up the struggle altogether.

What then is to be done? Arouse yourself to meditate, as much upon the promises of God, which ought to serve as ladders to raise us up to heaven, and make us despise this transitory and fading life, as upon threatenings, which may well induce us to fear his judgments. When you do not feel your heart moved as it ought to be, have recourse, as to a special remedy, to diligently seeking the aid of him without whom we can do nothing. In the meantime, strive to your utmost, blaming coldness and weakness, until you can perceive that there is some amendment. And in regard to this, great caution is required so as to hold a middle course, namely to groan unceasingly, and even to woo yourself to sadness and dissatisfaction with your condition, and to such a sense of misery as that you may have no rest; without, at the same time, any doubting that God in due time will strengthen you according to your need, although this may not appear at once.

—Correspondence

O Zion, that bringest good tidings, get thee up into the high mountain; O Jerusalem, that bringest good tidings, lift up thy voice with strength; lift it up, be not afraid; say unto the cities of Judah, Behold your God!   Isaiah 40:9

"That bringest tidings." Yet we ought carefully to observe this commendation which God bestows on his Church, that it may not be without a clear mark of distinction; for an assembly in which the preaching of heavenly doctrine is not heard does not deserve to be reckoned a Church. In this sense also, Paul calls it (I Tim. 3:15) "the pillar and ground of truth"; for although God might have governed us by himself, and without the agency of men, yet he has assigned this office to his Church, and has committed to it the invaluable treasure of his Word. For the same reason it will be called in another passage, "the mother of all believers" (Is. 54:1; Gal. 4:26). Hence it follows that nothing is more absurd and wicked than for dumb idols to boast of the name of the Church.

We are likewise taught that the Church has not been instructed of God in order that she may keep her knowledge hidden within herself, but that she may publish what she has learned. Besides, he commands that grace shall be freely and boldly proclaimed, that prophets and teachers may not speak with timidity, as if it were a doubtful matter, but may show that they are fully convinced of the certainty of those things which they promise, because they know well that "God, who cannot lie" (Tit. 1:2) is the Author of them. He enjoins the witnesses of his grace to proceed from Zion, that they may fill with joy the whole of Judea. — *Commentaries*

*Thus saith the Lord of hosts; In those days it shall
come to pass, that ten men shall take hold out of all
languages of the nations, even shall take hold of the
skirt of him that is a Jew, saying, We will go with you:
for we have heard that God is with you.*

Zechariah 8:23

The prophet at the same time not only commends humility,
but also exhorts all God's children to cultivate unity and concord. For whosoever tears asunder the Church of God, dis-
unites himself from Christ, who is the head, and who would
have all his members to be united together.

We now then understand that God ought to be sought in
order to be rightly worshipped by us; and also that he ought
to be thus sought, not that each may have his own peculiar
religion, but that we may be united together, and that every
one who sees his brethren going before, and excelling in many
gifts, may be prepared to follow them and to seek benefit from
their labors. It is indeed true that we ought to disregard the
whole world, and to embrace only the truth of God; for it is
a hundred times better to renounce the society of all mortals
and union with them than to withdraw ourselves from God;
but when God shows himself as our leader, the prophet teaches
us that we ought mutually to stretch forth our hand and
unitedly to follow him. — *Commentaries*

*Jesus saith unto her, Mary. She turned herself, and
saith unto him, Rabboni; which is to say, Master.*

John 20:16

"Jesus saith unto her, Mary." That Christ allowed Mary, a
short time, to fall into a mistake, was useful for confirming her
faith; but now, by a single word, he corrects her mistake.
He had formerly addressed her, but his discourse seemed to be
that of an unknown person; he now assumes the character of
the Master, and addresses his disciple by name, as we have seen
that the good shepherd calls to him by name every sheep of
his flock (John 10:3). That voice of the shepherd, therefore,
enters into Mary's heart, opens her eyes, arouses all her senses,
and affects her in such a manner that she immediately sur-
renders herself to Christ.

Thus in Mary we have a lively image of our calling; for the
only way in which we are admitted to the true knowledge of
Christ is when he first knows us, and then familiarly invites us
to himself, not by that ordinary voice which sounds indis-
criminately in the ears of all, but by that voice with which he
especially calls the sheep which the Father has given him.
Thus Paul says, After that you have known God, or rather,
after that you have been known of him (Gal. 4:9).

—*Commentaries*

Unto Timothy, my own son in the faith: Grace, mercy, and peace, from God our Father and Jesus Christ our Lord. I Timothy 1:2

But mark here the order which we must keep. It is this: that first of all it would please God to receive us into his grace, and then to send us those things which are profitable and necessary for us. True it is that our nature will always draw the contrary way, even as a sick man will be more tormented with his pang than with the cause of his disease. In like sort, when we pray to God, we desire him to give us bread to eat, and that he would send us whatsoever is necessary for us; if we be sick, that he would heal us; and if we want anything, that he would send it to us. See how stubbornly we approach God. We forget that which is most important, namely his love and his grace, and rely on things of baser sort and less account. One will crave to be rich, another would have whatsoever his lust leads him to. To be short, we are so froward in our desires that we know not what is good for us. And for this cause, let us follow the rule which is here set down, that when we call upon God, we crave of him especially and above all things that it may please him to be merciful to us, and forgive us our sins and take us to himself; and afterward to govern us and be our leader in all ways. — *Sermons*

*For he shall give his angels charge over thee, to keep
thee in all thy ways. They shall bear thee up in their
hands, lest thou dash thy foot against a stone.*

Psalm 91:11, 12

But the Scripture principally insists on what might conduce most to our consolation, and the confirmation of our faith — that the angels are dispensers and administrators of the Divine beneficence towards us; and therefore it informs us that they guard our safety, undertake our defense, direct our ways, and exercise a constant solicitude that no evil befall us. The declarations are universal, belonging primarily to Christ the head of the Church, and then to all the faithful; "He shall give his angels charge over thee, to keep thee in all thy ways. They shall bear thee up in their hands, lest thou dash thy foot against a stone." Again, "The angel of the Lord encampeth round about them that fear him, and delivereth them." In these passages God shows that he delegates to his angels the protection of those whom he has undertaken to preserve. Accordingly, the angel of the Lord consoles the fugitive Hagar, and commands her to be reconciled to her mistress. Abraham promises his servant that an angel should be the guide of his journey. Jacob, in his benediction of Ephraim and Manasseh, prays that the angel of the Lord, by whom he had been redeemed from all evil, would cause them to prosper. But whether each of the faithful has a particular angel assigned to him for his defense, I cannot venture certainly to affirm.

—*Institutes*, I, xiv, vi

That thou keep this commandment without spot, un-
rebukeable, until the appearing of our Lord Jesus
Christ: Which in his times he shall shew, who is the
blessed and only Potentate, the King of kings, and
Lord of lords;   I Timothy 6:14,15

Unbelievers take us for fools and witless idiots; and Saint
Peter says that this must be fulfilled in us. As Isaiah complained of it in his time, the Christians must endure the like
at this day. And in the meantime we see that we are afraid of
very little things; if a mouse but run before our eyes, we are
all amazed. And again, we are tied fast by the legs in this
world, for when we see the pomp of earthly princes, when we
see the boasting of the world, we are by and by possessed with
a false judgment; we know no more what the kingdom of God
means; we quite forget that. And what is the cause of it?
That we do not listen to what Saint Paul says here. For we
might easily defy all these earthly principalities when they lift
up themselves against God, if we were well persuaded that God
is supreme Prince, King of Kings and Lord of Lords. If this
were well imprinted on our minds, all the pelting trifles of
this world would be nothing to astonish us. That is what I call
whatever men are able to bring to make war against God.
Though they are able to do much, and can if they wish be
jolly fellows; yet because they match themselves against God's
majesty, whatsoever they are able to attempt is nothing but
smoke. And therefore let us mark well what Paul says, namely
that to be well confirmed in the fear of God, not to have our
eyes dazzled with the vanities of the world, nor carried away
with the allurements of Satan, nor to be overcome with any
temptation, nor to be made afraid with any earthly pomp and
loftiness we must give this sovereign empire to God, so that all
knees bow down to him and do him homage. — *Sermons*

*For John truly baptized with water; but ye shall be
baptized with the Holy Ghost not many days hence.*

Acts 1:5

That is frivolous which some gather out of this place,
namely that the baptism of John and the baptism of Christ
were different. For he does not dispute concerning baptism
in this place, but only makes a comparison between the person
of John and the person of Christ. When John says that he
baptized with water only, he does not reason of what sort
his baptism was; but what he himself was, lest he should
claim that to himself which was proper to Christ. As also the
ministers in these days ought not to speak otherwise of themselves; but they must acknowledge Christ to be the author of
all those things which they prefigure in the outward baptism,
and leave nothing to themselves except only the outward ad-
ministration. For when these titles are attributed to baptism,
namely that it is the washing of regeneration, a washing away
of sins, the fellowship of death, and burying with Christ, and a
grafting into the body of Christ, it is not declared what man,
being the minister of the outward sign, does; but rather what
Christ does, who alone gives force and efficacy to these signs.
We must always hold fast this distinction, lest, while we adorn
man too much, we rob Christ. — *Commentaries*

OCTOBER 12

Set a watch, O Lord, before my mouth; keep the door of my lips.   Psalm 141:3

Immediately thereafter he explains himself to mean, that he would not desire to strive with them in wickedness, and thus make himself like his enemies. Had that monk of whom Eusebius makes mention duly reflected upon this, he would not have fallen into that silly fallacy of imagining that he had shown himself the perfect scholar by observing silence for a whole term of seven years. Hearing that the regulation of the tongue was a rare virtue, he betook himself to a distant solitude, from which he did not return to his master for seven years; and being asked the cause of his long absence, replied that he had been meditating upon what he had learned from this verse. It would have been proper to have asked him at the same time whether during the interim he had thought nothing as well as spoken nothing. For the two things stand connected — being silent and being free from the charge of evil thoughts. It is very possible that although he observed silence, he had many ungodly thoughts, and these are worse than vain words.

In committing himself to the guidance of God, both as to thoughts and words, David acknowledges the need of the influence of the Spirit for the regulation of his tongue and of his mind, particularly when tempted to be exasperated by the insolence of opposition. If, on the one hand, the tongue is liable to slip and be too fast of utterance, unless continually watched and guarded by God; on the other, there are disorderly affections of an inward kind which require to be restrained. What a busy workshop is the heart of man, and what a host of devices is there manufactured every moment! If God do not watch over our heart and tongue, there will confessedly be no bounds to words and thoughts of a sinful kind — so rare a gift of the Spirit is moderation in language, while Satan is ever making suggestions which will be readily and easily complied with, unless God prevent. — *Commentaries*

O Lord, rebuke me not in thine anger, neither chasten
me in thy hot displeasure.   Psalm 6:1

We see how thoughtless and insensible almost all men are
on this subject; for while they cry out that they are afflicted
and miserable, scarcely one among a hundred looks to the hand
which strikes. From whatever quarter, therefore, our afflictions
come, let us learn to turn our thoughts instantly to God, and
to acknowledge him as the Judge who summons us as guilty
before his tribunal, since we, of our own accord, do not anticipate his judgment.

David does not simply ascribe to God the afflictions under
which he is now suffering, but acknowledges them to be the
just recompense of his sins. He does not take God to task as
if he had been an enemy, treating him with cruelty without
any just cause; but yielding to him the right of rebuking and
chastening, he desires and prays only that bounds may be set
to the punishment inflicted upon him. By this he declares God
to be a just Judge in taking vengeance on the sins of men.
But as soon as he has confessed that he is justly chastised, he
earnestly beseeches God not to deal with him in strict justice,
or according to the utmost rigor of the law.

The meaning therefore is this: "I indeed confess, O Lord,
that I deserve to be destroyed and brought to nought; but as I
would be unable to endure the severity of thy wrath, deal not
with me according to my deserts, but rather pardon my sins,
by which I have provoked thine anger against me." As often,
then, as we are pressed down by adversity, let us learn, from
the example of David, to have recourse to this remedy, that we
may be brought into a state of peace with God; for it is not
to be expected that it can be well or prosperous with us if
we are not interested in his favor. — *Commentaries*

Lo, children are an heritage of the Lord: and the fruit of the womb is his reward.   Psalm 127:3

In order to set forth this blessing of God — to have off-spring — in a clear light, Solomon commends a virtuous and generous disposition in children. The similitude introduced for this purpose is, that as an archer is armed with a well-furnished bow, so men are defended by their children, as it were with a bow and an arrow. The Prophet means that those who are without children are in a manner unarmed; for what else is it to be childless but to be solitary? It is no small gift of God for a man to be renewed in his posterity; for God then gives him new strength, that he who otherwise would straightway decay, may begin as it were to live a second time.

It is also to be added that unless men regard their children as the gift of God, they are careless and reluctant in providing for their support, just as on the other hand this knowledge contributes to encourage them in bringing up their offspring. Farther, he who thus reflects upon the goodness of God in giving him children, will readily and with a settled mind look for the continuance of God's grace; and although he may have but a small inheritance to leave them, he will not worry unduly on that account.

He teaches, then, that the children which we ought to wish for are not such as may violently oppress the wretched and suf-fering, or overreach others by craft and deceit, or accumulate great riches by unlawful means, or acquire for themselves tyrannical authority, but such as will practise uprightness, and be willing to live in obedience to the laws, and prepared to render an account of their life. Farther, although fathers ought dili-gently to form their children under a holy discipline, yet let them remember that they will never succeed in attaining the object aimed at, save by the pure and special grace of God.

—*Commentaries*

Therefore will I divide him a portion with the great,
and he shall divide the spoil with the strong; because
he hath poured out his soul unto death: and he was
numbered with the transgressors; and he bare the sin
of many, and made intercession for the transgressors.
Isaiah 53:12

After all this, he adds: *he prayed for the wicked.* This is
especially added to show that in his death and passion,
Jesus Christ bore the priestly office. Without this we should
not have everything necessary for the assurance of our salvation. It is true that, since the death and passion of our Lord
Jesus Christ is the sacrifice by which our sins are wiped out,
his blood is our cleansing, the purpose of his obedience is to
abolish all our rebellions and to win righteousness for us.
We have something to rejoice at in this. But it is not all;
for we are told that when we call upon the name of God we
shall be saved. But how can we have access to God? What
boldness it is, to come to pray to him! yes, to call him plainly
and openly our Father. Is it not too great presumption for us
to come so familiarly to God, and to boast that we are his
children, unless we have one who is our spokesman? And
where shall we find an advocate or attorney who could do so
much for us, until we come to Jesus Christ? This, then, is
what the Prophet wanted to add to round off what he is saying
— *Jesus Christ prayed for the wicked.*

When we are humbled like this, we can come to our Lord
Jesus Christ in the knowledge that it is he who is spokesman
for us, and that it is also through him that we can boldly call
ourselves the children of God. So when we come to pray, and
say: "Our Father, who art in heaven," we must recognize
that, as far as we are concerned, our lips are unclean, and we are
not even worthy to call him God our Creator, let alone being
so presumptuous as to regard ourselves as his children. But
in spite of this, our Lord Jesus Christ is our spokesman, and
our prayers and intercessions are sanctified by him, just as

it says in the last chapter of the Epistle to the Hebrews, that it is through him that we render to God the sacrifices of praise and all our prayers, and that he is our Mediator and today we call upon God our Father in his Name. We can indeed boldly glory that he regards us as his children.

—Sermons

290　OCTOBER 16

Therefore say thou unto them, Thus saith the Lord of hosts; Turn ye unto me, saith the Lord of hosts, and I will turn unto you, saith the Lord of hosts.

Zechariah 1:3

We must bear in mind that according to the common usage of Scripture, whenever God exhorts us to repentance, he does not regard what our capacity is, but demands what is justly his right. Hence the Papists adopt what is absurd when they deduce the power of free-will from the command or exhortation to repent; God, they say, would not have commanded what is not in our power to do. This is a foolish way of reasoning; for if everything which God requires were in our power, the grace of the Holy Spirit would be superfluous; it would not only be as they say a waiting-maid, but it would be wholly unnecessary; but if men need the aid of the Spirit, it follows that they cannot do what God requires of them. But it seems strange that God should bid men to do more than what they can. It seems so indeed, I admit, when we form our judgment according to the common perception of the flesh; but when we understand these truths — that the law works wrath — that it increases sin — that it was given that transgression might be made more evident; then the false notion — that God requires nothing but what men can perform — comes to nothing. But it is enough for us to know that God in exhorting us to repentance requires nothing but what nature dictates ought to be done by us. Since it is so, however short we are in the performance, it is not right to charge God with too much strictness, that he demands what is beyond our power.

—Commentaries

*And he hath made my mouth like a sharp sword; in
the shadow of his hand hath he hid me, and made me
a polished shaft; in his quiver hath he hid me;*
Isaiah 49:2

The present question is not about the person of Christ, but
about the whole body of the Church. We must indeed begin
with the Head, but we must come next to the members; and
to all the ministers of the Word must be applied what is here
affirmed concerning Christ; for to them is given such efficacy
of the Word, that they may not idly beat the air with their
voices, but may reach the hearts and touch them to the quick.
The Lord also causes the voice of the gospel to resound not only
in one place, but far and wide throughout the whole world. In
short, because he faithfully keeps them under his protection,
though they are exposed to many attacks, and are assaulted on
every side by Satan and the world, yet they do not swerve
from their course. We ought to have abundant knowledge of
this from experience; for they would all to a man have been
long ago ruined by the conspiracy and snares of adversaries, if
the Lord had not defended them by his protection. And indeed,
amidst so many dangers, it is almost miraculous that a single
preacher of the gospel is permitted to remain. The reason of this
is that the Lord guards them by his shadow, and "hides them
as arrows in his quiver," that they may not be laid open to the
assaults of enemies and be destroyed. — *Commentaries*

*Now the end of the commandment is charity out of a
pure heart, and of a good conscience, and of faith unfeigned:*
I Timothy 1:5

Now let us fall down before the face of our good God,
acknowledging our faults, desiring him that it would please
him to cleanse us, and touch us so to the quick that we may

learn to renounce whatever is of this world and of our flesh, and that we may take pains to come to him; yea, and that in such a sort that he may receive us as his children. And seeing it has pleased him to bring us to faith, by the knowledge of his truth, that it would please him to guide us even to the end, and hold us fast by the hand, that we never may be turned away from his holy calling. — *Sermons*

293   OCTOBER 19

Therefore will not we fear, though the earth be removed, and though the mountains be carried into the midst of the sea;   Psalm 46:2

"Therefore will not we fear, though the earth be removed." He concludes by way of inference that the faithful have no reason to be afraid, since God is always ready to deliver them, nay, is also armed with invincible power. He shows in this that the true and proper proof of our hope consists in this, that, when things are so confused, that the heavens seem as it were to fall with great violence, the earth to remove out of its place, and the mountains to be torn up from their very foundations, we nevertheless continue to preserve and maintain calmness and tranquillity of heart. It is an easy matter to manifest the appearance of great confidence, so long as we are not placed in imminent danger; but if, in the midst of a general crash of the whole world our minds continue undisturbed and free of trouble, this is an evident proof that we attribute to the power of God the honor which belongs to him. When, however, the sacred poet says, "We will not fear," he is not to be understood as meaning that the minds of the godly are exempt from all solicitude or fear, as if they were destitute of feeling, for there is a great difference between insensibility and the confidence of faith. He only shows that whatever may happen they are never overwhelmed with terror, but rather gather strength and courage sufficient to allay all fear. "Though the earth be moved and the mountains fall into the midst of the

sea" are hyperbolical modes of expression, but they nevertheless denote a revolution, and turning upside down of the whole
world. — *Commentaries*

294   OCTOBER 20

*The eyes of your understanding being enlightened;
that ye may know what is the hope of his calling, and
what the riches of the glory of his inheritance in the
saints,*   Ephesians 1:18

We clearly perceive how utterly destitute man is of every
good, and in want of all the means of salvation. Wherefore, if
he seek for relief in his necessities, he must go out of himself, and obtain it from some other quarter. It has been stated
also that the Lord voluntarily and liberally manifests himself
in his Christ, in whom he offers us all blessedness instead of
our misery, and wealth instead of our poverty; in whom he
opens to our view the treasures of heaven, that our faith may be
wholly engaged in the contemplation of his beloved Son, that
all our expectation may depend on him, and that in him all
our hope may rest and be fully satisfied. This, indeed, is that
secret and learned philosophy which cannot be extracted from
syllogisms; but is well understood by those whose eyes God
has opened, that in his light they may see light. But since we
have been taught by faith to acknowledge that whatever we
want for the supply of our necessities is in God and our Lord
Jesus Christ, in whom it has pleased the Father all the fulness
of his bounty should dwell, that we may all draw from it, as
from a most copious fountain, it remains for us to seek in him,
and by prayers to implore from him, that which we have been
informed resides in him. Otherwise to know God as the Lord
and Giver of every good, who invites us to supplicate him,
but neither to approach him nor to supplicate him, would be
equally unprofitable as for a man to neglect a treasure dis-
closed to him buried in the earth. — *Institutes*, III, xx, i

Behold, as the eyes of servants look unto the hand
of their masters, and as the eyes of a maiden unto the
hand of her mistress; so our eyes wait upon the Lord
our God, until that he have mercy upon us.

Psalm 123:2

"Behold! as the eyes of servants look to the hand of their masters." This similitude is very suitable to the present case. It implies that without the protection of God true believers have no comfort, are completely disarmed, and exposed to all manner of wrongs, have neither strength nor courage to resist; in short, that their safety depends entirely upon aid derived from another. We know how shamefully servants were treated in ancient times, and what reproaches might be cast upon them, whilst yet they dared not move a finger to repel the outrage. Being therefore deprived of all means of defending themselves, the only thing which remained for them to do was, what is here stated, to crave the protection of their masters. The same explanation is equally applicable to the case of handmaids. Their condition was indeed shameful and degrading; but there is no reason why we should be ashamed of, or offended at, being compared to slaves, provided God is our defender, and takes our life under his guardianship; God, I say, who purposely disarms us and strips us of all worldly aid, that we may learn to rely on his grace, and to be contented with it alone. It having been anciently a capital crime for bondmen to carry a sword or any other weapon about them, and as they were exposed to injuries of every description, their masters were wont to defend them with so much the more spirit, when anyone causelessly did them violence. Nor can it be doubted that God, when he sees us placing an exclusive dependence upon his protection, and renouncing all confidence in our own resources, will as our defender encounter and shield us from all the molestation that shall be offered to us. — *Commentaries*

Nevertheless among the chief rulers also many be-lieved on him; but because of the Pharisees they did not confess him, lest they should be put out of the synagogue: John 12:42

"Nevertheless, many even of the rulers believed on him." The murmuring and fierceness of the Jews, in rejecting Christ, having risen to such a height of insolence, it might have been thought that all the people, without exception, conspired against him. But the Evangelist says that amidst the general madness of the nation, there were many who were of a sound mind. A striking instance, truly, of the grace of God; for when ungodliness has once prevailed, it is a sort of universal plague, which infects with its contagion every part of the body. It is therefore a remarkable gift, and special grace of God, when, amidst a people so corrupt, there are some who remain untainted. And yet we now perceive in the world the same grace of God; for though ungodliness and contempt of God abound everywhere, and though a vast multitude of men make furious attempts to exterminate utterly the doctrine of the Gospel, yet it always finds some places of retreat, and thus faith has what may be called its harbors or places of refuge, that it may not be entirely banished from the world.

The word *even* is emphatic; for in the order of the rulers there existed so deep a hatred of the Gospel that it could scarcely be believed that a single believer could be found amongst them . . . . They who, swelled with arrogance, scarcely acknowledge themselves to be men, are not easily subdued by voluntary humility. Whoever, then, holds a high station in the world, will, if he is wise, look with suspicion on his rank, that it may not stand in his way . . . . On this account, persons who are placed in a low and mean condition ought to bear their lot with the greater patience, for they are, at least, delivered from many very bad snares. Yet the great and noble ought to struggle against their high rank, that it may not hinder them from submitting to Christ. — *Commentaries*

297   OCTOBER 23

*Now the end of the commandment is charity out of
a pure heart, and of a good conscience, and of faith
unfeigned.*   I Timothy 1:5

Saint Paul shows that when God published his law he had
before his eyes a certain end at which we also must aim; and
when we do so, we shall have the true life of the law; it shall
not be a dead letter to us; and not that only, but having the
pure knowledge of what is contained in it, we shall be quickened. What we have to gather from the law is, in sum, love
out of a pure heart and out of a good conscience, and faith unfeigned. In another place it is said that Holy Writ is profitable
to teach and to reprove and to admonish, and to make the man
of God perfect. Likewise in this text he shows that it was
God's purpose to confirm us in godliness, when he gave us his
law. For it was not to tickle our ears at all, and to feed us
with vain trifles, but it contains a doctrine very profitable to
us. And in what does it consist? It is true that Saint Paul puts
love here in the first place, but yet he shows that love comes
from a higher fountain, that is to say, from faith, which carries with it a good conscience and a pure heart; and then love
is the fruit of it. — *Sermons*

298   OCTOBER 24

*Who hath believed our report? and to whom is the arm
of the Lord revealed?*   Isaiah 53:1

Isaiah does not include merely the men of his own time,
but all posterity to the end of the world; for, so long as the
reign of Christ shall endure, this must be fulfilled; and therefore believers ought to be fortified by this passage against
such a scandal. These words refute the ignorance of those who
think that faith is in the power of every person, because
preaching is common to all. Though it is sufficiently evident

that all are called to salvation, yet the Prophet expressly states that the external voice is of no avail, if it be not accompanied by a special gift of the Spirit. And whence proceeds the difference, but from the secret election of God, the cause of which is hidden in himself? — *Commentaries*

299   O CTOBER 25

He that believeth on him is not condemned: but he that believeth not is condemned already, because he hath not believed in the name of the only begotten Son of God.   John 3:18

We are reminded how acceptable and precious a sacrifice in the sight of God faith is. As nothing is more dear to him than his truth, so we cannot render to him more acceptable worship than when we acknowledge by our faith that he is true, for then we ascribe that honor which truly belongs to him. On the other hand, we cannot offer to him a greater insult than not to believe the Gospel; for he cannot be deprived of his truth without taking away all his glory and majesty. His truth is in some sort closely linked with the Gospel, and it is his will that there it should be recognized. — *Commentaries*

300   O CTOBER 26

The grass withereth, the flower fadeth: but the word of our God shall stand for ever.   Isaiah 40:8

"But the word of our God shall stand forever." This passage comprehends the whole Gospel in a few words; for it consists of an acknowledgment of our misery, poverty, and emptiness, that, being sincerely humbled, we may fly to God, by whom alone we shall be perfectly restored. Let not men therefore faint or be discouraged by the knowledge of their nakedness and emptiness; for the eternal word is exhibited to them by which they may be abundantly supported and upheld. We are likewise taught that we ought not to seek consolation from any other source than from eternity, which ought not to be sought anywhere else than in God; since nothing that is firm or durable will be found on the earth. Nothing is more foolish than to rest satisfied with the present state, which we see to be but fleeting; and every man is mistaken who hopes to obtain perfect happiness till he has ascended to God, whom the Scripture calls eternal, in order that we may know that life flows to us from him; and indeed he adopts us to be his children on this condition, to make us partakers of his immortality. But this would be of no avail if the manner of seeking him were not pointed out; and therefore he exhibits *the word*, from which we must not in any respect turn aside; for if we make the smallest departure from it, we shall be involved in strange labyrinths, and shall find no way of extricating ourselves. — *Commentaries*

301　　　　　**OCTOBER 27**

Fight the good fight of faith, lay hold on eternal life, whereunto thou art also called, and hast professed a good profession before many witnesses.

I Timothy 6:12

Therefore as God was not moved to give us hope of our salvation for any goodness that he saw in us, but because it pleased him, and pleased him of his mere mercy, so when he goes on still to guide us, until we be come to the haven of salvation, he does it because it pleases him. This is the cause of the free calling of God towards us continually; so that men are beaten down here and cannot rejoice in themselves in that it is said that we must make an end of our salvation. Thus God does not want us to be idle, but, notwithstanding, our activity must be with fear and trembling. And why? Because it is God who works in us, giving us the will, giving us the effect, and everything else according to his good pleasure. Let us do the best we can, but without presumption, without pride. Let us not think that we can do so well as to merit anything, or that man is worthy to be exalted against God; for by this means the grace of God would be darkened and made to be nothing.

—Sermons

302 OCTOBER 28

And when he is come, he will reprove the world of sin, and of righteousness, and of judgment: John 16:8

"He will convince the world." It ought to be observed that in this passage Christ does not speak of secret revelations, but of the power of the Spirit, which appears in the outward doctrine of the Gospel, and in the voice of men. For how does it come that the voice proceeding from the mouth of a man penetrates into the hearts, takes root there, and at length yields fruit, changing hearts of stone into hearts of flesh, and renewing men, but because the Spirit of Christ quickens it? Otherwise it would be a dead letter and a useless sound, as Paul says in that beautiful passage in which he boasts of being a *minister of the Spirit* (II Cor. 3:6), because God powerfully wrought in his doctrine. The meaning therefore is that though the Spirit had been given to the apostles, they would be endued with a heavenly and Divine power, by which they would exercise jurisdiction over the whole world. Now this is ascribed to the Spirit rather than to themselves, because they will have no power of their own, but will be only ministers and organs, and the Holy Spirit will be their director and governor.

—Commentaries

303 OCTOBER 29

And all that believed were together, and had all things common; Acts 2:44

But this place needs sound exposition, because of fanatical spirits who feign a commonalty or participation of goods, whereby all policy or civil government is taken away; as in this age the Anabaptists have raged, because they thought there was no Church unless all men's goods were put and gathered together, as it were, in one heap, that they might all one with another take thereof. Wherefore we must in this point beware of two extremes. For many, under color of policy, do keep close and conceal whatsoever they have; they defraud the poor, and they think that they are twice righteous, if only they take away no one else's goods. Others are carried into the contrary error, because they would have all things confused. But Luke surely notes another order when he says that there was choice made in the distribution. If any man object that no man had anything which was his own, seeing all things were common, we may easily answer. For this community or participation together must be restrained unto the circumstance which immediately follows; namely, that the poor might be relieved as every man had need. — *Commentaries*

304   **OCTOBER 30**

And ye shall seek me, and find me, when ye shall search for me with all your heart.   Jeremiah 29:13

For conducting prayer in a right and proper manner the first rule is that our heart and mind be composed to a suitable frame, becoming those who enter into conversation with God. This state of mind we shall certainly attain, if, divested of all carnal cares and thoughts that tend to divert and seduce it from a right and clear view of God, it not only devotes itself entirely to the solemn exercise, but is likewise as far as possible elevated and carried above itself. Nor do I here require a mind so disengaged as to be disturbed by no solicitude; since there ought on the contrary most anxiously to be kindled within us a fervency of prayer (as we see the holy servants of God discover great solicitude, and even anguish, when they say they utter their complaints to the Lord from the deep abysses of affliction and the very jaws of death). But I maintain the necessity of dismissing all foreign and external cares, by which the wandering mind may be hurried hither and thither, and dragged from heaven down to earth. It ought to be elevated above itself, that it may not intrude into the Divine presence any of the imaginations of our blind and foolish reason, nor confine itself within the limits of its own vanity, but rise to purity worthy of God. — *Institutes*, III, xx, iv

305   OCTOBER 31

Thus speaketh the Lord of hosts, saying, Execute true judgment, and shew mercy and compassions every man to his brother: Zechariah 7:9

"Thus saith Jehovah of hosts, Judge the judgment of truth and show kindness and mercies, every one to his brother." The people were so devoted to their ceremonies as to think that the whole of religion consisted in fasting and in similar exercises. And as we are by nature prone to this evil, we ought carefully to consider what the prophet has taught us — that fasting is not simply, or by itself, approved by God, but on account of the end designed by it. Having already shown to the Jews their error, in thinking that God could be pacified by ceremonies, he now reminds them of what God mainly requires in his law — that men should observe what is just and right towards one another. It is indeed true that the first part of the law refers to the service due to God; but it is a way which God has commonly adopted to test the life of men by the duties of the second Table, and to show what this part of the law especially requires. God then in this passage as in many others, does not command righteousness towards men so as to depreciate godliness; for as this far excels everything in the whole world, so we know that in rightly forming the life, the beginning ought ever to be made by serving God aright. But as the prophet had to do with hypocrites, he shows that they only trifled with God, while they made much of external things and at the same time neglected uprightness and the duties of love. — *Commentaries*

As for the beauty of his ornament, he set it in majesty:
but they made the images of their abominations and
of their detestable things therein: therefore have I set
it far from them.   Ezekiel 7:20

Whatever God has given to men is a testimony of his paternal favor; therefore God's liberality abounds in us when he enriches us with his gifts. If therefore riches are a glory and ornament, so also are bodily health, and honors, and things of this kind. Since therefore God wishes his favor to be conspicuous in all his gifts, by which he adorns and marks men out, the Prophet properly says that the Jews were adorned with gold and silver. But he accuses them of ingratitude because they turned such glory into pride. The Jews made their images, which were so many abominations before God, out of gold and silver. This was a second profanation of God's gifts; the former was in pride, when the Jews through wantonness and abundance began to be insolent against God, thus they profaned the glory with which they had been adorned. But another pollution is also added, namely, that they made their idols of gold and silver, and offered to them gifts and sacrifices; as God complains in Hosea (2:8) that they converted whatever he had conferred upon them into impious worship. I had given, said he, my corn and wine and oil; but they adorned their idols. This was their thanksgiving, that blind to my liberality they offered sacrifices to their idols of my corn and wine and oil. — *Commentaries*

*For men shall be lovers of their own selves, covetous,
boasters, proud, blasphemers, disobedient to parents,
unthankful, unholy.*   II Timothy 3:2

If any wrong be done us, if we sustain but the loss of a
penny, we can quickly say, "What wickedness there is nowadays!" But if we have what we would desire, and no man
trouble us, no man grieve us, we think all is well. But though
the honor of God be trodden under foot, all honesty completely banished, and men become as brute beasts, it is all the
same to us, as long as we sustain no hurt nor damage. And yet
if we are God's children, we must needs taste what he has
showed us here by his Spirit, that though all things go as we
desire, with respect to the goods of this world, we must not
cease for all that to sigh and be grieved unless God be served
and there be good order and sin be kept in check as it ought
to be.

If this be so, every man will do his duty. For they that are
in office will not think they have done their duty when they
have maintained some balance among men, so that none can
complain, but they will look further. They will see that faithfulness, upright dealing, and especially religion and such vir-
tues as are requisite for honest life shall flourish and be maintained. Moreover the ministers of the Word of God must not
be satisfied if men do not make open trouble, unless men
also live honestly, and God be honored, and matters be in
good state, or at least they labor to make them so. Yes, and
they that have no public charge must look to themselves. When
a man shall see his children evil nurtured and his servants
acting lewdly, he cannot be at rest; though it do him no hurt,
yet it grieves him, and torments him when he sees that his
house does not serve God. They that have taken pains to rule
their household well, when they go out into the streets, if they
see any villainies and disorders, they fall to sobbing and sigh-
ing. — *Sermons*

*Woe to the idol shepherd that leaveth the flock! the
sword shall be upon his arm, and upon his right eye:
his arm shall be clean dried up, and his right eye shall
be utterly darkened.*   Zechariah 11:17

We see that the whole strength of men depends on the
grace of God; and farther, that a sound mind proceeds from
his Spirit; for since it is he who takes away from men both
their strength and a right judgment, we hence conclude that
to give these things is also in his power. Let men then know
that in order to possess due courage and strength, they are
to rely on the hidden power of God; and let them also know
that in order to discern what is useful and profitable, they must
be governed by his Spirit; and let those especially who bear
rule be assured of this, that when they exercise power in peace,
it is God's singular gift, and that when they rightly govern
their subjects, and are endued with sound discretion, it is
wholly to be ascribed to an influence from above.

—*Commentaries*

*The writing of Hezekiah king of Judah, when he had
been sick, and was recovered of his sickness:*
Isaiah 38:9

"The writing of Hezekiah." Though sacred history gives us
no account of this writing, yet it deserves to be recorded, and
is highly worthy of observation; for we see that Hezekiah was
unwilling to pass in silence, or to bury in forgetfulness, so remarkable a blessing which he had received from God. By his
example he shows what all believers ought to do, when God
miraculously and in an unusual manner exerts his power on
their behalf. They ought to make known their gratitude, not
only to their contemporaries, but also to posterity; as we see

that Hezekiah did by this song, which may be regarded as a public record. We see that David composed many psalms on this subject, when he had been delivered from very great dangers, so that he took care to celebrate till the end of the world what was worthy of being remembered by all ages (Psalm 18:2; 27:1). Especially, the more eminent any man is, and the higher the station which he occupies, the more is he bound to consider himself as placed by God on a stage, and enjoined to perform his duty. Yet all men, whether they be of ordinary rank or nobles and great men, ought to beware of ambition, lest while they profess to imitate Hezekiah and David, they magnify their own name more than the name of God. — *Commentaries*

310   NOVEMBER 5

He shall dwell on high: his place of defence shall be the munitions of rocks: bread shall be given him; his waters shall be sure.   Isaiah 33:15

"Who shaketh his hands from accepting a bribe." Under the name of bribes, by which judges are corrupted, he likewise includes everything else. There is nothing by which the dispositions of men and righteous judgment are so much perverted; and therefore he bids them "shake their hands" so as to intimate in what abhorrence they should be held, and with what care they should be avoided by all, lest, if they only handled or were tainted by barely touching them, they should be drawn aside from what is just and right; for "bribes" have wonderful powers of fascination, so that it is very difficult for judges to keep their hands altogether clean and uncorrupted by them. What, then, can we think of those who always have their hands stretched out and ready to receive, and crooked nails ready to catch; and not only so, but, like harlots, openly hire themselves out for gain? Need we wonder if God thunders against them with unrelenting vengeance? — *Commentaries*

And when he had given thanks, he brake it, and said,
Take, eat: this is my body, which is broken for you:
this do in remembrance of me. I Corinthians 11:24

From the Lord's Supper pious souls derive the benefit of considerable satisfaction and confidence; because it affords us a testimony that we are incorporated into one body with Christ, so that whatever is his, we are at liberty to call ours. The consequence of this is, that we venture to assure ourselves of our interest in eternal life, of which he is the heir, and that the kingdom of heaven, into which he has already entered, can no more be lost by us than by him; and, on the other hand, that we cannot be condemned by our sins, from the guilt of which he absolved us, when he wished them to be imputed to himself, as if they were his own. This is the wonderful exchange which, in his infinite goodness, he has made with us. Submitting to our poverty, he has transferred to us his riches; assuming our weakness, he has strengthened us by his power; accepting our mortality, he has conferred on us his immortality; taking on himself the load of iniquity with which we were oppressed, he has clothed us with his righteousness; descending to the earth, he has prepared a way for our ascending to heaven; becoming with us the Son of man, he has made us, with himself, the sons of God. — *Institutes,* IV, xvii, ii

And they shall be mine, saith the Lord of hosts, in that
day when I make up my jewels; and I will spare them,
as a man spareth his own son that serveth him.
                                            Malachi 3:17

It must be observed that the prophet does not speak simply of the remission of sins; our salvation, we know, consists of two things — that God rules us by his Spirit and forms us anew in his own image through the whole course of our life — and also that he buries our sins. But the prophet refers here to the remission of sins, of which we have need as to our good works; for it is certain that even when we devote ourselves with all possible effort and zeal in God's service there is yet something always wanting. Hence it is that no work, however right and perfect before men, deserves this distinction before God. It is therefore necessary, even when we strive our utmost to serve God, to confess that without his forgiveness whatever we bring deserves rejection rather than his favor. Hence the prophet says that when God is reconciled to us, there is no reason to fear that he will reject us, because we are not perfect; for though our works be sprinkled with many spots, they will yet be acceptable to him, and though we labor under many defects, we shall yet be approved by him. How so? Because he will spare us; for a father is indulgent to his children, and though he may see a blemish in the body of his son, he will not yet cast him out of his house; nay, though he may have a son lame, or squint-eyed, or defective in some other way, he will yet pity him and will not cease to love him; so also is the case with respect to God, who, when he adopts us as his children, will forgive our sins. And as a father is pleased with every small attention when he sees his son submissive, and does not require from him what he requires from a servant; so God acts; he repudiates not our obedience, however defective it may be.

—*Commentaries*

313   NOVEMBER 8

And I will bring the blind by a way that they knew not; I will lead them in paths that they have not known: I will make darkness light before them, and crooked things straight. These things will I do unto them, and not forsake them.   Isaiah 42:16

"And I will lead the blind." It is often advantageous to us also to have no way open to us, to be straitened and hemmed in on every hand, and even to be blinded, that we may learn to depend solely on God's assistance and to rely on him; for, so long as a plank is left on which we think that we can seize, we turn to it with our whole heart. While we are driven about in all directions, the consequence is that the remembrance of heavenly grace fades from our memory. If, therefore, we desire that God should assist us and relieve our adversity, we must be *blind*, we must turn away our eyes from the present condition of things, and restrain our judgment, that we may entirely rely on his promises. Although this blindness is far from being pleasant, and shows the weakness of our mind, yet, if we judge from the good effects which it produces, we ought not greatly to shun it; for it is better to be "blind" persons guided by the hand of God, than, by excessive sagacity, to form labyrinths for ourselves. — *Commentaries*

314   NOVEMBER 9

Ask ye of the Lord rain in the time of the latter rain; so the Lord shall make bright clouds, and give showers of rain, to every one grass in the field.
Zechariah 10:1

The prophet no doubt includes here, under one kind, all things necessary for a happy life; for it is not the will of God to fill his people in this world as though they were swine; but his design is to give them by means of earthly things, a taste of the spiritual life. Hence the happiness of which Zechariah now speaks is really spiritual; for as godliness has the promises of the present as well as of the future life (I Tim. 6:8), so the purpose of God was to consult the weakness of his ancient people, and to set forth the felicity of the spiritual life by means of earthly blessings. — *Commentaries*

Flee also youthful lusts: but follow righteousness,
faith, charity, peace, with them that call on the Lord
out of a pure heart.   II Timothy 2:22

"Flee the lusts of youth." It is not as though he were a young man of twenty years, for he had been exercised in preaching the word of God now a good while; he was a doctor, not only of one church, but of the country round about him; as we know that Saint Paul had appointed him not only to preach in one place, but also to have an eye afar off, to warn the bishops and all that were in like charge as he was.

So then he was a man of some maturity and ripe years; on the other hand, God chose him from among others; yes, and he had received singular gifts; there was not only doctrine and prophecy in him, but his life was of like quality and he had great zeal to advance the honor of God. In short, he was an example to all men. Yet he has need to be humbled and to have some warning from Paul to the end that he not allow himself at some time to stray from the path and show the follies of youth. At what age? He must have been more than thirty years old.

But the Spirit of God by the mouth of Paul would show us here in the person of one man, though we have profited in God's school, and are governed by his Holy Spirit, and have taken pains a long time to do so, that we are still not perfectly framed and polished. Yes, and when we are come to the age of forty years, do we show that we are become men? You shall see us ready to resist whatsoever is taught us, especially if the question be of serving God, there will always be smoke and storming. And therefore we begin to decline, we shall still be rude and ill favored without any improvement in us; God must always be mending us, and give us now and then a blow with the hammer, and take pains to polish us, or else there will always be something wrong with us. — *Sermons*

Like sheep they are laid in the grave; death shall feed on them; and the upright shall have dominion over them in the morning; and their beauty shall consume in the grave from their dwelling.   Psalm 49:14

As the wicked must all be prostrated before the Lord Jesus Christ, and made his footstool, his members will share in the victory of their Head. It is stated that this will be in the morning — a beautiful and striking metaphor. Surrounded as we are by darkness, our life is here compared to the night, or to a sleep, an image which is specially applicable to the ungodly, who lie as it were in a deep slumber, but not inapplicable to the people of God, such being the dark mist which rests upon all things in this world, that even their minds, except in so far as they are illuminated from above, are partially enveloped in it.

Here we "see only as through a glass darkly," and the coming of the Lord will resemble the morning, when both the elect and reprobate will awake. The former will then cast aside their lethargy and sloth, and being freed from the darkness which rested upon them, will behold Christ the Sun of Righteousness face to face, with the full effulgence of life which resides in him. The others, who lie at present in a state of total darkness, will be aroused from their stupidity, and begin to discover a new life, of which they had previously no apprehension. We need to be reminded of this event, not only because corruption presses us downwards and obscures our faith, but because there are men who profanely argue against another life, from the continued course of things in the world, scoffing, as Peter foretold (II Peter 3:4) at the promise of a resurrection, and pointing, in derision, to the unvarying regularity of nature through the ages. We may arm ourselves against their arguments by what the Psalmist here declares, that, sunk as the world is in darkness, there will dawn ere long a new morning, which will introduce us to a better and an eternal existence. — *Commentaries*

*And Hezekiah was glad of them, and shewed them
the house of his precious things, the silver, and the
gold, and the spices, and the precious ointment, and
all the house of his armour, and all that was found
in his treasures: there was nothing in his house, nor
in all his dominion, that Hezekiah shewed them not.*

Isaiah 39:2

"And Hezekiah was glad." This is a remarkable example;
and it teaches us that nothing is more dangerous than to be
blinded by prosperity. It proves also the truth of the old
proverb, that "it is more difficult to bear prosperity than adversity." For when everything goes on to our wish, we grow
wanton and insolent, and cannot be kept in the path of duty by
any advices or threatenings. When this happened to Hezekiah,
on whom the Prophet had bestowed the high commendation,
that "the fear of God was his treasure" (Is. 33:6), we ought
to be very much afraid of falling into the same dangers. He
is carried away by idle boasting, and does not remember that
formerly he was half-dead, and that God rescued him from
death by an extraordinary miracle. Formerly he made a solemn
promise that he would continually celebrate the praises of God
in the assembly of the godly (Is. 38:20), and now, when he
sees that his friendship is sought, and that a powerful monarch
sends to salute him, he forgets God and the benefits which he
had received from him. When we see that this good king so
quickly falls and is carried away by ambition, let us learn to
lay upon ourselves the restraint of modesty, which will keep
us constantly and diligently in the fear of God. — *Commentaries*

*Then said I, Lo, I come: in the volume of the book
it is written of me,*   Psalm 40:7

"Then said I, Lo! I come." Here David indicates his readiness to yield obedience, as well as the cordial affection of his heart and persevering resolution. His language implies that he cordially preferred the service of God to every other desire and care, and had not only yielded a willing subjection, but also embraced the rule of a pious and holy life, with a fixed and steady purpose of adhering to it. This he confirms when he says that the Law of God was deeply fixed in the midst of his bowels.

It follows from this, first, that however beautiful and splendid the works of men appear, yet unless they spring from the living root of the heart, they are nothing better than a mere pretence; and, secondly, that it is to no purpose that the feet, and hands, and eyes, are framed for keeping the Law unless obedience begin at the heart. Moreover, it appears from other places of Scripture, that it is the peculiar office of the Holy Spirit to engrave the Law of God on our hearts. God, it is true, does not perform his work in us as if we were stocks or stones, drawing us to himself without the feeling or inward moving of our hearts towards him. But as there is in us naturally a will, which, however, is depraved by the corruption of our nature, so that it always inclines us to sin, God changes it for the better, and thus leads us cordially to seek after righteousness, to which our hearts were previously altogether averse. Hence arises that true freedom which we obtain when God frames our hearts, which before were in thraldom to sin, unto obedience to himself. — *Commentaries*

*At that day ye shall ask in my name: and I say not
unto you, that I will pray the Father for you:*
John 16:26

"In that day you shall ask in my name." Besides, when
Christ is said to intercede with the Father for us, let us not
indulge in carnal imaginations about him, as if he were on his
knees before the Father, offering humble supplication in our
name. But the value of his sacrifice, by which he once pacified
God towards us, is always powerful and efficacious; the blood
by which he atoned for our sins, the obedience which he rendered, is a continual intercession for us. This is a remarkable
passage, by which we are taught that we have the heart of the
heavenly Father, as soon as we have placed before him *the
name* of his Son. — *Commentaries*

*Mischief shall come upon mischief, and rumour shall
be upon rumour; then shall they seek a vision of the
prophet; but the law shall perish from the priest,
and counsel from the ancients.*   **Ezekiel 7:26**

In this way he advises the Jews that they should catch at
security in vain, as if, at the passing away of one evil, they
were already free. For the wicked, as soon as God withdraws
his hand, think themselves escaped from all trouble, and so
despise God more carelessly; for they fancy that God has done
with them just like a debtor who has paid a small sum to his
creditor, and thus has sustained a relaxation and is careless;
so the reprobate harden themselves when God grants them
some respite; for they think that they have an agreement with
him that he should not trouble them any more. But the
Prophet denounces that there would be such a heap of evils
that one calamity should have many companions, because God
would not cease to add evils to evils. — *Commentaries*

November 16

Jerusalem is builded as a city that is compact together:
Psalm 122:3

The mutual concord which reigns among the citizens of a city, and by which they are united to each other, is compared to buildings, compacted together by a skillful and elegant workmanship, so that there is nothing imperfect, ill-joined together, or rent, but throughout a beautiful harmony. By this David teaches us that the Church can only remain in a state of safety when unanimity prevails in her, and when, being joined together by faith and charity, she cultivates a holy unity.

Now as each of us in particular would perish miserably if the whole Church were to be involved in ruin, it is not surprising to find David recommending to all the children of God to cultivate this anxious concern about the Church. If we would order our prayers aright, let us always begin with pleading that the Lord would be pleased to preserve this sacred community. Whoever, confining his attention to his own personal advantage, is indifferent about the common weal, he not only gives evidence that he is destitute of all true feeling of godliness, but in vain desires his own prosperity, and will profit nothing by his prayers, since he does not observe the due order.

—Commentaries

November 17

And the Lord said unto him, Go through the midst of the city, through the midst of Jerusalem, and set a mark upon the foreheads of the men that sigh and that cry for all the abominations that be done in the midst thereof. Ezekiel 9:4

This is a remarkable passage, because from it we learn, first, that God effectually threatens the impious, so that he may have attendants always at hand to obey him; then, that even unbelievers make war under the direction of God, and are governed by his rod, and do nothing except at his will. But, thirdly, we are taught that God never rashly executes his vengeance without sparing his elect. For this reason in the slaughter of Jerusalem he has an angel, who opposes a shield, as it were, to the Chaldeans, lest their cruelty should injure them beyond God's pleasure. Therefore I said that the place was remarkable, because when God puts forth the signs of his wrath, the sky is as it were overclouded, and the faithful no less than the unbelieving are frightened, nay terrified with fear. For as to outward condition, there was no difference between them. Because therefore the sons of God are subject to that terror which obscures all sense of God's favor in adversity, so this doctrine must be held diligently, namely when God gives the rein to furious men, so that they dissipate, overthrow, and destroy all things, then the angels are always united, who restrain their intemperance with a hidden bridle, since otherwise they would never be moderate. — *Commentaries*

323 NOVEMBER 18

The burden of the word of the Lord for Israel, saith the Lord, which stretcheth forth the heavens, and layeth the foundation of the earth, and formeth the spirit of man within him. Zechariah 12:1

Since then what Zechariah says could hardly be believed, he prescribes to the Jews the best remedy — that they raise up their eyes and then turn them to the earth. The expanse of the heavens constrains us to admire God; for however stupid we may be, we cannot look on the sun and the moon and stars and on the whole bright expanse above without some strong emotions of fear and of reverence. Since then God exceeds all that men can comprehend in the very creation of the world, what should hinder us from believing even that which seems to us in no way probable? For it is not meet for us to measure God's works by what we can understand, for we cannot comprehend, no not even the hundredth part of them, however attentively we may apply all the powers of our minds.

Nor is it yet a small matter when he adds that God had formed the spirit of man; for we know that we live; the body of itself would be without any strength or motion were it not endued with life; and the soul which animates the body is invisible. Since then experience proves to us the power of God, which is not yet seen by our eyes, why should we not expect what he promises, though the event may appear incredible to us, and exceed all that we can comprehend?

—*Commentaries*

Not every one that saith unto me, Lord, Lord, shall enter into the kingdom of heaven; but he that doeth the will of my Father which is in heaven. Matt. 7:21

It is easy to perceive what we are to learn from the law; namely, that God, as he is our Creator, justly sustains towards us the character of a Father and a Lord; and that on this account we owe to him glory and reverence, love and fear. Moreover, that we are not at liberty to follow everything to which the violence of our passions may incite us; but that we ought to be attentive to his will, and to practise nothing but what is pleasing to him. In the next place, that righteousness and rectitude are a delight, but iniquity an abomination to him; and that, therefore, unless we will with impious ingratitude rebel against our Maker, we must necessarily spend our whole lives in the practice of righteousness. For if we manifest a becoming reverence toward him only when we prefer his will to our own, it follows that there is no other legitimate worship of him but the observance of righteousness, sanctity, and purity. Nor can we pretend to excuse ourselves by a want of ability, like insolvent debtors. For it is improper for us to measure the glory of God by our ability; for whatever may be our characters, he ever remains like himself, the friend of righteousness, the enemy of iniquity. Whatever he requires of us, since he can require nothing but what is right, we are under a natural obligation to obey. But our inability is our own fault. — *Institutes*, II, viii, i

Thou shalt not be afraid for the terror by night; nor for the arrow that flieth by day; Nor for the pestilence that walketh in darkness; nor for the destruction that wasteth at noonday.   Psalm 91:5, 6

Wherever you turn, all the objects around you are not only unworthy of your confidence, but almost openly menace you, and seem to threaten immediate death. Embark in a ship; there is but a single step between you and death. Mount a horse; the slipping of one foot endangers your life. Walk through the streets of a city; you are liable to as many dangers as there are tiles on the roofs. If there be a sharp weapon in your hand, or that of your friend, the mischief is manifest. All the ferocious animals you see are armed for your destruction. If you try to shut yourself in a garden surrounded with a good fence and exhibiting nothing but what is delightful, even there sometimes lurks a serpent. Your house, perpetually liable to fire, menaces you by day with poverty and by night with falling on your head. . . .

On the contrary, when this light of Divine providence has once shined upon a pious man, he is relieved and delivered not only from the extreme anxiety and dread with which he was previously oppressed, but also from all care. For, as he justly dreads fortune, so he ventures securely to commit himself to God. This, I say, is his consolation, to apprehend that his heavenly Father restrains all things by his power, governs all things by his will, and regulates all things by his wisdom, in such a manner that nothing can happen but by his appointment; moreover, that God has taken him under his protection, and committed him to the care of angels, so that he can sustain no injury from water, or fire, or sword, any further than the Divine Governor may be pleased to merit.

—*Institutes*, I, xvii, x and xi

Come unto me, all ye that labour and are heavy
laden, and I will give you rest.   Matthew 11:28

So we see that our Lord Jesus Christ only calls those who
are "heavy laden and travail." Therefore, he excludes all those
who slumber in their iniquities, who flatter themselves, or hurl
themselves without any fear of God into reckless living. Those
who have burst out into evil cannot approach our Lord Jesus;
that is certain. For what will bring us to him save the voice
by which he invites us? It is certain that the door is shut to
as many as blind themselves with their pride and presumption,
who make themselves believe they are righteous in themselves;
they cannot hope that our Lord Jesus Christ will bring them
any comfort. And why? "Come unto me," he says. But
who? "All the world?" It is true that he calls all the world;
but yet He makes a distinction: "You who are heavy laden
and travail." When he has called all who need his help, he
shows that none can have a share in it save him who is heavy
laden and labours. So when we feel our burden and groan beneath it, knowing that we can do no other, the road is prepared and opened up for us to come to our Lord Jesus Christ,
for he has his arms outstretched to receive us. Hereafter we
shall see also that he was sent to preach to the afflicted in
heart. So we must be sacrificed like this, if we are to be conformed to our Lord Jesus Christ. Truly, the sacrifice he offered
is our full hope — that is to say, we must not presume to add
anything of our own. Jesus Christ has fully won salvation for
us by being sacrificed to God his Father; but all the same we
must be menaced by the judgment of God, that we may learn
what an enormity it is that we poor worms of the earth should
come to rise up against the majesty of him who created us,
that we should violate his justice; especially bearing in mind
that we are in this world to serve and honour him. Let us,
then, feel that vividly, so that we may come to our Lord Jesus
Christ. — *Sermons*

*Praise the Lord, O Jerusalem; praise thy God, O
Zion.*   Psalm 147:12

The blessing of God enjoyed within is next spoken of, con-
sisting in this, that the citizens dwell prosperously and happily
in it, and are fed bountifully, even to satiety; which does not
mean that the children of God always wallow in abundance.
This might be the means of corrupting them, prone as our
nature is to wantonness; but it suggests that they recognize
the liberality of God in their daily food more clearly than others
who lack faith, and whom either abundance renders blind, or
poverty vexes with deplorable anxiety, or covetousness in-
flames with a desire that never can be satisfied. God's paternal
favor was shown more particularly to our fathers under the law
in the abundance of temporal provisions, it being necessary to
lead them forward to something higher by what was elemen-
tary. — *Commentaries*

*Simon Peter saith unto them, I go a fishing. They say
unto him, We also go with thee. They went forth,
and entered into a ship immediately; and that night
they caught nothing.*   John 21:3

"And that night they caught nothing." God permitted them
to toil to no purpose during the whole night in order to prove
the truth of the miracle; for if they had caught anything, what
followed immediately afterwards would not have so clearly manifested the power of Christ, but when after having toiled ineffec-
tually during the whole night they are suddenly favored with a
large take of fishes, they have good reason for acknowledging
the goodness of the Lord. In the same manner also God often
tries believers, that he may lead them the more highly to value
his blessing. If we were always prosperous, whenever we put
our hand to labor, scarcely any man would attribute to the

blessing of God the success of his exertions, all would boast of their industry, and would kiss their hands. But when they sometimes labor and torment themselves without any advantage, if they happen afterwards to succeed better, they are constrained to acknowledge something out of the ordinary course; and the consequence is that they begin to ascribe to the goodness of God the praise of their prosperity and success.

—*Commentaries*

329   **NOVEMBER 24**

He will not suffer thy foot to be moved: he that keepeth thee will not slumber.   Psalm 121:3

"He will not suffer thy foot to stumble." Here the Prophet, in order to recall the faithful to the right path, and to defeat the influence of all the allurements which are wont to distract their minds, affirms that whatever advantages worldly men are accustomed to desire or hope for from the world, true believers will find abundantly and at hand in God alone. He not only attributes power to God, but also teaches that he is so affectioned towards us, that he will preserve us in all respects in perfect safety. As often as the power of God is extolled, there are many who immediately reply, It is very true that he can do such and such things if he is so inclined, but we do not certainly know what is his intention. In this passage, therefore, God is exhibited to the faithful as their guardian, that they may rest with assured confidence on his providence. As the Epicureans, in imagining that God has no care whatever about the world, extinguish all piety, so those who think that the world is governed by God only in a general and confused manner, and believe not that he cherishes with special care each of his believing people, leave men's minds in suspense, and are themselves kept in a state of constant fluctuation and anxiety. In short, never will the hearts of men be led in good earnest to call upon God, until a persuasion of the truth of this guardianship is deeply fixed in their minds.

—*Commentaries*

Is any among you afflicted? let him pray. Is any merry?
let him sing psalms.   James 5:13

But though prayer is properly restricted to wishes and petitions, yet there is so great an affinity between petition and thanksgiving that they may be justly comprehended under the same name. The Scripture not without reason enjoins us the continual use of both; for we have elsewhere said that our want is so great and experience itself proclaims that we are molested and oppressed on every side with such numerous and great perplexities, that we all have sufficient cause for unceasing sighs and groans and ardent supplications to God. For though they enjoy a freedom from adversity, yet the guilt of their sins and the innumerable assaults of temptation ought to stimulate even the most eminent saints to pray for relief.

But of the sacrifice of praise and thanksgiving there can be no interruption without guilt; since God ceases not to accumulate on us his various benefits, according to our respective cases, in order to constrain us, inactive and sluggish as we are, to the exercise of gratitude. Finally, we are almost overwhelmed with such great and copious effusions of his beneficence; we are surrounded, whithersoever we turn our eyes, by such numerous and amazing miracles of his hand, that we never lack matter for praise and thanksgiving.

—Institutes, III, xx, xxviii

But continue thou in the things which thou hast
learned and hast been assured of, knowing of whom
thou hast learned them; And that from a child thou
hast known the holy scriptures, which are able to
make thee wise unto salvation through faith which
is in Christ Jesus.   II Timothy 3:14, 15

Timothy, even from his childhood, had learned the holy
Scripture. By this he means that Timothy had much more advantage than if he had but recently been brought to the faith
from heathendom. True it is that his father was a heathen,
but God of his gracious goodness made him follow the faith
of his mother and his grandmother. And therefore he had been
faithfully brought up, and instructed in the doctrine of God,
and in true religion, even from his mother's breast.

For if a man be sixty years old, being already old and
frail for the knowledge of the Gospel, still he must strive with
himself, seeing he has erred all his life long, to make up for
that which he has lost. But they that have received true and
pure doctrine from the beginning, what must they do? Are
they not much more bound to God?

Therefore let us mark well that Saint Paul warns all those
who from childhood have been rightly instructed; if they fall
away, they shall be less able to excuse themselves, and they
deserve double condemnation, seeing they fall away from the
doctrine in which they were so long instructed, and in which
they should have been well confirmed. — *Sermons*

Then he answered and spake unto me, saying, This
is the word of the Lord unto Zerubbabel, saying, Not
by might, nor by power, but by my spirit, saith the
Lord of hosts.   Zechariah 4:6

Here we are reminded that if we desire to become proficient in the mysteries of God, we must not arrogate anything to ourselves; for here the Prophet honestly confesses his own want of knowledge. And let us not at this day be ashamed to lie down at God's feet, that he may teach us as little children; for whoever desires to be God's disciple must necessarily be conscious of his own folly, that is, he must come free from a conceit of his own wisdom, and be willing to be taught by God.

The angel bears witness that the power of God alone is sufficient to preserve the Church and there is no need of other helps. For he sets the Spirit of God in opposition to all earthly aids; and thus he proves that God borrows no help for the preservation of the Church, because he abounds in all blessings to enrich it. Farther, by the word Spirit we know is meant his power, as though he had said, "God designs to ascribe to himself alone the safety of his Church; and though the Church may need many things, there is no reason why it should turn its eyes here and there, or seek this or that help from men; for all abundance of blessings may be supplied by God alone." And *host* and *might* are to be taken for all helps which are exclusive of God's grace. It is indeed certain that God acts not always immediately or by himself, for he employs various means and makes use in his service of the ministrations of men; but his design is only to teach us that we are very foolish, when we look around us here and there, or vacillate, or when in a word various hopes and various fears and various anxieties affect us; for we ought to be so dependent on God alone as to be fully persuaded that his grace is sufficient for us, though it may not appear; nay, we ought fully to confide in God alone, though poverty and want may surround us on every side. — *Commentaries*

Then will I teach transgressors thy ways; and sinners shall be converted unto thee.   Psalm 51:13

"I will teach transgressors thy ways." Here he speaks of the gratitude which he would feel should God answer his prayer and engages to show it by exerting himself in effecting the conversion of others by his example. Those who have been mercifully recovered from their falls will feel inflamed by the common law of charity to extend a helping hand to their brethren; and in general, such as are partakers of the grace of God are constrained by religious principle, and regard for the divine glory, to desire that others should be brought into the participation of it. The confident manner in which he expresses his expectation of converting others is not unworthy of our notice. We are too apt to conclude that our attempts at reclaiming the ungodly are vain and ineffectual, and forget that God is able to crown them with success. — *Commentaries*

Peter saith unto him, Thou shalt never wash my feet. Jesus answered him, If I wash thee not, thou hast no part with me.   John 13:8

"Thou shalt never wash my feet." Hitherto Peter's modesty was excusable, though it was not free from blame; but now he errs more grievously, when he has been corrected, and yet does not yield. And, indeed, it is a common fault that ignorance is closely followed by obstinacy. It is a plausible excuse, no doubt, that the refusal springs from reverence for Christ; but since he does not absolutely obey the command, the very desire of showing his respect for Christ loses its beauty. The true wisdom of faith, therefore, is to approve and embrace with reverence whatever proceeds from God, as done with propriety and good order; nor is there any other way, indeed, in which his name can be sanctified by us; for if we do not believe that whatever he does is done for a very good reason, our flesh, being naturally stubborn, will continually murmur, and will not render to God the honor due to him, unless by constraint. In short, until a man renounce the liberty of judging as to the works of God, whatever exertions he may make to honor God, still pride will always lurk under the garb of humility.

—*Commentaries*

335 NOVEMBER 30

I hate them with perfect hatred: I count them mine enemies. Psalm 139:22

"I hate them with a perfect hatred." Literally it is, I hate them with perfection of hatred. He repeats the same truth as formerly, that such was his esteem for God's glory that he would have nothing in common with those who despised him. He means in general that he gave no countenance to the works of darkness, for whoever connives at sin and encourages it through silence, wickedly betrays God's cause, who has committed the vindication of righteousness into our hands. David's example should teach us to rise with a lofty and bold spirit above all regard to the enmity of the wicked, when the question concerns the honor of God, and rather to renounce all earthly friendships than falsely associate with flattery to the favor of those who do everything to draw down upon themselves the divine displeasure. We have the more need to attend to this, because the keen sense we have of what concerns our private interests, honor, and convenience, makes us never hesitate to engage in contest when any one injures ourselves, while we are abundantly timid and cowardly in defending the glory of God. Thus, as each of us studies his own interest and advantage, the only thing which incites us to contention, strife, and war, is a desire to avenge our private wrongs; none is affected when the majesty of God is outraged. On the other hand, it is a proof of our having a fervent zeal for God when we have the courage to declare irreconcilable war with the wicked and them who hate God, rather than court their favor at the expense of alienating the divine favor.

We are to observe, however, that the hatred of which the Psalmist speaks is directed to the sins rather than the persons of the wicked. We are, so far as lies in us, to study peace with all men; we are to seek the good of all and, if possible, they are to be reclaimed by kindness and good offices; only so far as they are enemies to God we must strenuously confront their resentment. — *Commentaries*

336 **DECEMBER 1**

Therefore I esteem all thy precepts concerning all things to be right; and I hate every false way.
Psalm 119:128

Assuredly when we see that the ungodly mock God with such effrontery, at one time rising up audaciously against him, and at another perverting every part of the law, it becomes us to be more inflamed with zeal, and to be the more courageous in maintaining the truth of God. The extreme impiety of our age especially demands of all the faithful that they should exercise themselves in this holy zeal. Profane men strive to outdo each other in scornfully aspersing the doctrine of salvation, and endeavor to bring God's sacred Word into contempt by their derisive jeers. Others pour forth their blasphemies without intermission. We cannot, therefore, avoid being chargeable with the crime of treacherous indifference, if our hearts are not warmed with zeal, and unless we burn with a holy jealousy. The Prophet not merely says that he approved of God's law wholly and without exception, but he adds that he hated every way of lying, or every false way. And, undoubtedly, no one subscribes in good earnest to the law of God, but he who rejects all the slanders by which the wicked taint or obscure the purity of sound doctrine. — *Commentaries*

Lift up your eyes on high, and behold who hath created these things, that bringeth out their host by number: he calleth them all by names by the greatness of his might, for that he is strong in power; not one faileth.   Isaiah 40:26

"Lift up your eyes on high." We ought to observe that we are so wicked and ungrateful judges of the divine power, that we often imagine God to be inferior to some feeble man. We are more terrified frequently by the empty mask of a single man than we are strengthened by all the promises of God. Not in vain, therefore, does the Prophet repeat that God is defrauded of his honor, if his power does not lead us to warm admiration of him; nor does he spend his labor in what is superfluous, for we are so dull and sluggish that we need to be continually aroused and excited.

Men see every day the heavens and the stars; but who is there that thinks about their Author? By nature men are formed in such a manner as to make it evident that they were born to contemplate the heavens, and thus to learn their Author; for while God formed other animals to look downwards for pasture, he made man alone erect, and bade him look at what may be regarded as his own habitation. This is also described beautifully by a poet, "While other animals look downwards towards the earth, he gave to man a lofty face, and bade him look at heaven, and lift up his countenance erect towards the stars." The Prophet therefore points out the wickedness of men who do not acknowledge what is openly placed before their eyes concerning God, but, like cattle, fix their snout in the earth; for, whenever we raise our eyes upwards, with any degree of attention, it is impossible for our senses not to be struck with the majesty of God. — *Commentaries*

Then said Jesus unto Peter, Put up thy sword into the
sheath: the cup which my Father hath given me,
shall I not drink it?   John 18:11

"Shall I not drink the cup which my Father hath given to
me?" In the same manner we, too, ought to be prepared for
enduring the cross. And yet we ought not to listen to fanatics,
who tell us that we must not seek remedies for diseases and any
other kind of distresses, lest we reject the cup which the
heavenly Father presents to us. Knowing that we must once
die (Heb. 9:27), we ought to be prepared for death; but the
time of our death being unknown to us, the Lord permits us
to defend our life by those aids which he has himself appointed.
We must patiently endure diseases, however grievous they may
be to our flesh; and though they do not yet appear to be mortal,
we ought to seek alleviation of them; only we must be careful
not to attempt anything but what is permitted by the Word of
God. In short, provided that this remain always fixed in our
hearts, "Let the will of the Lord be done" (Acts 21:14), when
we seek deliverance from the evils which press upon us, we
do not fail to drink the cup which the Lord has given us.

—*Commentaries*

For whether we live, we live unto the Lord; and
whether we die, we die unto the Lord: whether we live
therefore, or die, we are the Lord's.   Romans 14:8

If the account I have heard of the death of your good brother and mine have been the occasion of joy to me, as, indeed, there was good reason for it, you who have known better the whole matter, have, assuredly, far more ample matter for rejoicing, not for that you wished to be deprived of so excellent a companion, on which account both you and I have good ground for regret — all the more that the number of those who in the present day walk constantly in the fear of God is so small and rare, but because of the singular grace which God had conferred upon him, of perseverance in the fear of his name, the faith and patience which he has manifested, and other tokens of true Christianity. For all that is as a mirror in which we may contemplate the strength wherewith our kind heavenly Father assists his children, and most of all, out of their greatest difficulties. Then, also, we may conclude that his death was indeed happy and blessed, in the face of him and of all his angels.

At the same time, you must reflect that it is a fine example for you, lest it be converted into a testimony against you, to make you inexcusable before God, the great Judge. For inasmuch as he, dying as a Christian, has shown you how you ought to live, it is certain that God would not have such a testimony to be useless. Know, then, that the death of your brother is as God's trumpet, whereby he would call upon you to serve him alone, and this far more loudly than if your brother had lived ten years longer to exhort you; while, besides, the pious exhortations which he addressed to you are ever sounding in your ears, that his zeal may glow in your hearts, that his earnest and instant prayers may quicken you, to draw you towards him to whom he has been gathered and restored as one of his own.

—Correspondence

Yet it pleased the Lord to bruise him; he hath put him to grief: when thou shalt make his soul an offering for sin, he shall see his seed, he shall prolong his days, and the pleasure of the Lord shall prosper in his hand.

Isaiah 53:10

And furthermore, each one of us ought to apply this to himself and not doubt that, although we may trail our wings and be still held captive under sin, God will nevertheless deliver us from our captivity, and will perfect what he has begun in us and correct what is still at fault. And how? We must come to our Lord Jesus Christ; for it is he who puts his hand to the work since the charge of it has been committed to him and he has received this office from God his Father. So let us be satisfied that because he is ordained the minister of our salvation, there will be nothing lacking or unaccomplished by this means, seeing it is thus determined. Now moreover, let us apply all this to what St. Paul adds in the passage we have quoted, so that we may participate in the fruit of the death and passion of our Lord Jesus Christ: that is, to hear the message which is daily brought to us. For it is not enough that Jesus Christ suffered in his person and was made a sacrifice for us; but we must be assured of it by the Gospel; we must receive that testimony and doubt not that we have righteousness in him, knowing that he has made satisfaction for our sins. And therefore let us look to God to continue his work by this Redeemer and to continue it in such a way that it grows more and more until he has brought it to its end and conclusion. — *Sermons*

*Paul an apostle of Jesus Christ by the commandment
of God our Saviour, and Lord Jesus Christ, which is
our hope;* I Timothy 1:1

"God our Savior and Jesus Christ our hope." True it is
that this word Savior is often ascribed to the Son of God,
because it is he who has fulfilled and perfected whatever was
requisite to our salvation. He shed his blood, to the end that
we should be washed and made clean from our filth and
loathsomeness; he abolished the curse that was upon us; he
delivered us and set us at liberty from the slavery of death;
he utterly put sin to flight. We see then that we must seek our
salvation in our Lord Jesus Christ and that with good reason
he is called our Savior.

But still it is not without good cause that Paul gives
God the Father this title; and why? Let us see whence Jesus
Christ came to us. He was sent us from God his Father, for
so the Scripture witnesses; God so loved the world that he gave
his only begotten Son, delivering him to death for us (John
3:16, I John 4:9). Therefore, whenever we see our salvation
in the person of our Lord Jesus Christ, we must come to the
very head and fountain from which he came to us, that is to
say, from this love which God had for mankind. This is the
reason why Saint Paul calls God our Savior; teaching us by
this word that as often as we think on the profit which Jesus
Christ has brought us, and we have gotten by him, we should
lift up our hearts and know that God, taking pity on the lost
flock of Adam, made provision for it, and therefore gave this
remedy; namely, our Savior Jesus Christ, who came to draw us
out of the bottomless pit of death in which we were. — *Sermons*

But thou, O man of God, flee these things; and follow after righteousness, godliness, faith, love, patience, meekness.   I Timothy 6:11

Why are we Christians? Why are we baptized? Why do we call upon God? Is it only to live in this world and to have our pleasures and delights? No, no, but to climb up higher, and to know that we must drive to the kingdom of heaven, knowing that our inheritance is in heaven, whereunto we must run, and pass through this world, not delaying in it at all.

Considering that our condition is such that we have no certain and abiding dwelling place here, but we must go higher, and God calls us daily to come to him; if we be given to covetousness, shall we be excused, I ask you? If we remain still entangled in these worldly things after God has showed us the brittleness and shortness of our life, are we not worse than mad? And yet we see what pleasure covetous men take in it to plunge and drown themselves in this world; and again, though they be reminded of their temporary life, they think they shall live a hundred years after their death; there is no end nor measure with them; their desires are not to be satisfied.

But on the contrary, if we consider that our Lord sets us here as poor strangers, who are but passengers; and moreover that we must fight continually; this is enough to rid us of all covetousness. And again we must consider that we cannot push on to the kingdom of heaven unless we mortify and kill our fleshly affections. It is said, Where thy treasure is, there will thine heart be also. If our treasures are in heaven, it is certain that this devilish rage will be quickly quenched, and we shall mortify and kill all that which hinders us from coming to God; all that will be beaten down, and we shall from day to day labor to cut off all these needless things which abuse us here beneath. — *Sermons*

*And the women also, which came with him from Gal-
ilee, followed after, and beheld the sepulchre, and
how his body was laid. And they returned, and prepared spices and ointments; and rested the sabbath
day according to the commandment.* Luke 23:55, 56

Consider what was the courage and constancy of women at
the death of our Lord Jesus Christ; when the apostles had forsaken him, how they continued by him with marvellous constancy, and how a woman was the messenger to announce to
the apostles his resurrection, which the latter could neither believe nor comprehend. If he then so honored women, and endowed them with so much courage, think you that he has less
power now, or that his purposes are changed? How many
thousands of women have there been who have spared neither
their blood nor their lives to maintain the name of Jesus Christ
and announce his reign! Has not God caused their martyrdom
to fructify? Has their faith not obtained the glory of the world
as well as that of the martyrs?

And without going so far, have we not still before our eyes
examples of how God works daily by their testimony, and
confounds his enemies, in such a manner that there is no
preaching of such efficacy as the fortitude and perseverance
which they possess in confessing the name of Christ? Do you
not see how deeply rooted in their hearts is this saying of our
Lord, He who denies me before men, him will I deny before
God my Father; and he who confesses me, him also will I
confess, and avow before God my Father? They have not
feared to quit this perishable life to obtain a better, full of
glory and everlasting. Set before you, then, these noble examples, both ancient and recent, to strengthen your weakness,
and teach you to repose on him who has performed such great
things by weak vessels; and recognize the honor which he has
done you, in order that you may suffer yourselves to be led by
him, being confident that he is powerful to preserve your life, if

he wishes yet to make use of it, or if it is his will to exchange it for a better, you are most blessed in employing this perishable existence for his glory at so high a price, and with the assured hope of living eternally with him. For to that end have we been sent into this world, and illuminated by the grace of God, to glorify him, both in our life and in our death, and be finally united to him. May the Lord grant you the grace to meditate attentively on these things, and impress them on your hearts, in order that you may conform yourselves wholly to his holy will.

—*Letter* (to the women detained in prison at Paris)

344   **DECEMBER 9**

But he was wounded for our transgressions, he was bruised for our iniquities: the chastisement of our peace was upon him; and with his stripes we are healed.   Isaiah 53:5

When we consider the works of God throughout the world, they tell us that he ought to be praised for his majesty and greatness; but when we come to the person of our Lord Jesus Christ, we must learn to glorify God in his abasement. So there is a twofold way of praising God. On the one hand, we must exalt him because he shows us his goodness, righteousness and infinite power in all that he has created and done, and by ordaining and disposing everything. (I say "exalt him," not because we can add to his greatness, but because the Scripture speaks in this way to teach men that they must lift up their minds above all the world if they want to glorify God as he deserves.) And on the other hand, since our Lord Jesus Christ, in whom dwells all the fulness of the Godhead, was not only degraded for our salvation but was willing to be brought to the lowest depths — more, did not refuse to suffer the pangs of death, as if he had entered into hell — God deserves to be glorified more than for his greatness apparent throughout the world. But as the Prophet continues his argument, we must always keep this object in view: that whereas unbelievers are surprised that Jesus Christ was afflicted at the hand of God his Father and make it an occasion of stumbling to alienate themselves from him, we ought to be the more stirred to seek him; and we ought to be completely carried away by his love, seeing that he did not spare himself but was willing to bear all our burdens and relieve us of them. So when we see that our Lord Jesus Christ made such an exchange for us, and was willing to make complete payment of all our debts so that we might be cleared of them; that he was willing to be condemned in our name and, as it were, in our person so that we might be absolved — all this ought to draw us to him, indeed, set us on fire to find our rest in him. — *Sermons*

345   DECEMBER 10

And the inhabitants of one city shall go to another, saying, Let us go speedily to pray before the Lord and to seek the Lord of hosts: I will go also. Yea, many people and strong nations shall come to seek the Lord of hosts in Jerusalem, and to pray before the Lord.   Zechariah 8:21, 22

Faith then only produces its legitimate fruit when zeal is kindled, so that every one strives to increase the kingdom of God, and to gather the straying, that the Church may be filled. For when any one consults his own private benefit and has no care for others, he first betrays most clearly his own inhumanity, and where there is no love the Spirit of God does not rule. Besides, true godliness brings with it a concern for the glory of God. It is no wonder then that the Prophet, when describing true and real conversion, says that each would be solicitous about his brethren, so as to stimulate one another, and also that the hearts of all would be so kindled with zeal for God that they would hasten together to celebrate his glory.

We must observe that the Prophet in speaking of God's worship sets prayer in the first rank, for prayer to God is the chief part, the main thing, in religion. It is indeed immediately added, "and to seek Jehovah." He explains the particular by the general; and in the next verse he inverts the order, beginning with the general. However the meaning continues the same, for God seeks nothing else but that we should be teachable and obedient, so as to be prepared to follow wherever he may call us, and at the same time carefully to inquire respecting his will, as we have need of him as our leader and teacher, so that we may not foolishly go astray through winding and circuitous courses; for if we deem it enough to take presumptuously our own say, the effort to seek God will be fruitless. It must then be observed that God is then only really sought when men desire to learn from his Word how he is to be worshipped. But the Prophet adds prayer here, for the design of the whole truth respecting salvation is to teach us that our life depends on God, and that whatever belongs to eternal life must be hoped for and expected from him. — *Commentaries*

346   DECEMBER 11

> . . . *they shall see the glory of the Lord, and the excellency of our God.*   Isaiah 35:2b

"They shall see the glory of Jehovah." Till men learn to know God, they are barren and destitute of everything good; and consequently the beginning of our fertility is to be quickened by the presence of God, which cannot be without the inward perception of faith. The Prophet undoubtedly intended to raise our minds higher, that we may contemplate the abundance and copiousness of heavenly benefits; for men might be satisfied with bread and wine and other things of the same kind, and yet not acknowledge God to be the Author of them, or cease to be wretched; and indeed men are often blinded and rendered more fierce by enjoying abundance. But when God makes himself visible to us, by causing us to behold his glory and beauty, we not only possess his blessings, but have the true enjoyment of them for salvation. — *Commentaries*

And it shall come to pass in that day, saith the Lord
of hosts, that I will cut off the names of the idols
out of the land, and they shall no more be remem-
bered: and also I will cause the prophets and the un-
clean spirit to pass out of the land.   Zechariah 13:2

We may deduce that the Word of God not only shows the
way to us, but also uncovers the delusions of Satan; for hardly
one in a hundred follows what is right, unless he is reminded
of what he ought to avoid. It is then not enough to declare
that there is but one true God, and that we ought to put our
trust in Christ, unless another thing be added, that is, that
we warn men of those intrigues by which Satan has from the
beginning deceived miserable mortals. Even at this day he has
by various means withdrawn the simple and unwary from the
true God and entangled them in a maze of superstitions. Unless
therefore men be thus warned, the Word of God is made
known to them only in part.

This also ought to be carefully observed; for we see at this
day how some unprincipled men adopt this sentiment — that
the Church is not free unless every one is allowed with impunity
to teach whatever he pleases, and that it is the greatest cruelty
to punish a heretic; for they would have all liberty to be given
to blasphemies. But the Prophet here shows that the Church
cannot be preserved in a pure state, and, in a word, it cannot
exist as a healthy and sound body, except the rashness and
audacity of those who pervert sound and true doctrine be restrained. — *Commentaries*

That the saying of Jesus might be fulfilled, which he
spake, signifying what death he should die.

John 18:32

"That the word of Jesus might be fulfilled." The Evangelist
adds that it was necessary that this should be done, in order
that the prediction which Christ had uttered might be fulfilled, "The Son of Man shall be delivered into the hands of
the Gentiles" (Matt. 20:19). And indeed if we wish to read
with advantage the history of Christ's death, the chief point
is to consider the eternal purpose of God. The Son of God is
placed before the tribunal of a mortal man. If we suppose that
this is done by the caprice of men, and do not raise our eyes
to God, our faith must necessarily be confounded and put to
shame. But when we perceive that, by the condemnation of
Christ, our condemnation before God is blotted out, because
it pleased the heavenly Father to take this method of recon-
ciling mankind to himself, raised on high by this single consideration, we boldly and without shame glory even in Christ's
ignominy. Let us therefore learn, in each part of this narra-
tive, to turn our eyes to God as the Author of our redemption.

—*Commentaries*

Let the word of Christ dwell in you richly in all wis-
dom; teaching and admonishing one another in psalms
and hymns and spiritual songs, singing with grace in
your hearts to the Lord. Colossians 3:16

Now let us fall down before the face of our good God, with
confession of our faults, praying him to pluck us out of the
vain confidence of our fleshly mind, and that we may serve

him in such sort that we may be wholly given to him. And seeing it has pleased him to be so gracious to us as to give us his Word for our rule, let us be content to be ordered by it and to be instructed there more and more, and let it be always our goal to be fully built up in him; and in the meantime we may make him offerings and sacrifices both of our souls and bodies. And let us be consecrated and dedicated to him in such a way that he may dwell in us as in his true temples and that he may reign there, and that his image may shine there; to the end that we may at length be partakers of his immortal glory which he has prepared for us. And let us pray that he may be thus gracious, not unto us only, but to all people and nations of the world. — *Sermons*

350   DECEMBER 15

He shall not fail nor be discouraged, till he have set judgment in the earth: and the isles shall wait for his law.   Isaiah 42:4

"He shall not faint, nor be discouraged." I remember that there were in a populous city two preachers, one of whom boldly and loudly reproved vices, while the other endeavored to gain the favor of the people by flatteries. This fawning preacher, who was expounding the Prophet Jeremiah, lighted on a passage full of the mildest consolation, and having found, as he imagined, a fit opportunity, began to declaim against those harsh and severe reprovers who are accustomed to terrify men by thunderbolts of words. But on the following day, when the Prophet changed his subject and sharply rebuked wicked men with his peculiar vehemence of style, the wretched flatterer was constrained to encounter bitter scorn by retracting the words which were fresh in the recollection of all his hearers. Thus the temporary favor which he had gained speedily vanished, when he revealed his own disposition and made himself abhorred by the good and the bad. — *Commentaries*

And I thank Christ Jesus our Lord, who hath enabled me, for that he counted me faithful, putting me into the ministry; Who was before a blasphemer, and a persecutor, and injurious: but I obtained mercy, because I did it ignorantly in unbelief.   I Timothy 1:12, 13

Hereby both great and small are reminded of their duty. If we would exalt the grace of God, as is fitting, we have to confess what we are, and what would become of us if God did not help us. This is hard to do, seeing men seek nothing so much as to make themselves seem like something. Although they confess that they believe completely in God, yet they gladly obscure this knowledge, and will never come to a plain, free, and simple confession unless they are constrained to it. This is especially the case when it concerns revealing our shame, and rebuking ourselves, that our sins may be manifest, and so humbling ourselves that we are utterly condemned unless the Lord of his infinite mercy draws us out of condemnation. Whenever men must be thus humbled, they will not come to it, but will draw back as far as they possibly can, and use all sorts of hiding places, so that if they cannot wholly justify themselves, at least they may seek some closets to lurk in, that their shame and filthiness may not be known. So much the more we have to note this passage of Saint Paul. For he does not make a general confession, as hypocrites do, which says, "I am a man, I am a sinner." But he sets down in plain terms what he was; I was, says he, a persecutor of the Church of God; I was a blasphemer of his truth. He did not seek to cover himself with the name of the weakness of a man, but leaves to every man the confession of his own faults, and for his own part confesses his own. — *Sermons*

*For I am the Lord thy God, the Holy One of Israel,
thy Saviour: I gave Egypt for thy ransom, Ethiopia
and Seba for thee.*   Isaiah 43:3

"I have given the price of thy redemption." We too may
readily acknowledge, if we are not worse than stupid, that the
same providence and infinite mercy of God have been manifested toward us, when tyrants who would have wished to destroy us, and who joined in opening their mouths with eagerness to devour us, are made by him to engage in wars against
each other, and when the rage with which they burned against
us is directed by him to another quarter; for by doing so he
preserves us, so as to give them as the price of our redemption.
When we see irreligious men, amidst the uproar and confusion
of mutual wars, pause in their efforts to destroy us, while it is
manifest that they do not pause of their own accord, let us
lift up our eyes to heaven, and learn that God, in order to
spare us, miraculously substitutes others in our place, for we
were "like sheep appointed for slaughter" (Psalm 44:22),
swords were drawn on every hand, if he had not snatched them
from the hands of wicked men, or given them a different direction.

Hence we ought to draw a general doctrine, that the Lord
takes such care of all believers (I Peter 5:7) that he values
them more highly than the whole world. Although therefore
we are of no value, yet let us rejoice in this, that the Lord sets
so high a value on us and prefers us to the whole world, rescues
us from dangers, and thus preserves us in the midst of death.
If everything were at peace with us, and if we had no troubles,
we should not see this grace of God; for when a thousand
deaths appear to hang over us, and when there appears no
way of escape, and when he suddenly drives back the tyrants,
or turns them in another direction, we then know by experience what the Prophet says, and perceive God's invaluable
kindness toward us. — *Commentaries*

DECEMBER 18

Therefore did my heart rejoice, and my tongue was
glad; moreover also my flesh shall rest in hope:
Acts 2:26

Joy of the soul, gladness of the tongue, and quietness of
the whole body, result from sure hope and confidence. For
unless men are quite past feeling they must be anxious and
sorrowful, and, consequently, miserable and tormented, as
long as they feel themselves destitute of the help of God. But
that sure trust which we repose in God not only delivers us
from anxiety, but also replenishes our hearts with wonderful
joy and gladness. This is the joy which Christ promised to his
disciples should be full in them and which he testified could
not be taken away from them. — *Commentaries*

354 **DECEMBER 19**

Preach the word; be instant in season, out of season;
reprove, rebuke, exhort with all longsuffering and doc-
trine. II Timothy 4:2

First of all, we are not to take up the Word of God for
mere recreation, or listen to him merely when we have
leisure. This is far from yielding to him that obedience which
he desires. Every one of us must strive to profit. And as God
protests that morning and evening his arms are stretched out,
not only to receive us, but also to call us afar off, and seeks
nothing but to have us under his wings and to govern us, and
peaceably to enjoy us; so on our part we must take pains to
run to him when he calls us, and cut off all hindrances which
might turn us aside. We see that every man thinks himself
exempt if he has any business to do. "Surely I would gladly
go to the sermon, but I cannot. I have other business; I must
do this, and I must do that." Let us not think that God will
take such vanities for payment. Jesus Christ shows us this

when he mocks at those who say one has married a wife, another has bought a farm, and another will go to his vineyard or his field. This is very common in men's mouths, but the Son of God who is our Judge shows that he will not reckon with it. And so when we see the nets laid, and how the devil, when he cannot wholly draw us away from God, seeks to lay such stumbling blocks in our way that we cannot run as speedily as required; let us learn to break those nets and to exhort ourselves, as we see the holy God exhorting us to it. — *Sermons*

355   DECEMBER 20   •

And the Word was made flesh and dwelt among us,
(and we beheld his glory, the glory as of the only
begotten of the Father,) full of grace and truth.
John 1:14

"And the Word was made flesh." The word *flesh* expresses the meaning of the Evangelist more forcibly than if he had said that he was made man. He intended to show to what a mean and despicable condition the Son of God, on our account, descended from the height of his heavenly glory. When Scripture speaks of man contemptuously, it calls him flesh. Now, though there be ever so wide a distance between the spiritual glory of the Word of God and the abominable filth of our flesh, yet the Son of God stooped so low as to take upon himself that flesh, subject to so many miseries. The word *flesh* is not taken here for corrupt nature, as it is often used by Paul, but for mortal man; though it marks disdainfully his frail and perishing nature, as in these and similar passages; for he remembered that they were flesh (Psalm 78:39); all flesh is grass (Is. 40:6). We must at the same time observe, however, that this is a figure of speech in which a part is taken for the whole; for the lower part includes the whole man. — *Commentaries*

And they were both righteous before God, walking in
all the commandments and ordinances of the Lord
blameless.   Luke 1:6

Although praise is bestowed on Zacharias and Elisabeth
for the purpose of showing us that the lamp, whose light went
before the Son of God, was taken not from an obscure house,
but from an illustrious sanctuary, yet their example shows to us,
at the same time, the rule of a devout and righteous life. In
ordering our life, therefore, our first study ought to be to
approve ourselves to God; and we know that what he chiefly
requires is a sincere heart and a pure conscience. Whoever
neglects uprightness of heart, and regulates his outward life
only by obedience to the law, neglects this order. For it
ought to be remembered that the heart, and not the outward
mask of works, is chiefly regarded by God, to whom we are
commanded to look. Obedience occupies the second rank;
that is, no man must frame for himself, at his own pleasure, a
new form of righteousness unsupported by the Word of God,
but we must allow ourselves to be governed by divine authority.
Nor ought we to neglect this definition, that they are *righteous* who regulate their life by the *commandments* of the law;
which suggests that, to the eye of God, all acts of worship are
counterfeit, and the course of human life false and unsettled,
so far as they depart from his law. — *Commentaries*

*Then said Mary unto the angel, How shall this be,
seeing I know not a man?*   Luke 1:34

"How shall this be?" The holy virgin appears to confine
the power of God within as narrow limits as Zacharias had
done; for what is beyond the common order of nature, she
concludes to be impossible. She reasons in this manner: *I
know not a man;* how then can I believe that what you tell
me will happen? We ought not to give ourselves very much
trouble to acquit her of all blame. She ought immediately to
have risen by faith to the boundless power of God, which is
not at all fettered to natural means, but sways the whole world.
Instead of this, she stops at the ordinary way of generation.
Still, it must be admitted that she does not hesitate or inquire
in such a manner as to lower the power of God to the level
of her senses; but is only carried away by a sudden impulse of
astonishment to put this question. That she readily embraced
the promise may be concluded from this, that, though many
things presented themselves on the opposite side, she has no
doubt but on one point. — *Commentaries*

Then Joseph her husband, being a just man, and not willing to make her a public example, was minded to put her away privily.
Matthew 1:19

The reason why this mystery was not immediately made known to a greater number of persons appears to be this. It was proper that this inestimable treasure should remain concealed, and that the knowledge of it should be imparted to none but the children of God. Nor is it absurd to say, that the Lord intended, as he frequently does, to put the faith and obedience of his own people to the trial. Most certainly, if any man shall maliciously refuse to believe and obey God in this matter, he will have abundant reason to be satisfied with the proofs by which this article of our faith is supported. For the same reason, the Lord permitted Mary to enter into the married state, that under the veil of marriage, till the full time for revealing it, the heavenly conception of the virgin might be concealed. Meanwhile, the knowledge of it was withheld from unbelievers, as their ingratitude and malice deserved. — *Commentaries*

*And there were in the same country shepherds abiding
in the field, keeping watch over their flock by night.*
Luke 2:8

"And there were shepherds." It would have been to no purpose that Christ was born in Bethlehem, if it had not been made known to the world. But the method of doing so, which is described by Luke, appears to the view of men very unsuitable. First, Christ is revealed to but a few witnesses, and that too amidst the darkness of night. Again, though God had, at his command, many honorable and distinguished witnesses, he passed by them, and chose shepherds, persons of humble rank, and of no account among men. Here the reason and wisdom of the flesh must prove to be foolishness; and we must acknowledge that "the foolishness of God" excels all the wisdom that exists, or appears to exist, in the world. But this too was a part of the "emptying of himself"; not that any part of Christ's glory should be taken away by it, but that it should lie in concealment for a time. Again, as Paul reminds us that the gospel is mean according to the flesh, "that our faith should stand" in the power of the Spirit, not in the "lofty words of human wisdom" or in any worldly splendor; so this inestimable treasure has been deposited by God, from the beginning, "in earthen vessels," that he might more fully try the obedience of our faith. If then we desire to come to Christ, let us not be ashamed to follow those whom the Lord, in order to cast down the pride of the world, has taken, from among the dung of cattle, to be our instructors. — *Commentaries*

And she brought forth her firstborn son, and wrapped
him in swaddling clothes, and laid him in a manger;
because there was no room for them in the inn.

Luke 2:7

"Because there was no room for them in the inn." We see
here not only the great poverty of Joseph, but the cruel tyranny which admitted of no excuse, but compelled Joseph to
bring his wife along with him, at an inconvenient season,
when she was near the time of her delivery. Indeed, it is probable that those who were the descendants of the royal family
were treated more harshly and disdainfully than the rest.
Joseph was not so devoid of feeling as to have no concern about
his wife's delivery. He would gladly have avoided this necessity; but, as that is impossible, he is forced to yield, and
commends himself to God. We see, at the same time, what
sort of beginning the life of the Son of God had, and in what
cradle he was placed. Such was his condition at his birth, because he had taken upon him our flesh for this purpose, that he
might "empty himself" on our account. When he was thrown
into a stable, and placed in a manger, and a lodging refused
him among men, it was that heaven might be opened to us,
not as a temporary lodging, but as our eternal country and
inheritance, and that angels might receive us into their abode.

—*Commentaries*

*And the shepherds returned, glorifying and praising
God for all the things that they had heard and seen,
as it was told unto them.* Luke 2:20

"Glorifying and praising God." This is another circumstance
which is fitted to be generally useful in confirming our faith.
The shepherds knew with certainty that this was a work of
God. Their zeal in *glorifying and praising God* is an implied
reproof of our indolence, or rather of our ingratitude. If the
cradle of Christ had such an effect upon them as to make them
rise from the stable and the manger to heaven, how much more
powerful ought the death and resurrection of Christ to be in
raising us to God? For Christ did not only ascend from the
earth, that he might draw all things after him; but he sits at
the right hand of the Father, that, during our pilgrimage in
the world, we may meditate with our whole heart on the
heavenly life. When Luke says, that the testimony of the
angel served as a rule to the shepherds in all that they did, he
points out the nature of true godliness. For our faith is properly
aided by the works of God, when it directs everything to this
end, that the truth of God, which was revealed in his word,
may be brought out with greater clearness. — *Commentaries*

*Which in his times he shall shew, who is the blessed
and only Potentate, the King of kings, and Lord of
lords; Who only hath immortality, dwelling in the
light which no man can approach unto; whom no man
hath seen, nor can see: to whom be honour and power
everlasting. Amen.*   I Timothy 6:15, 16

Men's knowledge is not certain. They know not that men
were made to the image of God, and that God provided an inheritance for them above in the heaven. All the wise men in
the world could never devise this doctrine. Yet we are so
stuffed and filled with all the vanities of the world that we
cannot cast our eyes toward heaven. Even when we have confessed that our true happiness is in heaven, and that we are
pilgrims here beneath, and that we have no abiding place but
with God; when we have confessed all this, and that without
dissembling and hypocrisy but as those who are thoroughly persuaded; yet we do not cease to be entangled in this world and
lie grovelling here as though we should remain here forever.
We see what pains men take and how they torment themselves.
If a man ask them, "Is there no better life?" every man will
confess, and that without hypocrisy, that there is. For they
know it to be so. But yet they become beasts because their unbelief has gotten a firm hold on them, and their affections are
out of line, and they cannot so master them as to withdraw
themselves from those things that are nothing. — *Sermons*

*As soon then as he had said unto them, I am he,
they went backward, and fell to the ground.*

John 18:6

"It is I." We may infer from this how dreadful and alarming
to the wicked the voice of Christ will be, when he shall
ascend to his throne to judge the world. At that time he stood
as a lamb ready to be sacrificed; his majesty, so far as outward
appearance was concerned, was utterly gone; and yet when he
utters but a single word, his armed and courageous enemies fall
down. And what was that word? He thunders no fearful ex-
communication against them, but only replies, "It is I." What
then will be the result, when he shall come, not to be judged
by a man, but to be the Judge of the living and the dead; not
in that mean and despicable appearance, but shining in heavenly
glory, and accompanied by his angels? — *Commentaries*

*Seeing then that we have a great high priest, that
is passed into the heavens, Jesus the Son of God, let us
hold fast our profession. For we have not an high
priest which cannot be touched with the feeling of
our infirmities; but was in all points tempted like as we
are, yet without sin. Let us therefore come boldly unto
the throne of grace, that we may obtain mercy, and
find grace to help in time of need.*

Hebrews 4:14-16

But since there is no one of the human race worthy to present himself to God, and to enter into his presence, our heavenly
Father himself, to deliver us at once from shame and fear,
which might justly depress all our minds, has given us his Son
Jesus Christ our Lord to be our Advocate and Mediator with
him; introduced by whom we may boldly approach him, con-

fident, with such an intercessor, that nothing we ask in his name will be denied us, as nothing can be denied to him by his Father. And to this must be referred all that we have hitherto advanced concerning faith; because, as the promise recommends Christ to us as the Mediator, so, unless our hope of success depend on him, it deprives itself of all the benefit of prayer. For as soon as we reflect on the terrible majesty of God, we cannot but be exceedingly afraid, and driven away from him by a consciousness of our unworthiness, till we discover Christ as the Mediator, who changes the throne of dreadful glory into a throne of grace; as the apostle also exhorts us to "come boldly unto the throne of grace, that we may obtain mercy, and find grace to help in time of need." — *Institutes*, III, xx, xvii

365   **DECEMBER 30**

For I am now ready to be offered, and the time of my departure is at hand. I have fought a good fight, I I have finished my course, I have kept the faith:
                                   II Timothy 4:6, 7

In the first place, I render thanks to God, not only because he has had compassion on me, his poor creature, to draw me out of the abysss of idolatry in which I was plunged, in order to bring me to the light of his gospel and make me a partaker of the doctrine of salvation, of which I was altogether unworthy, and continuing his mercy he has supported me amid so many sins and shortcomings, which were such that I well deserved to be rejected by him a hundred thousand times — but what is more, he has so far extended his mercy towards me as to make use of me and of my labor, to convey and announce the truth of his gospel; protesting that it is my wish to live and die in this faith which he has bestowed on me, having no other hope for refuge except in his gratuitous adoption, upon which all my salvation is founded; embracing the grace which he has given me in our Lord Jesus Christ, and accepting the merits of his death and passion, in order that by this means all my sins may be buried; and praying him so to wash and cleanse me by the blood of this great Redeemer, which has been shed for us poor sinners, that I may appear before his face, bearing as it were his image.

I protest also that I have endeavored, according to the measure of grace he has given me, to teach his word in purity, both in my sermons and in my writings, and to expound faithfully the Holy Scriptures; and moreover, that in all the disputes I have had with the enemies of the truth, I have never made use of subtle craft nor sophistry, but have gone to work straightforwardly in maintaining his quarrel. But alas! the desire which I have had, and the zeal, if so it must be called, has been so cold and so sluggish that I feel myself a debtor in everything and everywhere, and that, were it not for his excellent goodness, all the affection I have would be but as smoke, nay, that even the favors which he has accorded me would render me so much the more guilty; so that my only recourse is this, that being the Father of mercies, he will show himself the Father of so miserable a sinner.

—Calvin's *Last Will and Testament*

366   DECEMBER 31

I have fought a good fight, I have finished my course, I have kept the faith: Henceforth there is laid up for me a crown of righteousness, which the Lord, the righteous judge, shall give me at that day: and not to me only, but unto all them also that love his appearing. II Timothy 4:7, 8

In these combats where men torment themselves out of measure, what do they hope for? A crown of leaves and nothing else. But we have a far better reward. For our Lord calls us to the inheritance of the kingdom of heaven. He will make us partakers of his immortality and of his glory. And yet we hardly move a foot or an arm for this end. Do we not show that we give small honor to God and that we think little of his promises?

For in those days those who were going to fight ate nothing but biscuit, and did not eat their fill. Thus these poor fools, for a little worldly praise, that men should say, he is a nimble fellow, or he wrestles well; for this commendation they fasted and risked their lives. They pined away all their lives, they dared not drink their fill even of water, they abstained from delicate meats, they kept a precise diet; and all this was only to have a little fame, and to have men clap their hands and say, Ho, there is a noble lad; he is worthy to have a dozen leaves; he has fought manfully; he shall be crowned.

And behold our God calls us not only to have a word of commendation in this world; but having chosen us to himself, shows us that our wages is ready, that we shall not miss the crown of glory, and that the angels of Paradise clap their hands for us. To be short, the holy fathers, the holy prophets, apostles, and martyrs shall receive us in the latter day; ought not this to encourage us to walk faithfully and to fight constantly to the end?

This is the reason why Saint Paul uses this figure, when he says that he had fought a good fight. It is as if he had said, "As for them who travail according to the world for ambition or covetousness, let them please themselves and brag of their combats as much as they wish. But as for me, I have to content myself when I serve my God; I shall not lose one foot, but all shall come into account before him. The angels of Paradise rejoice in that I have been an instrument to perform in God's name that which he committed to me for the advancement of the kingdom of his Son." — *Sermons*

TOPICAL INDEX

Printed in the United States
68976LVS00002B/412-459